A road of her own.

DATE			

A ROAD OF HER OWN

A ROAD OF HER OWN

Women's Journeys in the West

EDITED BY
MARLENE BLESSING

FULCRUM PUBLISHING
GOLDEN, COLORADO

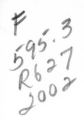
Library of Congress Cataloging-in-Publication Data
A road of her own : women's journeys in the West / edited by
  Marlene Blessing.
    p. cm.
  ISBN 1-55591-307-5 (hardcover)
  1. West (U.S.)—Description and travel. 2. Women travelers—West (U.S.)
I. Blessing, Marlene, 1947–   .
F595.3.R627 2002
917.804'082—dc21

                               2002008172

Editorial: Marlene Blessing, Linda Gunnarson
Cover and interior design: Kate Thompson
Cover photograph: Road, Comanche National Grassland, Colorado, © Stephen Collector.

Fulcrum Publishing
16100 Table Mountain Parkway, Suite 300
Golden, Colorado 80403
(800) 992-2908 • (303) 277-1623
www.fulcrum-books.com

Printed in Canada
0 9 8 7 6 5 4 3 2 1

For Blessing, whose love travels with me always

And for Robert, who shares the journey ahead

A Special Note

A Road of Her Own is written by women who have traveled widely and, through such travels, expanded their understanding of the world and themselves. A major portion of the book's royalties will be donated to the Rocky Mountain Multiple Sclerosis Center in Denver, Colorado, a research-based non-profit that is in the forefront of seeking a cure for those women and men who suffer the ravages of M.S. Many of those who are afflicted with this disease have lost their ability to journey independently. It is our hope that in some small way this contribution will serve as a sign of support and an acknowledgment of the rare gift our freewheeling travels are.

Contents

Acknowledgments

Lest this list of thank-yous inflates into a life story, I will try to stick to the primary people who first prepared me for the road, who then urged me toward discoveries on it, and who now support me as the road goes on.

First, my odd thanks to a remote and isolated mother, whose increasing distance from the world only made me hungry to know it. Her battles with multiple sclerosis, which raged more than forty years, showed me early in life how suddenly one's life can detour, as well as how important it is to seize every moment of discovery available.

Then there are the teachers, too many to honor. Two stand out among the rest. Mrs. Parlato, the second-grade teacher who skipped me to a higher grade, taught me about the flight of the mind by showing me the many worlds in books. Much later, the late Richard Blessing, professor, poet, fiction writer and, eventually, husband, picked up where Mrs. Parlato left off. Because of him, I have an editing career and life as a writer. Also, because of him, I will always tell stories.

Friends, both the writers and the nonwriters, have been central to this project. My love and affection to all of you, and most especially to those with whom I am closest: Constance Bollen, Andrea Jarvela, Valerie Trueblood, Brenda Peterson, Linda Hogan, Maggie Edgar, Deb Easter, Janet Thomas, Brad Matsen, Ray Troll, and luminous poet and friend Gwen Head. Family, too, have played an important role, and I extend gratitude beyond words to my sister, Deborah Loop, my brother, Bruce Loop, and my amazing stepson, Craig Blessing.

The writers who have helped create *A Road of Her Own* are my angels. Most of the essays in this collection, thanks to them, are original, never-before-published stories. And those several essays that were previously published are gems that also add to the richness within. Additionally, Kate Thompson, artist, writer, hip sister, and graphic designer extraordinaire, has made this book a beautiful object. My everlasting thanks to you all.

Finally, I am privileged to work for a publisher I love and admire, Bob Baron. He challenged me to make this long-festering dream of a book of women's road trips into a reality when he signed the contract for the book. Additionally, my colleagues at Fulcrum Publishing are a joy to work with. Those with whom I work most closely and depend upon without hesitation are Dan Forrest-Bank, Cyndie Chandler, Nancy Duncan-Cashman, Dianne Howie, and Ellen Wheat.

Most importantly, I thank my life's companion, Robert Sheldon, for his excess of love and for his unwavering devotion.

Introduction: Daughters of the Road

As a young girl growing up in the Seattle of the 1950s, I had three life ambitions. Why I made such a list at the age of ten, I don't know. But these three choices have held up better than some of my more mature dreams. I wanted to learn to type, to play the piano, and to drive a car. The first ambition sprang out of a direct and potent experience. In the basement apartment of our rental house in West Seattle lived a freelance writer named Ruby. She wasn't big on children, especially talkative, nosy ones such as myself. But every now and then, she granted me an exclusive audience. The *plunk-plunk-plunk* of her Underwood typewriter would cease and she'd motion me through her door with her red-nailed, charm-braceleted hands, and wrists.

As she told me stories of her writing assignments, Ruby took long draws on her unfiltered cigarettes and blew smoke rings, and I'd follow the wispy clouds of it out the window and beyond to Puget Sound. It seemed to me that all her plunking at the typewriter led directly to her freedom to enter other lives and other worlds at will. How could I resist a vehicle that would take me farther than my fat-tired bicycle?

By contrast, my ambition to play the piano was short-lived, derailed by my teacher's alcoholism and my boredom with practicing scales. But my passion for the road has been a constant, fueled early by one parent's love affair with travel. My father loved to drive. He was a bus driver when I was a preschooler and often let me ride with him for his entire route around Alki Beach to Fort Lawton, in the Magnolia neighborhood. About midway, we'd hit downtown Seattle, and I'd see the busy city and its busy people (especially the glamorous hookers on First Avenue). In later years, Dad occasionally drove trucks for piecework, sometimes deadheading a semi with trailer cross-country to New York, sometimes delivering fresh produce from the Kent Valley to the Pike Place Market, and sometimes pruning and topping trees and hauling the cuttings to the dump.

But the driving he really loved was the kind that involved hitting the open road to go hunting, to golf or fish, to visit relatives in the Skagit Valley, or simply to wander just outside the city limits, no destination in mind, experiencing the joy of "being one with the car" and looking out at a world in motion. I inherited both his love of a long, meditative drive and his restless curiosity about places beyond.

From my mother I inherited something altogether different. While I can't speak for the wonderful contributors to this collection, I can hazard a guess that many had an experience similar to mine. Mothers seldom drove cars or initiated road trips—that was the province of our mobile, breadwinning fathers. This is not today's experience. Even "soccer moms," who are plagued with fast-moving daily routines of chauffeuring kids around in minivans, have more time at the wheel than did most mothers before the sixties. In fact, from the sixties and beyond, not only did our encounters with feminist politics have our heads spinning, but it had our wheels spinning as well. We took to the roads in record numbers. And we often did it with the knowledge that our journeys were a departure from our mothers' common experience.

The first essay in this book, "Detours," is by Brenda Peterson, and it speaks very directly to the stifled dreams of travel that our mothers passed on to us, usually in an indirect or subliminal way. She begins thus: "Since childhood, when they were next-door neighbors and best friends, my mother and Aunt Helen plotted a girls' road trip. Now in their seventies, knees in need of replacement, many dreams deferred by wifely duties and mothering, both women at last hit the road west on their first road trip together." In the stories that follow, readers will have many chances to learn about the varied adventures that we post-sixties women have had and continue to have on the open roads of the West. Perhaps, as I have, you'll find yourself forming a question that can't be answered. In Peterson's words, the question might be about "…what the West would have become if more women had explored the landscape, naming the rivers, valleys, mountains, if we made maps with a feminine geography."

But the stories within do not merely chart an external geography. The roads also lead inward, and several of the roads traveled are not at all literal in nature. For example, Susan Tweit confronts the newly diagnosed onset of her life-threatening chronic disease, as she hikes through the Rockies with only a dog, her fears, and her resolve as companions. While Chickasaw writer Linda Hogan gives us an intimate view of a traditional healing ceremony, one meant to restore humans' connection with the animal world. And Teri Hein's visit to a Montana Hutterite community takes her into an alien world, one that leaves her unsettled, with questions she cannot answer.

Traveler's tales are what we cannot get enough of in this age of expansiveness for women. And they are a talisman we all need. My own mother carried one tale for her entire life, a tale as deep and poignant as that of a fragile plant carried by an immigrant into the New World. Mother grew to young womanhood on a small farm in Minnesota, the thirteenth child of a Norwegian couple. Her mother died when she was only sixteen, and her father followed just a few years after. I don't know what my mother dreamed of as she gazed out over those fertile Midwestern fields with the family dog at her side, but I've speculated plenty since seeing a picture of her from that time. She looks wistful in the black-and-white snapshot. She's wearing an airman's leather jacket and slacks, her brown hair is cropped and tousled, and she has an air of happy distraction.

It cannot have been too long from the time of this uncharacteristic snapshot (all others from this time are posed portraits) that her older brothers gathered to decide to ship her west to relatives in Tacoma, Washington, who could help her find a job and, eventually, a suitable Lutheran husband. I doubt that these fine Norwegian brothers gave her desires much thought. And perhaps she never voiced them. These sensible men were keenly aware that the farm and the small town of Rothsay in which it stood could not support either my mother's need for income or for romantic love.

Mother's story is that the brothers butchered a cow and sold its meat to buy a one-way railroad ticket for her to Tacoma. That would have been in the late thirties. As she sat upright in a passenger car for the four days that the trip would have taken, the landscape outside her window would shift dramatically. Imagine growing up with green alfalfa and soybeans and people who themselves remained green Americans by clinging to Northern European tongues and traditions. Imagine a woman who had never seen the craggy and majestic mountains of the West or felt the salt spray of the Pacific Ocean on her face. Those experiences alone could be enough to make a sheltered woman of her time feel weightless, floating in a balloon like Dorothy of Oz, only heading *away* from Kansas and the softer Midwest.

This was my mother's longest solo adventure. In fact, it was her only solo adventure. I have never been sure whether it was a journey that she came to see more as a leaving than as an arrival. But the latter surely prevailed. Although she lived the heady World War II years in Seattle as a single working woman, happy with career and friends, eventually she surrendered this independence for a husband and three children, with the weekly neighborhood coffee klatch her consolation. I never saw her walk or run far, much less slip into our '53 Mercury for a drive. And after she was diagnosed with multiple sclerosis, her world shrank even further.

■ ■ ■

By 1966, when I would fly, for the first time, to the Philippines to marry my serviceman sweetheart, I still had not learned to drive a car. When my husband returned to the states soon after, where he was to serve in the Bremerton shipyard for the final year of his enlistment, he received a change of orders. He was to be sent to Vietnam. In the trauma of the days before his leaving, he determined that he would teach his teenage bride to become a licensed driver in the two weeks that remained to us. The lessons themselves are a blur—although I remember clearly his adamant instructions about never swerving to avoid hitting an animal in the road. I do recall how many fights we had in those few days—he cursing the fact that I couldn't do everything as instructed the first time through, I crying because my longtime dream seemed futile.

In the small North Cascades town of Concrete, not far from where my in-laws lived, I took the driver's test. Why there? Because my skills were questionable, and I might not pass a test in the big city of Seattle. In that little town, with a single double-lane road heading through it, I just might be able to perform adequately. The officer who sat in the passenger seat next to me as I completed the exam kept asking me to do the thing I do best: imagine. "First, imagine that there is a stoplight and it's just turned red." I stopped on a dime. "Next, imagine that you are about to turn left on the road." I signaled about a block in advance, slowed to a stop, and pretended to wait for an opening in busy traffic to turn onto a crossroad. "And finally, imagine that you are parallel parking between two vehicles." (Those, too, had to be imagined.) I passed my imagining exam with flying colors and left with a real driver's license in hand. I would never be the same thereafter.

In the years that have followed, I have logged many miles in cars, alone and with friends, family, and lovers. Like my fellow writers in this collection, I live in the West, a place where there are still long reaches of not-so-populated land that can't be traversed easily without driving a car. Try crossing Arizona, or heading for a hiking trip to the Olympic Peninsula, or winding down the coast of Oregon to walk its spectacular beaches, or visiting your friend in Salida, Colorado, without getting behind the wheel.

But this challenge is just a smokescreen. Truth is, the automobile is our faithful steed, the horse that allows us independent women to gallop through breathtaking landscapes—coast, mountain, prairie, desert. The true stories in *A Road of Her Own* are not merely about exhilarating adventures. Often, there is the shadow of danger or heartbreak. In Kim Barnes's "The Clearwater," for example, we are immersed in the experience of a mother with young children who has veered off into an unfamiliar place alongside a familiar Idaho river. After picnicking on the bank of the river with her children and feeling anger over a friend's betrayal dissipate with the flowing water, Barnes suddenly faces the fact that her car is stuck and she may not be able to negotiate the pitched and muddy path back to the highway. Fear fills her heart. In her words, "I felt suddenly and awfully alone, not because of the isolation, but because I was a woman where I should not be, having risked too much for the river."

We shiver with knowing when we read Linda Hasselstrom's gripping "Beulah Land," a story that encapsulates the risks women face when traveling alone. From one setting to another, she is assailed by the comments of men who find her solitary travel both enticing and outrageous. More than once she is questioned thusly: "What are you doing out here by yourself in the middle of the night, anyway?" Clearly her tough South Dakota resoluteness has helped her survive the tens of thousands of miles she's driven over the years: "My preparations for bad weather and bad people have become second nature, but I travel cheerfully as well as alertly."

"Cheerfully" and "alertly" are key expressions here, cohabiting in the emotional and psychological universe of any traveling woman. We will not be deprived of the pleasures of our journeys, nor will we cease to have them. There are picaresque romps down the road for us, as well as escapes and blowing-off-steam episodes to be had. Trips of bonding also await, far more enduring and sane than the Thelma-and-Louise suicide variety. And there are thrilling explorations in nature ahead, trips in which a majestic hawk is seen gliding on a western thermal, blue sky and billowing clouds an ocean above.

When you've traveled all the roads within the pages of this book, I hope you will have glimpsed even more intimately the world we women travelers of the West now claim as our own. I also hope you will share my sense that our mothers, and their mothers before them, in some measure paved these roads for us with their unfulfilled dreams. They deserve our thanks for the lived stories we pass to our own free daughters. We also owe an enormous debt of gratitude to generations of Western women before us. Their legacy of independence in a wild and free land may well have made it inevitable that the Western states would lead the nation in giving women the vote. I like to believe those women still smile on us as we journey along the open highways and solitary back roads of our chosen land.

—Marlene Blessing, 2002

 **Detours**

BRENDA PETERSON

Since childhood, when they were next-door neighbors and best friends, my mother and Aunt Helen plotted a girls' road trip. Now in their seventies, knees in need of replacement, many dreams deferred by wifely duties and mothering, both women at last hit the road west on their first road trip together.

Mother and Aunt Helen packed up Helen's beloved black 1992 Mazda, a car that was to be my family's gift to me. We all met midcontinent in Denver, Colorado.

"It looks just like a Jaguar," my Aunt Helen had told me on the phone when I was debating whether or not to accept my parents' unexpected gift. "Sleek and elegant. And safe."

"You'll love it," my mother took up the car cause. When she talks on the phone cross-country to me in Seattle, she always shouts exuberantly, as if to make up for the distance. "It's so much better than that old rattletrap you're driving."

Mother had bought the Mazda from Aunt Helen with a modest inheritance from her cousin Martha, a woman who worked for TWA and had jetted around the globe, never married.

I was a devoted old-model-Saab girl, happily hugging countless Wild West back roads and switchbacks with a car that had sensual curves of her own—*and* front-wheel drive. More than my hesitation about taking this mobile family inheritance, I struggled over the self-image that might be imposed on me, as if my mother were once again insisting I buy a purple prom dress, a polyester first interview outfit, or a chiffon formal gown for their fiftieth anniversary. Purple is Mother's favorite color. Mine is gray. In a flamboyant family, I've learned to be subversive. My secret plan for the family Mazda was to sell it as soon as I got to Seattle and buy a Saab newer than my 1986 hatchback.

It is telling that my family's idea of a present would also involve a road trip to receive it. We are nomadic. A soundtrack to my childhood was the old white spiritual, "This world is not my home, I'm just a' passing through." Until I finally clung for four years to the same University of California college—against my parents' wishes, I had attended fourteen different schools in sixteen years. I am the only one in my immediate family who has continued to claim the West. They are all finally settled in the south of Florida and northern Virginia.

But the West is where I was born and where my mother, at seventy-two, dreams of returning—at least to summer in a Colorado family cabin—if my seventy-five-year-old father ever does make good on his promise of retiring. My mother always says that her year of college at University of Colorado, Boulder in 1948, where she boldly majored in journalism and minored in theater, was one of the most wonderful years of her life. The other memorable years were 1945–1948, when at sixteen she lied about her age and ran off to work as a telegrapher for the Wabash Cannonball in Iowa.

"The good old Wabash was desperate for station agents because of the war," Mother tells the story with pleasure and conscious pride. "I'd 'decorate the platform,' watching as those trains roared by at eighty miles per hour. I'd look for smoking journals on the train wheels. If I saw smoke, I'd hold my nose and point so the engineer could stop the train and check for fire." She laughs, "Mostly I just got a lot of burns on my hands from smoking cinders while I held up the trains' orders on a wooden V-stick so the engineer and conductor could snatch the orders as they passed the station. Not many women working the rails in those days."

My mother's hands are still dotted with tiny white cinder-scars like constellations. And she still rues the mistake of switching tracks on a train in St. Louis. "You should have seen that engineer's face as he sailed by the station on the *wrong track!*"

I wonder now whether my mother was on the right track when she married at twenty-one, leaving the railroad for my forester father and, nine months later, me. When my parents moved way out west to a remote national forest lookout station in the High Sierras, Mother began writing her first novel, *All Aboard,* about her girls' life running trains. She was pregnant with me.

Sometimes I imagine I can still hear the first sounds reaching me from inside my whooshing watery womb. There is afternoon music, the Mills Brothers, "Downtown Strutters' Ball" and "Mood Indigo"; there are elk bugles and screech hawks at midnight around our forest cabin; and every morning there is the rapid *tap-tapping* of my mother's fast, telegrapher-trained fingers on the typewriter, as if still sending out code to save our country. To keep trains on time. What she was trying to save was the writer in her who would soon be swallowed up by family life. She would give birth to "babies instead of books," as she told me all my childhood. Even now, after years of writing my own books, I glance down at my agile fingers on the keyboard and recognize my mother's hands.

■ ■ ■

When my Mother and Aunt Helen met me in Denver with their elegant car, the Mazda looked as if it was packed for a 1940s prom. "Glenn Miller and Great Hits of the 1940s" audiotapes all over the backseat, makeup cases as big as suitcases, Coca Cola cans, paper towels for spills, and brightly colored hair bonnets to keep their bouffants from blowing in the wind.

"Wait till you hear the sound system," Aunt Helen smiled. "Like being surrounded by an entire orchestra."

I had to grin at stories of my mother and aunt driving over the speed limit, sipping Coca Cola, singing "I'll be down to get you in a taxi, honey!" or "Pack up all your cares and woe, here we go, singing low…" as they roared across flatlands of green Kansas wheat and eastern Colorado plateau, where prairie madness and dustbowls once drove women to the edge.

"So, how was your first road trip together?" I asked them as we all admired the subtle and, yes, sleek lines of Aunt Helen's Mazda. Studying my aunt's car, I abandoned my secret plan to sell it. I surrendered to their gift; in fact, I was overwhelmed by it.

"I'll bet you two just wanted an excuse to finally take your road trip west together," I said. I was so moved I did not know how to thank them.

"Ohhhhh…now…" Mother said with an expression of delight and mischief. I knew that look well—it's how women of her generation kept any sense of self in a "Father Know's Best" world. It is the same "up-to-no-good-honey-can-I-still-please-you" comic grin of Lucille Ball conniving with sidekick Ethel to outwit the dim, good-natured Fred and the bewildered but still princely Ricky Ricardo. All their lives my mother and aunt had longed for this trip; it still had to take the form of family service. "We did get in a glorious day of shopping here in Denver before you arrived," Mother grinned. "Got you a Rocky Mountain elk antler key chain for the new car."

We ran our hands along the lustrous curves of the beautiful sedan. "Don't you think it looks like a race car?" Aunt Helen giggled. I had imagined my aunt driving a sensible luxury gas-guzzler, but I should have known better. Like my mother, Aunt Helen was blessed with jet-black curly hair and wild blue eyes as attentive and wary as any wolf's.

Neighbor girls growing up in a small Missouri town, they would marry brothers from the backwoods, men keenly intelligent and eager to travel the world with pretty girls as their wives. My mother and Aunt Helen have always kept their looks. Aunt Helen took our reunion as an opportunity to advise me on cosmetics and aging skin. She has the unwrinkled face of a much younger woman.

"After a certain age, forget the dabbing," she said, politely noting my fifty-year-old crow's-feet, "you just *slather* on face cream."

"We're having the time of our lives!" Mother enthused as we pulled into Kittredge, Colorado, a mountain tourist trap of a town boasting a Wild West cafe and tavern. "Can't believe we had to wait so long for our girls' road trip."

"Just *all our lives*," Helen said. They exchanged a conspiratorial glance, like escaped prisoners.

"You two are like Thelma and Louise," I teased, "if they'd lived to be grandmothers."

"Didn't they have to drive off a cliff to escape their husbands?" Mother asked.

I smiled. "Why did it take you two so long, anyway?"

"Well," Mother said, "there was always someone else who insisted on riding along. You kids, or husbands, or you name it. We just never were free. Not like you modern gals."

I remember the last road trip Mother had made with women friends. It was in the '60s when she and several churchwomen crashed the Virginia State Southern Baptist convention and took the floor to filibuster for a woman's right to vote in Southern Baptist churches. They succeeded in their quest to see a brief feminine flowering of women's rights in the church. Now forty years later, the same Southern Baptist convention is dominated by far-right fundamentalists, who command women to "submit themselves" to their husbands.

"Stealth-Southern-Baptists," Mother calls them. "Those right-wingers railroaded the convention when the moderates weren't looking. Nothing we could do to stop them."

I wondered about how people, passions, and belief get railroaded or detoured. Certainly my mother and aunt had been "deflected," as the Russian poet Anna Akmathova writes, from their "true course." How was it that a girl who ran off to work underage at the Wabash Cannonball had so changed tracks from wartime adventurer to stay-at-home wife and mother? Who or what had switched the track? I pondered their lifelong wait—a girls' road trip that after fifty years became a grandmothers' road trip.

I glanced around the Wild West cafe and faux gunslinger bar. It was decorated with elk trophies and "Wanted" posters. Bar "girls" dressed in miniskirts with sheriff's posse silver stars on their leather vests took our tame orders. It occurred to me then that in another century, it was not only risky, but rare for women to travel together. Mail-order brides, prostitutes, schoolteachers, settlers were the roles allowed our foremothers in the Western expansion. But before the European settlers, did women travel alone or together in small bands? Were there Native women scouts, geographers, warriors, and explorers before Lewis and Clark followed Sacajawea, whom Western history records as an all-but-forgotten guide for great men?

My Mother, Aunt Helen, and I visited my friend Linda Hogan, a Chickasaw writer in the Rockies. After more tips on skin care, we fell into talking about history and women traveling together. "Of course there were many Native women explorers besides Sacajawea," Linda said. "And warriors like Lozen, Geronimo's brilliant military strategist, scout, and diviner."

I wondered what the West would have become if more women had explored the landscape, naming the rivers, valleys, and mountains, if we had made maps with a feminine geography. Would we have given place-names to so many soldiers or European royalty who had never even seen this New World? I like to believe that women, like many Native people, would have named nature less after great men of war or politics and more after the spirit of the place itself. So instead of naming the great volcanic peaks of the Northwest after Hood and Rainier, they might have called Mount Rainier *Changer* or Puget Sound *Whulge*, its Salish name, which sounds so like the *shushing* waves of this intimate, inland sea.

But the power of naming nature—like recording history itself—has long been denied women's vision. Women traveling together and narrating the West is an untold story, until very recently. This road trip by grandmothers to give a beautiful vehicle to a daughter, who would then drive even farther, to the Northwest, felt historic.

The first thing I had to do was name the new car. *Jaguar.* Or *Jag*, for short. When I slipped behind the wheel, my mother and aunt turned up the stereo six-CD player to "Ghost Riders in the Sky" as the car prowled around mountain switchbacks through Bear Creek canyon. I marveled at its smooth power and subtle steering.

"This *is* a race car, Aunt Helen!"

"Now you see why it's so hard for me to give it up for one of those sensible four-wheel drives in the snow."

Aunt Helen had to part with her car to better navigate black-ice roads on her almost daily trips to visit her 102-year-old father who still worked his own farm. As I said good-bye to my mother and aunt, I felt a poignancy to our parting. Wouldn't it be wonderful if they could both join me on my road trip back to Seattle? We could harmonize to Gershwin songs and stop at hole-in-the-road motels. They could tell me stories of growing up together and how they dreamed of one day traveling out west together. But Mother had to get home for a knee replacement surgery and Aunt Helen, who had already had both her knees replaced, had an ailing husband who needed her care.

"Oh, honey, wish we could join you," Mom said. "But that would be some big detour in our lives."

As I drove them to the airport, it struck me that my whole life, by their terms, was a detour from the typical woman's road. Though I'd had long-term partners, I'd always refused marriage, seeing how it had changed my mother—as an end, not a beginning. I'd chosen not to have children, though I'd helped raised stepchildren. This is my legacy, a mother who detoured from her own writing road, who never took a road trip with her best childhood girlfriend until she was in her seventh decade. A mother who even now still longs to buy a modest mountain cabin in Colorado with her small inheritance.

My mother's road is not the same one I choose to travel. Perhaps those first five years of my life in a Forest Service lookout cabin in the High Sierras, watching my mother slowly put away her writing as she took on the mission of motherhood, perhaps the memory of her typing endless Letters to the Editor, instead of her own book, perhaps the longing in her voice when she told me at the age of seventy-two, "Do you think I can go back to that book on a girl working the Wabash Cannonball I wrote when I was pregnant with you in the Sierras? Do you think at this late age I can still write?" Perhaps all of this in my mother's journey has determined for me a different life's map.

I saw my Mother eagerly memorizing the Colorado red rocks, jagged peaks of her Boulder college days, greening and fragile aspen, purple lupine, and red Indian paintbrush blooming alongside the mountain roads. "Oh," she murmured, "I was so happy here once."

I wondered whether she had ever again been so happy. She would, of course, assure me that she had. But something about that longing in her expression as she breathed in the wild rampage of Bear Creek running spring-time high and the wide horizon of perfect blue and big clouds gave me pause. At the Denver airport, Mother and I said good-bye to Aunt Helen, sending her back to Missouri. Then Mother and I had tea while awaiting an editor and friend Maureen, who was leaving husband and two daughters to come ride back home with me in the new Jaguar-car.

"Western women's road trip?" Maureen had answered without a beat when I'd proposed the journey. "Wahooo!" she said. "No stopping us!"

"I wish I could continue on with y'all," my mother said as we saw her to her plane. "You modern women. You just go wherever you please."

"We stand on your shoulders, Mom," I told her as we embraced. "Thanks again for the beautiful car."

"You take this trip for me," Mother said and held me tighter. "And you tell me all about it. Promise?"

"I've got an assignment to write about," I said. "I'll tell you the story of our trip," I promised.

But as I sat down to write what happened next after we left my mother and aunt at the airport, I looked at my own hands and remembered my mother's typing, her untold story, her unbought Colorado cabin, her inheritance given to her children. I knew that the real story was not what Maureen and I, modern women, did on our continued trip out west, over Rockies and Cascades, through Wyoming high chaparral and Montana wildflower meadows, lingering at the Little Big Horn where Native history was detoured and forced into a footnote of the history of western Manifest Destiny.

The farther I drove west from having met my aunt and mother midcontinent, the closer their own road trip seemed to me. I found evidence of them everywhere, like ghost riders—from the neat Kleenex box in the backseat to the brightly colored afghan in the trunk knitted by my Grandmother Virgie. These women in my family followed me west to a place they have briefly lived and rarely traveled, as if the West belongs to a feminine future long denied them. A future where women took to the road whenever they liked.

I thought this road trip story would lead with Mother and Aunt and then the real part would begin—when my friend and I hit the road. But as in traveling, the real stories are often what we first believe are detours.

If my mother had not switched tracks from her own writing, would I have been born? Would I have become a writer? If my mother had found her mountain cabin when she was a college student in Boulder, would she have met and married my father in Missouri? If she and Aunt Helen had taken that Wild West road trip when they were young girls, would they ever have returned?

"We're going to do this again, Helen and I," my mother assures me still. "We're going to travel out west and look at Colorado mountain property. Who knows? One day we'll all have a family reunion way out there! Will you meet us again, if we do?"

"Wahooo," I assured her. "No stopping us."

The People of the Salmon

NATALIE FOBES

State Route 14 winds next to the water on the Washington side of the Columbia River Gorge. Trucks and cars rumble along the potholed and patched pavement laid over the path walked by explorers Meriwether Lewis and William Clark. On a spring day in 1986, I retraced their footsteps on my way to meet the descendants of the Indians they had encountered more than 180 years before.

I drove past the first sailboarders of the season, enthusiasts from around the world who migrate to the gorge to be challenged by the alliance of gale-force winds and dammed water. About the time their vans arrive in the town of White Salmon, the spring chinook make their way up the rivers. In the old days, the Indians say, the appearance of swallows and gulls heralded the return of the life-giving salmon. Today it's the sailboarders and biologists.

Now is the time for many Yakama Indians to load poled nets atop their Chevys and Fords and return to the Klickitat River to fish in the ways of their ancestors.

I was nervous. I wasn't sure how I would be received by the Indians. After the court battles of the seventies resulted in affirming tribal fishing rights, mistrust had heightened between Indian and non-Indian fisherman during the court battles over tribal fishing rights. Two years before, a newspaper photographer friend of mine had been "encouraged" to leave the Klickitat Canyon by the barrel of a fisherman's shotgun. I wasn't working on a story for a newspaper or magazine. I was working on my own with a grant from a journalistic foundation. I couldn't promise the Indians that their photographs, words, and stories would ever be published. I could only promise them that I wanted to listen and I wanted to learn.

I almost missed the turn to the canyon. The road was a couple of ruts leading into heavy brush. My car bottomed out repeatedly for the next mile, and branches scraped its sides. Until I saw the rusty pickups lining the dusty pullout, I wasn't even sure I was on the right road.

I pulled in beside a Chevy. Beyond the near-empty parking lot littered with pop cans, boulders and ankle-breaking rocks jumbled into cliffs. Beyond them, the water of the Klickitat blasted through an opening maybe fifteen yards wide. Corroded cables held weathered wood scaffolds over the falls. Heat waves radiated from the rocks. Sweat popped from my pores. A crow sat on a branch, its black eyes bobblin'. It seemed to laugh at me. I wanted to go home.

Across the river an old man stood alone on one of the platforms hung high above the river. He dragged his dipnet upstream through the rapids. On the upswing, he saw me. I waved. He watched. I smiled. He motioned toward a two-by-three-foot plywood box hung with pulleys from a cable strung across the river. I tried not to look down as he pulled me to the other side. As I jumped out, a camera slipped from my shoulder. He caught it and he smiled.

We didn't say much that first afternoon. I told him a little about me. Leonard Dave Sr. told me a little about fishing. We watched the swallows wing through the canyon. We watched the salmon break through the foam at the base of the falls. We watched the sun journey across the sky.

Dusk and night are the best times to fish, Leonard told me as the scaffolds filled with fishermen. The salmon can't see your shadow and they can't see the net.

It's also a dangerous time to fish. On moonless nights, a man can easily walk off the platform's edge. If he is fortunate, the rope tied around his waist holds until his buddies can pull him back up. Sure, he might be embarrassed by the story of him dangling like a bug over the water as it is retold for weeks, months, or even years. But he is alive.

If he is not lucky, his body may turn up in a gillnet downstream. Most every season, fishermen are lost to the river, Leonard told me. Some might have had alcohol or drugs clouding their vision. For others, it was just their time, he said.

Leonard's son and namesake climbs onto the platform twenty feet above the rapids. Dipnet fishing is better suited to a young man's body. The weight of the net and the bent-over position cause back muscles to spasm and arms to shake. Very few women fish this way, and I understand why. After months of weight training I could hardly lift the pole.

Leonard Jr. caresses the stream bottom with his thirty-four-foot dipnet, pulling hand under hand, pushing hand over hand, pacing five steps from one end of the platform to the other. He searches the bottom. Downstream from the falls, beneath the foam, between the rocks and out of the current are the hidey-holes where salmon rest.

Years of fishing this same spot have taught him the location of those rocks. He tries not to hit them: The sound will scare the salmon. Leonard Jr. swings the net from the water and repositions it a few yards downstream and to the left. He tries to keep the net behind the fish; the sight will cause the salmon to bolt. During the peak of the season, he says, a man is lucky to get a salmon once every twenty or thirty tries. During the rest of the season, he's lucky to get one every couple hours. It is the end of the season and luck has left the canyon.

The last light fades from the sky. The rush of the river swallows up all other sound. The Yakamas fish. Some are talking; I can see their lips move. Some are smoking; it curls around their baseball caps. The fishermen become ghost-shadow forms, slow-dancing with their poles. Now and again the sound of a salmon fighting in a steel-meshed net somehow punctures the river roar. And sometime near midnight, the rocks give up the day's warmth. From then until dawn, the river's coolness claims the valley's air as its own.

"Salmon was a way of life, my ancestor's way," Leonard Sr. says quietly. "My parents, my grandparents, and their grandparents have always fished here. If some of these old trees standing here, if some of these big rocks could only talk," he says, "many a story could be told. Things that happened, ancient things, parts of history," he continues. "I'd sure like to hear it all myself.

"The trees and rocks would speak of an old way of life. Of respect for the Creator's gifts. Of the abundance of salmon and the absence of hunger if the Creator's rules were followed. Of the Indians using every fishing technique we use today." But just as steel wire replaced animal sinew in the nets, Indian life changed.

The vast number of salmon astounded and frustrated the first European explorers. One complained that the splashing of migrating salmon kept him awake at night. Another wrote that his horse refused to cross a stream because its belly was constantly bumped by thirty-pound fish. Wilbur Slokish Jr., a Klickitat River fisherman, told me of the time the Lewis and Clark Expedition came to his ancestors' village. It was a story passed down through the generations, a tale long told and long enjoyed within his family.

"The villagers welcomed the expedition members with songs, dances, and a great feast worthy of a visiting chief," Wilbur said. "The women worked especially hard to prepare the freshly caught salmon. When the fish was finally presented to the honored guests, the explorers shook their heads. Much to the amazement of the villagers, the explorers pointed instead to the villagers' dogs."

Wilbur shook his head as we laughed. "Can you imagine?" he asked. "They wanted to eat the dogs."

What I would have given to have seen the expressions on the faces of the Indian hosts and heard the words that passed among them as they discussed the explorers' request. Did their desire to be good hosts overcome their sense that the white guys were crazy? Wilbur wasn't sure how it worked out. He didn't know if they cooked the dogs. After I wiped away my tears of laughter, I was struck by the sense of immediacy with which Wilbur had told the story. It was as if it happened just a few years ago and not at the beginning of the nineteenth century.

■ ■ ■

On a trip a few years later, I set up my tent in a campground on the Oregon shore of the Columbia River. Behind me semi-trucks and RVs blasted by on Interstate 84. Before me, The Dalles Dam rose from the still water of its reservoir. Just as I couldn't see the end of the freeway, I couldn't see the end of the reservoir. Hard to believe and sad to think that drowned under the reservoir was one of the greatest geographical and cultural sites in the West.

Celilo Falls marked one end of an eight-mile-long canyon where the Columbia was forced into a narrow channel full of eddies and islands. The Indians hung scaffolds from the rocks to dipnet and spear adult salmon returning to their spawning grounds upriver.

The Indians called it Wyam, which translates as "Echo of Falling Water" or "Sound of Water Upon the Rocks." It was the center of trade for Northwest Indians. Each spring, tribes traveled from the shores of the Pacific Ocean, from the mountains of the Cascades and Olympics, from the plains of what are now Washington, Oregon, Montana, and Idaho. They came by canoe. They came by horseback and they came by foot to fish, to trade oysters, clams, roots, and skins, and to talk. If you were rich, you brought all you could afford to trade. If you were poor, you brought what you could. Overseeing the commerce were the flat-headed Chinook Indians who developed a 300-word jargon used in negotiations. (The Chinook flattened their heads by placing padded boards against the foreheads of their infants. The goal was a wedge-shaped head that sloped back from the eyebrows.)

What a sight it must have been. Of all the places I wish I could have seen before the settlers came, of all the cultures I wish I had known, this is the one that tops my list. Celilo draws me. It haunts me. It saddens me to know it is gone forever.

A few years back, there was a proposal to draw down the reservoir and expose Celilo Falls. When I heard about the plan, I felt like someone had hit me in the stomach. Exposing this holy place would be like digging up the bones of my mother long after she was buried. I know the spirit, and I remember it as if with some bit of flesh-knowledge: the fishermen fishing from rocks or scaffolds, giving thanks for every salmon they pull in; the children lying on their bellies over still pools of water, holding lines with carved bone hooks; women, babies strapped to their backs, kneeling over the fresh catch of fish, stripping the roe and splitting the flesh with their bone or slate knives. I am there on the bank, the sun radiating into my skin, the sweat drying on my face.

I see the racks full of split crimson salmon drying in the wind and in the smoke of the fires. I hear the staked salmon's oil spitting into the flames as it cooks. I taste the hot flesh. And I feel the satisfaction of a full belly after a hard day's work.

As I slipped into sleep, the roar of the interstate gave way to the spirit song of the ages-old river. The song that reunites all who listen with those who have come before.

My vision cleared with the harsh light of morning and the bawling of kids in the RV next to my tent. The monolithic concrete, steel, and cabled Dalles Dam has turned Celilo Falls into a distant dream. Today the canyon lies under a hundred feet of water that backed up when the dam was completed in the fifties. Newspaper reports of the day describe the tribes' last longhouse ceremony, a memorial service attended by scores of Indians. They were all there, standing on the same bluff where I was decades later—the Wishrams, the Wascos, the Wyams, the Yakamas, the Klickitats, the Nez Perce, the Warm Springs, and the Colvilles—watching as the dam's last gate closed.

The Columbia roared in rebellion. It assaulted the man-made barrier. Again and again it attacked, until the roar of the waves drowned out all other sound. A small wave grew at the base of the dam, became a wall of water, and then raced upstream.

The newspapers describe the cheers of the non-Native onlookers and the silence of the Indians as the water approached Celilo Falls. They tell of the moments the rapids refused to submit to the reservoir. And they report that as the water finally drowned Celilo Falls, tribal leaders turned their backs.

■ ■ ■

In 1865 and 1866, the Indians signed eleven treaties with Washington Territorial Governor Isaac Stevens. The treaties did not give rights to the Indians as most people think. The Indians gave limited rights to the settlers. The elders were adamant that the tribes reserved the right of food gathering. They insisted on clauses upholding their exclusive right to fish on their reservation's waters as well as "the right of taking fish, at all usual and accustomed grounds and stations…in common with all citizens of the Territory." Those words assumed critical importance in court decisions nearly 120 years later.

During the intervening years, almost everything changed.

Indian fishing grounds were increasingly used by non-Indian sport and commercial fishermen. Commercial nets stretched from bank to bank on some rivers. Traps and wheels worked with deadly efficiency until they were outlawed in the late 1930s. Watersheds were logged and mined. Rivers were dammed. Towns grew into cities. The number of Indian fishermen plummeted. Fewer fish returned to most rivers. On others, no salmon returned.

The United States, acting as trustee for several tribes, sued Washington State in 1970, seeking reactivation of Indian treaty fishing rights. At that time, Indians caught only 5 percent of the harvestable fish and owned less than 1 percent of the state's 6,000 commercial fishing licenses.

For more than three months, U.S. District Judge George Boldt heard testimony from anthropologists, biologists, fisheries managers and tribal leaders about the importance of salmon to the Indians, the biology of the fish and commercial and sport fisheries. Tension built as the entire Northwest fishing community—both Native and non-Native—awaited his decision.

Most old-timer fishermen can remember what they were doing on February 12, 1974. Some were repairing nets for the upcoming season, others were working on their boats, a few were just hanging out at home. They remember the swirl of emotions and thoughts they had as they got the news from the radio, the television, or an old fishing buddy. The moment is captured like a still photo in their memory because that was the day their world imploded.

On that day, Boldt presented his decision: The twenty tribes that had signed the original treaties were entitled to half the harvestable return of salmon at all their historic fishing areas. The environment of streams running through their reservations could not be impinged. This edict was to receive priority second only to the conservation of the salmon.

Boldt knew the treaties had been written in English and translated into the 300-word trading jargon of the Chinook. He surmised that Governor Stevens's aides certainly knew the meaning of the key phrase "in common." So Boldt consulted dictionaries from the 1860s and found "in common" defined as "shared equally…with many." Boldt determined that the fish should be divided equally among treaty tribes and non-Native fishermen.

Few fishermen were interested in the finer points of how Boldt reached his decision. The salmon war had begun. Seasons closed. Tempers flared. Boats were rammed and set on fire. During confrontations between treaty and non-Native fishermen, people on both sides were threatened, beaten up, and, in one case, shot. The state's Department of Fisheries and Department of Game refused to comply with the decision and appealed. Eight times, treaty fishing rights were appealed, including twice before the U.S. Supreme Court. Eight times those rights were upheld.

The state agencies faced a daunting task. In order to divide the fish as ordered by the court, they had to know how many salmon returned to Washington State rivers. The agencies didn't have a clue. Fishing seasons had been determined not on biological data but on the number of days the season had been open in prior years.

Agency biologists were shocked when they finally tallied the size of the runs. Almost all had declined precipitously and some had become extinct. Even the most historically productive river in the state, the Columbia, was a disaster. In 1884, as many as 16 million salmon fought their way through the rapids. In 1984, only 2.5 million returned. The state agencies set up to protect the resource had contributed to the dramatic decline of salmon runs.

"The best thing that happened to the resource was the Boldt decision," former Yakama Nation biologist Larry Wasserman told me. "The state was finally forced to become accountable for the salmon." Washington Department of Fisheries and Game spokesman Tony Floor, himself a veteran of the salmon wars, agreed. "It was the first turning point in bringing responsible management back to Washington State."

In the years since the Boldt decision, the number of Indian fishermen has doubled, while the number of non-Indian fishermen has declined by more than a third. Treaty catches finally reached the 50 percent level in 1988 and are higher on some rivers. And while tribal and state leaders have been forced to form a sometimes easy, sometimes uneasy alliance, anger on both sides still runs deep.

"Why do we have to pay for the sins of our forebears?" a non-Native fishermen asked me in 1998 while leaning on the bow of his troller. A couple years before, he had fished from April to October. This year he fished only five days and didn't even make enough money to pay for his diesel fuel.

He was not the only one hit hard by the short season. Every third boat tied to the dock at Seattle's Fishermen's Terminal had either a bright orange "for sale" sign or a marshal's auction notice posted in the window. In some towns, he told me, the joke was that a person could have the choice of a toaster or a fishing boat when he opens a new account at the local bank.

"Our livelihood has been destroyed," he said. "We have to take second jobs to make ends meet. Our communities are dying. Our traditional way of life is gone," he said.

"Fishing regulations are chipping away at our seasons," one Yakama Indian told me. "These restrictions are a form of genocide," he said. "People accuse the Indians of not looking toward the future," he continued, "of not saving money in the bank or taking out insurance or making retirement plans. But we did plan ahead," he told me. "The Indian people preserved the earth and her creatures for future generations. Hundreds of years ago our ancestors were planning ahead for you and for me so there would be a world for all of us."

■ ■ ■

Rain sputtered through the ventilation holes cut in the roof of the Tulalip longhouse near Marysville, Washington. Flames from three cedar fires turned the drops into eye-watering smoke. I pushed the wet hair from my forehead and warmed my hands over one of the fires. It was June of 1988 and it had been a long time since I had visited a house of worship, I thought. Within a few hours, I would be joined by more than 200 people, Indian and non-Indian alike, to celebrate the return of the salmon.

The elders of the Tulalip Tribe had felt that something of their culture had been lost. They had resurrected their ancient ceremony eleven years before, a ceremony that thanked the Creator and his creation—the salmon. Traditionally participants would eat of one salmon, but realities of the modern world dictate that many additional salmon would be brought from Coastal tribes. But the spirit of the gathering, the prayers, and the songs, date back hundreds of years.

In the old days, every family, every village, every band around the Pacific Rim believed the salmon was a sacred gift from the Creator. The stories these Native peoples tell about the salmon are remarkably similar. The names change but the theme remains the same.

In one legend, the salmon people lived in a beautiful mansion at the bottom of the ocean under the horizon where the sea meets the sky. Each year these spirit people would don their fish costumes and get ready to return to the rivers to sacrifice themselves for mankind. But first they would send a chief or scout to make sure the Indians still honored the salmon.

The first fish caught would be wrapped in cedar boughs and laid on a litter. Everyone in the village would dance, drum, and sing a welcome. The arrival of the first salmon meant life to the Indians; it was a celebration of thanksgiving, rebirth, and renewal.

No matter how many people were at the feast, all shared the first salmon's flesh. When it was finished, the villagers put the salmon skeleton back into the water. They hoped it would return to the underwater mansion to lead the rest of the salmon people to the stream.

The sound of a footstep on the dirt floor pulled me back to the present. My flame-blinded eyes slowly adjusted and I saw Raymond Moses sitting on the bleachers, highlighted in the swirling smoke by a shaft of light.

Raymond was the fire keeper of the longhouse and had been tending the fires since long before dawn. He welcomed me with a nod, then began tuning his drum, quietly at first, stopping to listen to the echoing tone of the stretched skin and adjusting the rawhide to tighten it. Finally he began a beat as steady as the rain.

I know I picked up my cameras. I know I worried about my exposure in the dark of the longhouse. I know I photographed him—I have the photographs to prove it. But my thoughts had scattered like a dream in the morning, until I was left with the warmth of knowing his soul.

I have no idea how long we floated on the notes from the drum. He asked to stop a couple times. I remember I pleaded with him to continue, for his drumming was filling the air with the song of life. On the edge of his song, new voices, new drums joined in. Their melodies embraced Raymond's, making it stronger, bolder.

The power of the song resonated through the longhouse. The longhouse amplified that power. We were insignificant. We were omnipotent. We were nothing and we were everything. And then, with no warning, the music stopped.

Replacing it was a quiet, a peace, an absence of sound, a void. I was exhausted. My heart was racing and my breathing shallow. I knew had been part of something, something unlike anything I had experienced before. Something I can't explain and seldom talk about with any but my closest friends.

I had journeyed into a place where there was no time. I had been led down a path that had no beginning, middle, or end. For a few moments (or was it a few days?), I had felt—no, believed—in the oneness of all creation. I had touched the energy that lies just outside the fires' circle of light. I had taken a step beyond, and I could never go back to who I was before I walked into that other world.

I've often wondered whether Leonard Dave Sr. foresaw what would happen to me in the course of this story. Years have passed since the time we sat on the rocks and watched the world revolve around the day. I remember what he said when I told him I had to go. And I remember the seriousness with which he spoke. "You can't leave now," he said. "You are one of us."

I remember the promise I made. A promise I have kept. Each spring when the days lengthen and the swallows return and the chinook salmon make their way up the rivers, I remember the stories of the People of the Salmon.

Rain in the Desert

PAULETTE JILES

The morning I left for the Dry Devil's River, a light rain started up. My husband helped me load the pickup with my camping equipment.

He said, "Polly, this is going to get a lot heavier. I think you should wait a day."

But I couldn't wait a day: the city life was driving me crazy and I wanted to get out to the wild places. Jim and I are restoring an 1883 stone house in the San Antonio Historic District, which means we are downtown, and the soundscape is a riotous weave of sirens, trains, and traffic helicopters. I had planned to camp out for two weeks at the most remote State Natural Area in Texas, on the Dry Devil's River, and I was on my way. The Dry Devil's River was about 150 miles west and south of San Antonio and I wanted to get there early and set up camp before dark. I put my notebooks and papers in the cab with me, and everything else in the bed of the pickup, kissed Jim good-bye, and started out, despite his misgivings. Then as I was driving out of San Antonio, it began to rain as heavily as I have ever seen it rain.

It had been a rainy spring and the ground was already saturated. By the time I got to the outskirts of the city, every major highway into San Antonio was flooded. Highway 10, which I was heading westward on, flooded at Camp Bullis Road where Leon Creek had come over its banks. Highways 281 and 90 were also flooded. I couldn't have turned back if I wanted to.

I kept thinking it had to slow down sometime. Thirty-two miles northwestward on Highway 10, I came to the immense highway cuts just outside of Kerrville. Ahead, I saw Texas State Patrol cars with their lights flashing and slowed down. In the downpour, a rockfall of limestone boulders had spilled across the road and struck a small car. The patrolmen in their Stetsons and yellow slickers were talking to the driver and his passenger. I could see they weren't hurt, just wet and scared. After that, whenever I could, I drove in the middle of the highway as I came through the deeper cuts, thinking I might well be next.

The landscape changed as I drove west on Highway 10—as much as I could see of it through the downpour. The live oaks and cedar of the hill country gave way to smaller, scrubbier growth: mesquite, Spanish sword, the tough cedar elms. Rain swept over the landscape and washed it with pale watercolors. Eighteen-wheelers roared past me in wild waves of spray. I pulled over at a truck stop in Sonora and called Jim to tell him I was all right. I had to nearly shout over the noise of trucks and rain, but as we talked the intensity of the downpour began to lessen. The storm began to stalk off over the eastern horizon in long, separated columns.

Sonora is a small town on Highway 10, about 116 miles from San Antonio. This was where I was to leave Highway 10, a major four-lane, and turn south on 277. Highway 277 runs ninety miles straight south from Sonora to the border town of Del Río, and it is one of the loneliest stretches of highway in the world. Which is why I love it. It is a small two-lane highway used mostly by ranchers, and the Dry Devil's River camping place was about sixty miles south on 277, halfway between Del Río and Sonora.

However, there was a good chance that portions of it were now under water from the massive rains. As I walked out of the truck stop, I saw a car with a Coahuila, Mexico, license plate, so I knew the travelers had driven up Highway 277 from Del Río and Mexico. I ran over to them and made a "roll down your window" gesture. The driver rolled the window down and nodded inquiringly at me.

"Está inundado la carretera a Del Río?"

"Está bien, está bien, no problema! Se puede pasar!"

So I turned south on 277, the little two-lane highway that dipped and rolled through the tumbled semidesert landscape. The rain had now stopped completely, but in places I was driving through shallow standing water. I threw up wings of water on either side of my truck. I was the only person on the highway and I felt wonderful.

About halfway to the State Natural Area, a very long, substantial bridge has been built at the place where the highway runs alongside the normally dry Dry Devil for those rare times when it does flood. Crossing the bridge, I saw a most wonderful sight: the broad valley of the Dry Devil's River was entirely under water. A sheet of shining water slid along under the mesquite trees, around the Spanish sword. It looked as if the desert floor were plated with some sort of mercurial metal. After the bridge, the highway ran to one side of the valley at a higher level, and I had to stop and look at the flood for a long time. I knew it would be years before I saw anything like this again.

Ten miles farther on, I saw the sign for the entrance to the Dry Devil's River State Natural Area. The sign reads "Dolan Creek" and it is a dirt road. A mile or so down this dirt road, a park ranger waved me down.

"There's no way in," he said. "It's flooded out the road. You can't get across the river, but it will be down by tomorrow."

"Is there anyplace to stay around here, then?" I asked. "A motel or something?"

The ranger answered, "No, not unless you go all the way to Sonora or on down to Del Río. Me and my wife have started up that little store at Loma Alta back on the highway to Del Río. At least go back there and check in. Let her know which way you're going."

We introduced ourselves. He said their names were Evan and Marsha, and they lived at Loma Alta, and the resident rangers in the park were Paula and Bill.

I drove back down the dirt road to Highway 277, and turned south for a couple of miles. I passed a place that the map said was a little town called Vinegaroon, but that was actually an abandoned stone building and a sign saying *Vinegaroon*. Then I came to what the map said was a town called Loma Alta.

Loma Alta consists of a store, gas station, and the house where the ranger and his wife live when he's not on duty at the Dry Devil's River. It is the only gas station and store on the long stretch between Del Río and Sonora, and it is much frequented by ranchers and ranch hands. When I pulled in, I could see behind the store a row of rooms from an abandoned motel.

I introduced myself to Marsha and told her I had come to camp out at the Dry Devil, but couldn't get across the road until tomorrow. Marsha was a cheerful woman, with brown hair and a breezy way of making everyone who walked into the store feel welcome. She invited me to be seated at the little table in the store, where local people came to drink beer and eat tamales after they gassed up.

"I'd hate to drive all the way back to Sonora and stay in a motel and then drive back down here tomorrow morning," I said.

"We were thinking of trying to get that old motel behind this place fixed up and be able to offer people rooms," she responded, "but we haven't even got started on them."

"Well, I don't mind, I could stay there."

"But there's nothing in those rooms!" she said.

"I have everything," I said. "I have my airbed, battery lamp, propane cooker. I mean I was going to camp out anyway. It's too late to go back to Sonora or Del Río."

She laughed. "Hey, it's yours. And free, too."

I sat up that evening in the little store with Marsha and group of *vaqueros,* ranch hands from the area, all Mexican. They had come to buy beer and visit, to leave the isolated ranches where they worked. They needed beer, cheese, conversation, storytelling. They were men of the outdoors, with hands as hard as petrified wood, and their spurs jingled on the concrete floor. They had all come from across the river, from northern Coahuila. They kept asking me to translate for Marsha, but after a while I couldn't translate fast enough. Instead, I just sat and listened and laughed at their stories of wild horses and broken-down pickups, advice on where to buy a good hat in Villa Acuna, where to swim a horse across the Río Grande.

"Who can sing a song?" I asked. "Something that tells a story."

The oldest one had iron-gray hair and a battered straw cowboy hat, a pink shirt. The other men, who were all younger, sat back and looked at him. They gestured toward him as their elder, the man who knew all the words to the ballads. He threw his arms wide and sang,

> *Era su primera carrera*
> *La cosa estaba difícil*
> *De atinar una quiniela,*
> *Los dos fueron compañeros*
> *Criados en la misma tierra*
> *Rancho de Chapa Varela...*

It was one of the songs of Leonardo Yañez "El Nano," the border bal-ladeer. How good it was to hear his songs here in this remote place, around a table full of beery vaqueros, with the rain drawing off across the Dry Devil's River in scattering, moonlit clouds. I slept well that night in the abandoned motel. The next morning Marsha wouldn't hear of any payment.

She said, "Jeez, I should pay you for doing all the translating!"

She called Evan on his cell phone and he told her the river was down enough for my pickup to cross, so I waved good-bye and went on.

In a day, all that water had disappeared.

I drove to the ranger's office and paid up for two weeks of camping, and I met the resident ranger and his wife, Bill and Paula. She said, "I have never known anybody to come here and camp and stay for two weeks!"

"First time for everything," I said.

The two weeks I spent at the Dry Devil's River were dreamlike. Because of the rain, everything flowered. The cenizo bushes burst out in vermilion, the desert willow was covered in its orchid-like blooms, and the prickly pear was crowned with yellow and claret flowers. In the heat of the day I stayed in the shade of the tent, and in the cool mornings and evenings I wrote and read and listened to the radio or just to the silence.

The ranger's wife invited me to go with her in the Parks Department Land Rover to a remote wet-weather pool called José María Springs; the water was so clear and had risen so suddenly that at the bottom of the canyon pool brown-eyed susans still waved in the transparent currents. Paula and I jumped into the water at high noon when the temperature was more than a hundred degrees. It was almost like falling through blue air.

This rolling country was rocky, covered with low brush, except in the valley of the Devil's River, several miles away. Unlike the Dry Devil, the Devil's River ran year-around from a group of springs up toward Sonora. Paula and I drove down there, and as we came into the valley of the Devil's River, I suddenly found myself in the tropics: palms, wild cane, lush grasses, and indigo buntings.

At night I lay and watched out the tent screens as millions of fireflies swam among the cactus blossoms. I wrote by hand by the light of the battery lamp, and sometimes listened to the radio. My favorite program was, and still is, *El Rancherito del Aire* from Villa Acuna, across the river from Del Río. It's a radio station I can pick up almost anywhere in West Texas, and on all my camping trips I listen to it to find out what time it is (I don't carry a clock or a watch) and for good *ranchero* music. Sometimes the announcer would tell me it was two in the morning, while overhead the stars were brilliant right down to the horizon. Jackrabbits came to play among the cenizo bushes every evening at dusk. They actually danced standing up.

While I was encamped, a group of biology students and their professors arrived to look for scorpions. I was amazed at the amount of scorpions found, just around the campground.

"Oh, they usually won't bother you if you don't bother them," a student told me. "Just be sure to shake your shoes out every morning. Are you really staying out here for two weeks? We've never stayed for more than a few days!"

When life gets too crowded and hectic, when the news is terrible and I have heard one too many sirens streaking down Pereida Street in San Antonio, I think of Loma Alta, and of a vaquero singing the ballad of the poor boy who won the race on his lean and fragile colt. I picture the mouse-colored jackrabbits dancing among the cenizo, and fireflies lighting up the gold and burgundy cactus flowers. It's a place and a time I keep in my heart.

 **One Road**

PEGGY SHUMAKER

In 1985, I drove solo from Arizona to Alaska, to take a one-year job in Fairbanks. This is an excerpt from a longer essay.

I do my interviews over the phone and decide to trade four jobs in Arizona for one in Alaska. The one I choose is tenuous—a one-year sabbatical replacement, teaching at University of Alaska, Fairbanks—but I'll get paid for reading books and talking about them, for helping people with poems, stories, essays. Utter luxury.

I cram the essentials into my Honda and set out to drive solo from Arizona to Alaska. My friend Karla's shaken, scared for me. "Take someone with you," she worries.

"I want to go alone," I say. "Really."

"Take a gun," she insists.

"Not a chance," I say.

She gives me a can of mace as a going-away present.

My friends Tito and Lupita make me promise to call every night, so they can chart my journey, or so they can tell the Mounties where to start looking.

It's only a one-year job, no guarantee of anything beyond. But I see it as a chance to be a citizen of a wider world, a world beyond everything I've known.

I don't know a soul in Alaska. That means nobody knows my story, or my stories. They won't correct, can't add their slants, don't have any idea what roles I've played up till now. I can reveal whatever I want to, whenever I want to. I can write this new draft on a clean sheet of paper.

And the people I meet will help shape the story.

■ ■ ■

Copious good-byes. The worst are my nieces, their fierce marsupial hugs.

I head out for my grandmother's house in El Cajon, California. It's not so strange that just before I launch myself into the unknown, I aim for the one person who links me most closely to my past.

August 9, 1985. Heat rises in waves over pavement. I tuck a spray bottle beside my ankles and mist my feet when heat closes in. A Chinese poet says, "Think not that everything is too familiar" and goes on to describe that at the moment of death, we will each touch our own hair and body and wonder whose it is. Right now I feel oven air blasting past me, my skin salted tight, Ruben Blades and Son del Solar, hot salsa on the cassette deck.

I know this desert. We traveled it almost every year of my growing up. But this time I watch it carefully, another good-bye. The ocotillo's bare now, the saguaro sunken into its pleats. I watch two hawks and two turkey buzzards.

An eighteen-wheeler pulls up parallel. The driver holds up a scrawled sign: "Open your legs!" He waggles his tongue. I brake, but he stays with me. I speed up, but my four cylinders are no match for his diesel big rig. He stays parallel, leering. I feel my stomach turn. There's no town for miles, no respite. I smile and point to the next exit. He's salivating. I let him go first, wait for the come-cry of his jake brakes. Then I gun it. He can't react fast enough to catch me. For the next hour I watch my mirrors, knowing what's behind me.

It never occurs to me to reach for the mace.

■ ■ ■

Eight hours, through the desert, over the boulder-strewn Jacumbas, coasting down into The Box, El Cajon, walled in by mountains. In 1942 my grandparents bought a couple of acres and a little white house across from a dairy. Then they built the brown house and rented out the white one. My grandfather never made peace with his decision to sell the back part of the land, where chicken coops and walnut trees made way for apartment buildings. The neighborhood gobbled up pastures and barns until houses sprouted everywhere.

Hungry, hot, weary, I pull up into the shade of the mulberry tree my grandpa planted before I was born. We have pictures of each of the cousins roosting in that tree. I shower, cool down.

Grandma Moen is fretful but doesn't want to say so. Instead she talks about the morning my family left for Arizona, left from next door and drove to a place nobody'd been. I take down from her wall the picture she snapped that morning—my dad, impatient and chafing; my mom, tired already. I'm five, holding the leash of our boxer dog, Pepi. The little kids are messing around, Susie and Johnny arguing, Ginny flicking one of those wheels that zips inside, outside a long metal U, up and down, not going anywhere, but making good time. I remember asking my mom if the people in Arizona would speak English.

My grandma tells me how worried she was. My mom might have an asthma attack and she'd be alone with us kids in Tucson, far away where my grandma couldn't help her. Even then Grandma could predict that my mom would spend her marriage mostly solo.

My grandma says, guilty, "I advised her to stay in that marriage, for you kids."

I tell her, "Maybe you can let that go now." The marriage was no picnic, for anybody, but my mom has been dead now for sixteen years. "Depends, though. You get a bigger kick out of guilt or absolution?" Grandma smiles then and tucks away her sorrow in its special place.

When the time comes, we take deep breaths. Grandma walks me out, and we hold each other. I know she doesn't think this is a good idea, my going alone. Maybe she doesn't think my going so far away is exactly wise. But she never tries to make me somebody I'm not. Instead, she seems endlessly fascinated by the person I keep becoming, even when that person distresses her.

How will we stay close?

How do we manage to love those we love and still create our lives?

Her love is my prime example.

■ ■ ■

August 12. The Honda's odometer turns 100,000.

I think about the cost of staying.

My mom stayed. At first. She and my dad were spectacularly mismatched, but she stayed stubborn and tried to force him to develop some family feeling. He was always running away, from his religious-zealot father, from the cacophony of four kids.

My mother's life, one of those little wheels that zips inside, outside a long metal U, up and down, not going anywhere but making good time. Then he asked for a divorce, and she told her mother, "This may be the last thing I can give him."

My mother took up smoking, wheezing till her lips turned blue. She'd take me with her in the car when she had an asthma attack, so I could talk if she couldn't. If she blacked out, it was my job to keep us from crashing.

She worked two jobs and came home one night not quite in this world. She wasn't drunk; she was calm. She woke me (2:30 on a school night, damn) and took me outside to see the Toyota Land Cruiser she'd aimed directly into a sturdy palo verde. You could still see bean pods, green bark, feathery leaves stuck in the crush of canvas and metal. "Never took me anywhere I wanted to go," she said. The court had ordered my father to provide us transportation. A drafty four-wheel drive with no heat or air was his solution. My mom was eerie for three days. Then she stood up under an open cabinet, whacked her hard head, drew blood again. She couldn't stop crying. I couldn't help her. I just kept the little kids out of her way, tucked her in, brought her medicine. She had no clue how to get over the shattered glass of her life, no clue how to travel landscapes she never chose.

I question my own motives, hourly. Am I running, like my dad? Whenever love comes into it, I'm skittish and unsure. I can offer it. I have lots of trouble accepting it and all the obligations implicit in the bonds it forms. So unsettled, unsettling, the sense of being out of control. Flashes of panic not all that different from flashes of passion. If it were my job to hand out free samples of confusion, they wouldn't even need to supply me with stock.

August 14, Sacramento. Near the capitol building, monumental trees. One gargantuan ponderosa pine has to be guyed up so its own weight won't pull it over. I wonder about growing so large you can't sustain yourself.

August 15, to Portland. Mount Shasta! Stunning under its glaciers. Those are the first glaciers I've ever seen. That they're turquoise is news to me. Light rain at twilight, a gorgeous misty passage. Ashland is appealing. I picture Lear and Cordelia there.

August 16, Seattle. I arrive early at a friend of a friend's group house, near Green Lake. Negotiate very narrow, steep streets with planter circles barricading each intersection. Nobody home, so I read May Sarton's *Journal of Solitude.* Her journey staying home is not so different from mine going far away. Each trek ultimately leads inward. Sarton writes of the intensity of feelings magnified by solitude. I keep thinking, *I know this.*

Whenever I'm depressed, I think of Wayne. When it's most acute, my stomach twists about Wayne and Cynthia, how when we split, he chose a woman with no job, no education, no prospects, and immediately set about convincing her to make children. Tito says, "Maybe he just needed a break from you." Of course, and most of what they share has nothing to do with me. But it's galling. I indulge in tire-slashing fantasies, her beater hissing down into a low rider, rusting on its rims.

I think of how wrong they are as a couple, and worry about how Wayne will suffer. Maybe even more than he has by loving me.

■ ■ ■

At Marmot Mountain Works in Bellevue, I purchase a fabulous slinky green down sleeping bag for $156. It'll be my bed when I get to Alaska. Also, it'll be covers while I'm on the ferry. I didn't reserve a stateroom. It cost too much, and besides, I want to talk to people.

Seattle folks tell me stories of the Alaska Highway—strafed windshields, seven flat tires in two days. I worry about the story where six inches of mud oozes over the floorboards, the corduroy road a mosquito bog.

August 17. Up early, north into farmlands and orchards. A strong sense of leaving home as I near the border. I'm glad I didn't fly. I think stepping off a plane would never have given me this sense of vastness.

At the Canadian border, a girl asks me a few questions, hands me a green card, and tells me to park and go upstairs. I look down at my Artists in Education T-shirt, ripped at the neck, and realize that I have caused myself a few hassles. Upstairs, the man asks to see my driver's license, my cash ($200), my credit cards. He asks where I have worked, where I am going to work, whether my passage on the ferry is paid. He asks whether I've had any trouble with the law. Then he stamps my green card, sends me downstairs. A woman asks me about guns. No, I say. Then she tilts her head and says, "What about mace?" I admit Karla's gift, lift it from under the seat. She says, "You'll have to get rid of it. We don't allow it in our country." I consider that a good omen.

The official then tells me I'll have to empty out the mace, not just toss the can. She points to the place I should do this. I want to miss all living organisms, but she tells me it's better on the bushes than in the air. So I spray out the nasty stuff on some very sinister shrubs and push the can into the domed dustbin. My nostrils stay irritated for two hours, even though I take care to stand upwind and scrub up afterward.

The atmosphere in British Columbia is wide open, countrified. Imposing mountains, orderly farms. Signs warn drivers to watch for moose. I follow rivers all day long. Mozart matches this landscape. Every creek has water in it!

August 18. On to Smithers. British Columbia will not fit in my camera. Everywhere I turn is another lake, another island, river, forest. Unspoiled, overwhelming. I take a snapshot for Tito—Overwaitea Foods Bulk Foods. I don't think the brand name would fly in the United States.

At roadside rest areas the graffiti are just as graphic, the same obscene imperatives, but almost all of them here say "please."

I find a mom-and-pop motel for $37 Canadian. The grubby codger asks where my husband is. I say, "None of your business." He insists on carrying my bags up two flights to my room. I make sure there is a deadbolt, and I check for peepholes. That evening I ask at the front desk about nearby restaurants, and the old woman there, to my shock, is in her thirties, just beaten down. Her husband stops me outside and tells me he also has a motel in Prince Rupert. We could spend a few days there, a week maybe? I don't tell him that I'd rather be flayed and left on an anthill. I simply smile and ask, "Oh, you and me and your wife?" Then he backs off.

August 19. The road to Prince Rupert follows the Skeena River. Without equal, this is the most lavish, spectacular land I've seen. The day's drive begins at the foot of the Kathlyn Glacier, passes lakes with wooded islands and green cascades of water. Clear views of broken, jagged ranges of earth-edges cutting the sky.

I can measure my luck by how the sky looks at Prince Rupert. Thunderclouds gather in the early afternoon along the river, but then pass inland. At dinner I watch rafts of logs, some a mile long, floating en masse, corralled somehow.

August 20. I wake early—5:45, excited about going on the ferry. I pack, clean up, and ask where I can get a cup of chocolate. I'm forty-five minutes early for the three-hour advance check-in. Get directions, go to start the car. No response at all. Mild panic. I go back to the desk, call for help, and the clerk offers me tea.

We talk about Mexico, then about jaking—fishing without rod or bait, just dangling a hook on a line and pulling it up so the bottom fish go for it. She talks about isolation, how when rock slides close off the highway to Prince Rupert, nothing comes in, no fruit, no dairy, no people. She says one's perspective broadens with the awareness that there's not another settlement, not a village within 100 miles.

Bill from Rupert Esso finally arrives. We "boost" the battery, let it charge, and try to start 'er. Nothing. He fills the cells with water from the jug I lugged all the way from Mesa, cleans the terminals, and we try again. At last! I let it run for an hour.

In line for U.S. Customs, after buying a ticket—$286, Prince Rupert to Haines—I get up my nerve and shut off the car. Starts right up again. I'll sail Prince Rupert to Ketchikan today, about six hours, then disembark. Overnight in Ketchikan, then on to Haines tomorrow.

■ ■ ■

At U.S. Customs, the woman asks for ID, then about what I bought in Canada. Then she asks if I have alcohol, tobacco, citrus fruit. No, no, no. She asks for my purse. Snoops through, then sends me on my way. What a mess it could have been if an agent wanted to unpack the whole carload.

In line now, waiting to board ship, I see a huge totem pole. Most of the pigment has faded or disappeared. It's about four feet in diameter. Top face is a gray-black bird of prey, curved beak and wide eyes. The second resembles a ritual mask, geometric markings and a large scooped nose arcing upward. The third face is gentler, rich brown, maybe human, with thick eyebrows. Oddly, the back is split open, as if the hollowed original were reinforced with a new center. A metaphor for this moment in my life.

9:45 A.M. The far row of cars has rumbled down the ramp into the depths of the ship. Walk-on passengers, laden with bundles in both hands, cross over on the walkway. People in our line start their engines, wait for the signal. The ship's flying a maple leaf on one side and a deep blue banner with lighter markings on the other. We're moving!

10:25 A.M. The deep blue flag is spangled with gold stars, the Big Dipper, Alaska's flag. The deck is too cold right now. This morning's overcast, windy. People are picking out spots to pitch small tents. I'm more inclined to unroll my bag on the floor between seats. Less likely to wake up soggy.

We're on the M.V. *Aurora.*

During lunch, the people in the next booth say, "So what part of Arizona are you from?" I look down to see how it shows. They laugh and admit seeing my license plate while the ferry was loading. Win Green is supervisor of the Tongass National Forest, all 17 million acres. He and Sue and their children live in Ketchikan. They show me pictures. They have two eagle trees in view from their deck, plus bears more often than they care to. We get to talking and I ask their advice on where to stay. Sue says, "We have a couch." So I trust in the kindness of strangers, follow them right off the ferry, up the hill, home for my first night in Alaska.

Win shows me his collection of bear skulls, ranging from big to enormous to truly frightening. The fangs curve, longer than my fingers. They tell me to be sure to cache food far from where I'll sleep, to wash up meticulously, and never ever to bring food near my tent. I realize I am utterly unequipped to camp in bear country. The rules I know from the desert won't do anything but get me in trouble. They warn me not to drink from the streams, even clean water, or *Giardia* carried by beaver could be a long-lasting souvenir.

August 21. I see an eagle in flight! First Sue points out a patch of white, high in the bare branches of a snag. Then the bird unfurls its huge wings so delicately I think it will glide downward in a slow, sweeping arc. But no. It rises and banks, easing over the pilings at water's edge, brushing close to tips of the spruce, then settles back on its original perch. Sue takes me to the dump to see more eagles. She also needs to get rid of the fish guts smelling up her garage and increasing the danger of bears.

We find ravens instead. Ravens hop, pecking out what's shiny or delicious, choosing from the mountain of refuse the varied bits that give life.

■ ■ ■

Ravens, eagles, and cape fox are clan symbols for the Tlingit. I see them carved at Saxman, a village separate from the town of Ketchikan, though both share the same island.

At Saxman, the totem poles rise up three stories tall into mist. One pole shows a young boy crouching on his heels, his arm held fast in the mouth of another being—god or animal? They have at Saxman the largest collection of totems anywhere, and a huge work shed where Nathan Jackson is carving a new one. Two workmen hammer and saw up on scaffolds. They are busy raising the roof so even larger projects can be taken in. The poles are carved lying down, of course. A massive ceremony brings out large crowds for the raising of a new pole. Ropes attached for the lifting represent spirit lines. I think of the spirit paths in Navajo weaving.

I set out to explore on my own, but again, dead battery. I clean off the terminals with baking soda. No luck. Pop the clutch going downhill in reverse, and somehow it catches. Then dies. Sue pushes, and we get 'er rolling. Dies again at the junction of Sue's driveway and the main road. I ease out into traffic, hoping, and build just enough momentum to get going one more time. At the first gas station, they can't get to it before the ferry arrives. I have to check in at 12:30. The chevron guys come through, though. When they test the battery, the needle whips right over to REPLACE. So they do. With my new no-maintenance box bolted down and bungied in place for insurance, I should be in good shape the rest of the trip. Total bill: $87. A relief.

■ ■ ■

I sip a bowl of homemade soup at Jumbo's Corner Café, then walk down to Creek Street to watch salmon swim upstream. Fish so thick the river roils, more fish than water. Excited, I point. A local scoffs, "Them's just dog salmon." When I don't understand, he tells me people feed these to their dog teams. They're too mushy for people.

Every now and then an orange fluorescent tag swims by, a hatchery-marked sample, so counters can trace when and where the fish started out, and how well their generation's doing.

I head back to check in. Light rain wets everything. After an hour, I'm on board the M.V. *Matanuska,* a much larger vessel than the *Aurora* and much easier on the stomach. Though part of the stability comes from geography—we're in protected water now, all the way up the Inside Passage. Yesterday, Win pointed out the only sand beaches in Southeast Alaska. All other beaches, without pounding water to make sand, remain rocky.

I think about the trade-offs we make to stay in a landscape. Sue Green is a master equestrienne, breeder of Appaloosas, but she lives on an island where there is no place to ride. When she arrived, there were no horses at all on Ketchikan. Now there are seven. She organizes a horseless horse group. They groom horses, stroke them, feed them, muck out stables, even put tack on and take it off. But the forest here's too thick to welcome hikers, much less riders. Between trees in this rain forest, the muskeg's too marshy to support weight.

I think about the trade-offs we make to leave. What are the rates of exchange? What price to live lives of our own choosing?

■ ■ ■

August 22, 1985. Spume and flukes! Sighted whales this morning off Douglas Island. The mist was so thick at six o'clock I couldn't see a thing. By nine it lifted, revealing, inch by inch, waterfalls, glaciers, thick forest to timberline. Up above, the "high saeter"—the rocky, mossy mountain meadows from Grandpa Moen's stories of Norway.

■ ■ ■

I sleep quite comfortably between rows of seats. The new bag heats up just right as long as I leave the foot unzipped, so I can stick out bare toes.

■ ■ ■

Glaciers—light plays over ice, even when the sun's behind clouds. Blue cast to the ice field, deep brown or gray moraines, lateral, median, terminal. Dozens of Dall porpoises skim, splashing in arcing leaps through green water, starboard.

■ ■ ■

A motley crew composes group-effort postcards for Ole's girlfriend. Ole drives the Green Tortoise bus. My contribution: "I have a glacier in my heart 'cause you're not here." Others are worse, trust me. Green Tortoise is a tour group that clears out the seats from old buses, converts the space into sleeping quarters, and sells cheap tours. This group will spend four weeks in Alaska and Canada for about $1,000 per person, meals included. They curl up in their bunks at night while Ole drives them to the next stop. Then they stumble out, the cook rustles up some chow, and they go exploring.

The tour's heading to Dawson but will be in Fairbanks a few days after I get there. We promise to meet at the Howling Dog Saloon in Fox, Alaska.

August 23, 1985. The ferry arrives late, traffic jams up, and I don't hit the road until suppertime. At Haines, mountains rise right out of the water—no beach, no margin. So many powerful vistas, most with no safe spot to savor or photograph them. I drive north from Haines, set my watch on Alaska time. An eagle perches up close in the Chilkat Eagle Preserve. I make out its talons as it comes in feet first to land on a branch just above me.

For fifty miles past Haines, the road's velvet. Then good dirt—hard packed and well graded. The dirt lasts only from mile 50 to 96, not the ordeal everybody warned me about.

The Wrangell–St. Elias area overwhelms. I wonder if you need technical skills, belays, and crampons to go up there. Signs at the trailheads advise people how to avoid bear encounters. Wear bells, talk, sing. Make sure you don't surprise a bear. But if you do have a close encounter, don't say anything insulting. I drive along, thinking, *Bear, your mama's got marmot breath!* What would insult a bear?

Foolishly, I try to make Beaver Creek. I pass up a likely place to stay at Kluane Lake, the Bayshore Motel. Mountain sheep click across the highway, then up the cliffside, as though vertical and horizontal were identical.

Heavy mist, never-ending twilight. I decide that I will stop at full dark, my eyesight questionable, my fatigue unquestionable. Tension and a little fear keep me alert. I roll down the window, stay a little cold all the way. The music, steel drums. Andy Narrell's "Stickman" clicks over for the third play. It's after eleven. It occurs to me, much too late, that full darkness may not show up here for a month or two. Stupid! The Midnight Sun's for real.

I've been driving for sixty miles without seeing a sign. This is new territory for me, a place I don't know the rules. Or the landmarks. Or a soul. The map shows only one road, but could this be the wrong one? Or the wrong way?

I pull over, get out to stretch and hear a raucous voice from the trees. Raven, trickster. "Hey there," I call, recognizing a relative, even this far from home. He answers back.

Then, very welcome, I catch sight of a twenty-four-hour store/lodge/cafe. I had planned to stretch out beside the car in my new sleeping bag, but Win and Sue's bear stories cured me of that delusion. I pull in, grateful, to the Koidern River Fishing Lodge.

I make a pit stop, then find a pay phone. I've been calling Tito and Lupita at every stop, as promised, and call them now, even though it's way too late on a work night. Tito yells, "Peggy! We were worried. Where *are* you?"

"Somewhere in Yukon Territory," I mumble.

"Can you be more specific?"

"Probably not," I sigh. I tell him Koidern River Lodge. I tell him eagles and Green Tortoises and exhaustion. We tell each other miss and love.

I hang up, look around. Mostly plywood, this place. A very young, very tired man is tanking up on coffee, so he can "put in at least another hundred." Clearly a bad idea. I'm glad I won't be on the highway when he is.

The chalkboard menu has two entries: chili and split pea soup. I think, *What can they do to split pea soup?* Almost asleep, I order split pea and a glass of milk. The milk is oily, rank. I ask for water. The woman fixes me with a stare. Then she reaches into the microwave and pulls out a bowl of gray gelatinous glop. A guy behind me says, "Which one is that?" "Soup," I tell him. He says, "I'll have the chili." I munch the soda crackers, wash them down with warm water. Then I ask if they have a room to rent. I pay $35, and a guy shows me into a wide, plywood paneled longhouse with doors on either side. All along the corridor are animals—fox, bear, raccoon, wolverine, wolf—poorly stuffed, taxidermied into contortions. The lighting is bad. He puts one shoulder to the wall. A reluctant plywood slab scrapes open, and I step into the cell. There's no lock on the door, no knob. The shower stall, rusted and tipsy, yawns out from the wall. I'm too tired to go back out on the road, too wary to camp out with bears nearby, too disoriented to think. I thank the man, shut the door, and pile all my stuff against it, keys in a plastic mug on top so they'll clatter if anybody tries to shove the door. Then I fall onto the cot, into weird dreams.

Six hours later I wake, fully dressed. I chatter through a quick cold shower and slip back behind the wheel. All day I shiver. Can't shake the sense of having escaped.

August 24. Good omen—I start my period. Have to stop at a roadside rest area and clean up a little. Beginning lots of new cycles, physical, spiritual, artistic, emotional.

Taking a breather at Tok, I realize I'm at the crossroads of two classic stories: (1) a young woman leaves home in search of a mysterious grail, and (2) a stranger comes to town. I'm leaving and arriving all at once. I don't know yet what I'll bring back from the enchanted taiga, the forest of trees no bigger than cornstalks, scraggly dwarf trees tangled black and gray, stunted by permafrost. I don't know yet what I will offer this place.

When the vista opens, I can see along the riverbed. Gravel, wide, with just a few liquid paths. Why does the water cut such a wide swath? I can see where it has changed its course as it makes its way.

I pull into Fairbanks after a full day of pedal-to-the-metal. Find the housing office, check out my apartment in Yak Estates. One whole wall downstairs looks out into birch woods.

■ ■ ■

I roll out the green sleeping bag over floor pillows. Set out the objects that will help me make a home—pictures of family, of the desert. My samba mask, leather, and ribbons and glitter. The incised water spirit pot from Santa Fe. Molas. The fuchsia-blossom vase I bought when I couldn't afford food. I make a few notes about the circle of totems. Put on Hummel's trumpet concerto, lean back, close my eyes. Notice that I am shaking.

■ ■ ■

Will I have anything useful to share with the people here? Will the people in Alaska speak my language? Will I be able to learn theirs?

Will we introduce ourselves by citing our relatives? I am Peggy, daughter of Hanna, daughter of Harriet, daughter of Amy Zoe, daughter of Amy Holden.

Amy Holden taught school, as did Amy Zoe, resigning as required when they married. Harriet became a farm wife and mom at eighteen, and didn't go back to school till her husband retired. Famous family quotation, "I'm not staying home all day with you." Hanna always wanted more education, fought my dad to buy books. Every one of these women read every day. Every one of these women wrote poems, journals, letters.

I am the first of this line of readers to go to college, the first to graduate. With every poem I write, with every class I teach, they live through me, and I through them.

Maybe my nieces will tell their friends, "My aunt is a professor. My aunt writes books." Maybe wider possibilities will open to them. Yes, people like us can go to college. People like us can live a life of the mind in a world of ideas, art, poetry. It's vital for us to add our voice to the song, our step to the dance, our line to the poem.

■ ■ ■

Three nights later, I set out for the Howling Dog Saloon to meet up with the Green Tortoise folks. This tavern is legendary, a little microcosm of Fairbanks. I take the Steese Highway about eleven miles north of town. The Goldstream Valley spreads all around. To the right, the pipeline zigzags, dips underground, and parts the trees up some slopes. Eight hundred miles, from Prudhoe Bay to Valdez. There's a pull-off for tour buses, and people taking pictures of each other under the tube of rushing crude. Ravens dabble in roadkill, finding nourishment in the most unlikely scraps of fur.

Farther on, I see my first moose, knee deep in a marshy spot, antlers dripping with water weeds. I watch the blonder tips of his coat lifting in the breeze. His skin shivers to shuck off bugs.

■ ■ ■

The Howling Dog looks pretty shabby, mostly spray-painted plywood frosted with foam insulation, Day-Glo orange and yellow, dried out, and crumbly. I don't like bars much, and this one looks doubtful. A dozen custom Harleys ring the door. But I gather my courage, my ID, my keys, and step into gloom. Before my eyes adjust, I'm pretty blind. I back toward the near wall. Gradually, the line of guys at the bar comes into focus, a line of guys mostly big and bearded and tattooed. They're looking me over. They have chains. I see a rectangle of light out the far side, hear the slaps and grunts of some game. Then one of the bikers comes up behind me. I flinch. He puts his hand, his huge hand, on my shoulder, his arm around me.

"Don't worry. I'll look out for ya," he murmurs. His costume is scary—Hell's Angels colors, heavy cross in his pierced ear, stained jeans. Then I look closer. His face is well worn, his raven eyes lively.

"I'm meeting friends here," I say.

"Just did," he says. I relax, and he takes me over to a lopsided table. I can see now that the game outside is volleyball, the players on the near court serious. One team has the raw haircuts of low-ranking military guys, the other the shaggy look of students or professors.

The band's about ready to go, The Flyers. The biker, Michael, says, "Everybody's half in love with the bass player." I watch her long fingers warming up, see how her eyes close when she hits a tricky note. I can see why. She's graceful as new willow.

"That carpet there," Michael says, nodding toward the bandstand, "is one hundred percent pure Pope carpet." I look blank. "From when Reagan and the Pope shook hands out at the airport." The carpet is indeed the high-ranking red of formal welcome. I wonder if he's making this up.

He says, "New here?" I nod. He tells me to watch out for rental ads that use the word "rustic." That means an outhouse and no water. I tell him I already have a place, with plumbing.

"Can I come take a shower?" He's laughing. He gives advice about where to get a good parka, used, the kind they issue to workers on the North Slope. He looks at my sandals, and expounds on the virtues of Sorels (sturdy), moon boots (very cheap), felt boots (light and warm), and bunny boots (good for extreme cold). He gives me the number for a good mechanic who can winterize my car.

It'll need a headbolt heater, battery blanket, and 5-20 oil, if I want the Honda to start at anything colder than fifteen below.

He tells me to check out the permafrost house on Farmer's Loop Road, a sprawling California ranch house that melted the frozen earth beneath. It's now split into three pieces, none level.

The place is filling up. I can pick out European backpackers by their gestures, even before they speak German. A local couple dressed in long john tops and plaid boxers brag about their success dipnetting. I have no idea what that means. I overhear the careful English of students newly arrived from Asia. Alaska Natives, young, stake out one wall. Four clean-cut hockey players take up more room than they need. All shapes and sizes, all colors, creeds, political persuasions come together here. No little kids, but some teenagers no doubt using fake ID. Some old-timers, some newcomers.

By the time Ole and the Green Tortoise folks mosey in, I'm dancing on the rough planks, watching my uneven step.

Whatever this place is, I am a part of it.

Saturday Night with the Hutterites

TERI HEIN

"The girls would like to sing for you," Paul said, weaving his way through the adults in his sitting room. Bernie and I sat erect on our wooden chairs, as everyone there was, each of us waiting for another question to bob to the surface.

"What do you think about Mr. Bush? Will he be the president?" asked Susan, who lived across the sidewalk on the other side of the dining hall. She was somewhere between the age of twenty-five and forty-five, never had and never would vote in her life, but knew about the presidential election thanks to the one copy of the Great Falls, Montana, *Tribune* that came to the Hutterite colony every day. It was passed from person to person, its route dictated by the configuration of living units, a sort of string of townhouses that line the sidewalks.

I was surprised by the question, unaware that the Hutterites were attuned to national politics. "I am very scared by Governor Bush," I answered cautiously to this room full of farming people. "He is an oil man and I'm afraid he will not protect the environment." After these two days in the colony, I had learned to keep my responses short. A long answer landed on a conversation like a giant boulder dropped on a flat surface. It rolls nowhere. Long answers made people squirm and then offer us more food.

"Oh, we hate those environmentalists," chimed in Annie, as if to show agreement with me. She sat over in the far corner up against the wall on the old leather bus seat, another woman of ambiguous age. "They've made so many rules for us here on the colony—like our pig slurry, for example. We had to contain our pig slurry and that cost us so much money."

There was a silence.

"How's the weather there in Seattle?" John asked. He had followed us over from his home, where we had stopped earlier, as he'd requested, to answer questions.

"It rains a lot."

I had taught Paul's fourteen-year-old daughter Marie while she was in Seattle for cancer treatment the year before. More importantly, Bernadette, or Bernie, who had been Marie's nurse, was visiting. For the two days we stayed there, everyone invited us to come by, carefully counting out the doorways along the sidewalk. "I'm the seventh one down," one would say, extracting a promise from us to stop in. We approached each door imagining all those aches and pains waiting inside, as well as the questions about Seattle weather and had we ever visited a colony before and did we like it and would we like a snack.

It was always the same, a fact that became increasingly frustrating. We were hoping for a deeper conversation, even if we couldn't identify exactly how it would go.

I accompanied Bernie on all these home visits, although my medical expertise does not go beyond the placement of Band-Aids. It would have been rude to refuse these medical missions, in spite of the intended social nature of our visit. Besides, there was nothing else to do once we had toured the colony, a collection of metal buildings standing in rigid rows on a hilltop above Belt, Montana. Most were connected and served as living units, although another long row contained the church, dining hall, kitchen, day care, and Laundromat. The schoolhouse sat off from the rest, a stark building where the twenty-four colony children attended classes together through eighth grade—their progress monitored by Mr. Prete, a teacher sent in by the state. Eighth grade marked the end of their formal education, the boys then learning to farm with men, and the girls learning to cook and sew with the women.

There were also the barns, one right after another, housing a collection of every farm animal Old MacDonald could imagine, as well as galvanized metal sheds with computer systems to organize the products, from the dozens and dozens of eggs shipped daily down to Great Falls to the gallons of milk and the hundred turkeys butchered right before Thanksgiving every year. In the woodshop, Lazarus, a man I guessed to be in his late forties, made coat hangers and mirror frames for the soon-to-be-married couple, Marie's brother and his girlfriend. Their house was almost finished, and the furnishings Lazarus made were identical to the ones he had been making for twenty years—his shellacked cabinets and dressers sat clonelike in each of the homes. In the garage sat the colony vehicles—all the trucks needed for farming, and the van used for the rare trips into Great Falls for doctor appointments or supplies. There was a smokehouse for making sausage and the baking kitchen, stocked with giant walk-in ovens and huge industrial machines for mixing the bread dough.

Pleasant Valley Colony sits at the top of the hill, built fifteen years before when the Chalmer Colony—located 200 miles to the north—had grown past the ninety-five-person mark and the two groups split in two, as Hutterite colonies do, like cells dividing as they continue to grow. Their growth is rapid in this twenty-first century, with families still averaging eight or nine children. The new colony had to find 5,000 acres—the minimum needed to support a colony. Montana is one of the few places where 5,000 acres are available and partially explains why the state is dotted with Hutterite groups.

First the men built the buildings—identical floor patterns and furniture for each living unit. Then the elders drew straws to determine which families moved to the new colony and which families stayed. "It was a terrible, terrible time," Lydia told us. "Some people wanted to go and some people wanted to stay. But it was up to the elders to determine this." She had come to Great Falls in the van with her ancient, ailing father, Jake, who was taken to the doctor before Lydia and Jake, along with Paul, picked Bernie and me up at the airport. Lydia was a tall, thin woman who, like her sister, Susan, had never married, and now the two sisters lived their life caring for their widowed father. "Splitting the colony was a sad time for us. We had to divide everything in two. You know always somebody thinks something isn't fair."

During our visit, many people spoke of this fifteen-year-old event as if it had occurred yesterday.

John was the first person we met when we arrived. He seemed to be waiting in the colony's parking lot for us, a handsome, fit older man who announced upon meeting us that it was important we stop by his house during our visit because he had some questions. He uttered the word "questions" as if they were dollars in a bank account—stored up and imperative. We asked him about the colony name: Pleasant Valley. "I got nothing against pleasant things but, in case you didn't notice, we're not in a valley. We're on the top of a hill." But the elders had liked the sound.

From the top of that hill was a stark, distant view of the October fields, plowed sections, and prairie lands that seemed to stretch out forever. There are few natural trees on this gray landscape, and at night the lights of Great Falls, twenty miles away, startle one with their nearness. In the day, when the town is not so easy to make out in the distance, I felt a million miles from anywhere familiar.

The colony buildings were clustered together on top of the hill, huddled as if for protection from all that openness, all that exposure to the world. Ten or fifteen seedling trees, just a few inches tall, had been planted that year. Every time we walked the sidewalk a different person drew our attention to them—something important to this colony, fifteen years young. Only now, it seemed, after all the work of building and settling, were people ready for some shade. I asked Paul, our host, why they hadn't planted the trees when they had first started the colony. He seemed puzzled by the question.

My question seemed as odd to him as his lack of response seemed to me. For me, a tree planted fifteen years before would now be giving him the shade he so desired. For him, my fifteen-year rush for shade was really no time at all when he had much more important work to do before tree planting could be accomplished.

Next I asked him about the family lockers in the cold storage room. "Paul, if everyone owns everything communally and everyone believes in sharing and sharing alike, why does each family have its own locker and, more importantly, why does each locker have a padlock on it?"

Again, the same quizzical look. I think the look was because the padlocks were not about security from each other. They were just about having padlocks because, for some reason, they had them. The need for security was a question from my world, not his.

There are few natural trees on this gray landscape, and at night the lights of Great Falls, twenty miles away, startle with their nearness. In the day, when the town is not so easy to make out in the distance, I felt a million miles from anywhere familiar.

The Hutterites are part of the Anabaptist tradition, originating in the 1500s in southern Austria, which helps explain the spoken German that thrives in this Montana landscape. The Anabaptists' unwillingness to be Catholic or Lutheran, not to mention their refusal to fight wars, meant they were booted around Europe for centuries, ending up in Russia in the late 1700s, thanks to Catherine the Great's willingness to let them be. When Czar Nicholas took over a hundred years later, however, the party was over. He insisted they go to war and they went instead to what would later become South Dakota.

Thanks to a shunning of birth control, there are now 434 North American colonies with about 36,000 Hutterites inhabiting them. The Hutterites pride themselves on their large families. "Sugars and Peppers, that's what we call them," Rebecca told us, referring to girls and boys. Today's Hutterites are still living much like their ancestors did in Europe—speaking German with a Tyrolean dialect, speaking English with a German accent, letting the men run the show, and sharing everything, both assets and work, communally. The division of chores—milking, making bread, canning, butchering, plowing, sewing, cooking—is all determined along gender lines, and then the elders appoint each person to specific tasks. It didn't seem that anyone ever questioned the assignment received. This was the way it was done. James had been working with pigs for five years. "I hate pigs," he told us, his handsome thirty-something face ruddy in the cold Montana air. "But I won't have to do this forever. I think in ten years or so, I'll be moved over to milking. I'm really looking forward to that."

■ ■ ■

"The girls are downstairs waiting for you," Paul urged us. Everyone gathered in the sitting room looked disappointed about our leaving the room, even though the conversation had stalled out several times as we struggled to discover new topics after two days in the colony. Everyone there had known each other all their lives. Their conversations tended to be about the cow with anthrax or the blown fuse in the bread-baking oven, topics in which neither Bernie nor I could hold our own.

The steps down to where the girls awaited us in the party room, as it was called, were lined with teenage boys. It was clearly Saturday night. They wore special clothes—V-necked multicolored polyester shirts that shone a bit in the light. Polished cowboy boots, cowboy hats, and the acrid smell of aftershave underlined that this was not a work night, although many of these boys would get up at 4:00 A.M. to do the milking. There, in the basement, where the walls were lined on three sides with plastic kitchen chairs, sat the girls, all seven of them—the sum total of the teenage girl population in this colony. Unlike their male counterparts, they didn't seem to don anything different from what they wore every day. If each had a closet like Marie's, it was crammed full of handmade dresses, vests, and *kupf-tiechles,* the black-and-white polka-dotted scarves all the women wear. Each piece of their clothing is meticulously handsewn right down to the decorative stitching where the ties attach to the scarves. The girls wore combinations of these clothes for work and for play, certainly always keeping their bonnets on, so as not to bare their heads to the heavens. Whether seven, seventeen, or seventy, each one's clothing was the same—long skirts, vests over blouses, bonnets, and practical shoes. Only recently had they begun to buy readymade shoes.

But the boys dressed up on weekend nights, shedding their worn work jeans, flannel shirts, and work boots. Bernie and I had marveled earlier when Paul Jr. and Thomas appeared in the sitting room, decked out in their cowboy clothes. "Where are you guys going?" we asked. They blushed a deep red that moved up their cheeks like a tide. "We're goin' out girl watching."

Girl-watching consisted of going to someplace, say the dining hall, and closely watching the very girls they had worked side by side with that day, not to mention gone to school with for eight years and did know and would know forever. Outsiders never move to the colony. It is just too different.

■ ■ ■

The colony's interest had been piqued by Bernie's and my arrival, even though in just about every way we represented everything they consciously chose not to be. We are career women who rarely go to church, we travel by ourselves, don't take orders from men, wear pants, and swear at will. I live with my boyfriend and have for years with no particular intention of marrying. But the differences didn't seem to matter. There was not one moment in which we felt judged or viewed with even a whisper of contempt.

For the several months that Marie and her family were in Seattle for her cancer treatment, Marie and I quizzed each other about our disparate existences. I was forthcoming with the circumstances of my life, as I quizzed her about hers. I was constantly surprised and delighted when her family was not disappointed in my personal life choices. People come from all over the country to the hospital, and I think some fundamentalists have soured me unfairly toward other fundamentalist religions.

I found the Hutterites to be a kind, tolerant, remarkably accepting group of people—from the bottom of their hearts, or so it seemed to me. I think they emphasize the love-thy-neighbor part of Jesus' teaching. Since the church service we attended at the colony was conducted in German, I don't really know, though.

After that service, we filtered out of church and into the dining room. The men and women sat separately, as they do during services—men on the left side, women on the right, with the youngest in the front and the oldest in the back. All meals, we noticed, were eaten at breakneck speed, and people rarely seemed interested in mealtime conversation. It detained them from getting back to work, a seeming obsession, surprising even to us who came from the breakneck world of dot.com Seattle. When they weren't kneading bread or darning socks, the women were ripping up polyester shirts bought at the Goodwill in Great Falls—using the strips to make rag rugs or other craft projects. The men seemed to relax a bit more, although all put in more hours per day than any Microsoft worker I know.

But they weren't universally content to stay. Thomas, Marie's brother and Paul and Rebecca's oldest son, had run away once. "It happens often with the boys when they get to their early twenties and aren't yet married," Paul said. In fact, another son, Ed, is away now. "They go off to work the oil rigs in Texas or the cotton fields in Oklahoma. It's not considered a travesty by the colony, although it's certainly frowned upon, and the boys write home often. "But they always come back," Paul said. Paul had done it himself. Then he came home. "We know where we belong."

One evening Thomas said to me, in that same out-of-the-blue way these people asked their Governor Bush and weather questions, "I asked a girl to dance in Texas."

"How'd it go?"

"She said no." He smiled.

Later that evening he came into the sitting room and asked Bernie and me if we wanted to go to the tavern in Belt that night. We were confused. "I've got the pickup tonight because Phillip's plowing and I have to go pick him up at eleven. We could go," he said, his face flushed and mischievous.

We looked at Paul. Thomas laughed and walked off. "The minister would have all your heads if you went to Belt," Paul quickly informed us. Belt was three miles away. Thomas is twenty-three years old. "Hey, if I want to go to a bar, I go to a bar," Bernie reminded Paul. Paul shrugged and smiled.

■ ■ ■

The teenage girls were awkward and squirmy when we took our seats in the party room. In spite of what Paul had said, there was no indication that they wanted to sing for us. The boys hung on the stairs, as if unwelcome down below. Maybe the party room was for girls only on this night. John entered the room and sat down—he seemed to follow us everywhere. We had gone to his house earlier that day to fulfill our promise made on that first day: to drop by and answer his questions. It turned out that John has a mysterious tremor in his hands, a cause of great concern to him and something that propelled him to avidly seek Bernie's advice. She insisted she was a children's cancer nurse and had given him a phone number in Seattle to call about his condition. But he seemed to feel that proximity to her was curative.

We all continued to sit awkwardly, the silence growing larger. John left when it seemed that the girls were going to postpone singing. The teenage boys on the steps receded. We had seen the girls several times over the past two days, but of any group at Pleasant Valley, they seemed the most uncomfortable around us. Even Marie, who had begged us via mail to come visit, had hung back.

Finally, Judy, a tall girl sitting in the middle, broke the silence. "First you two have to sing us a song," she challenged. There was an edge to her.

"We've never sung together in our lives," Bernie answered.

"How do you like the colony?" another girl asked.

I sighed. Another mazelike conversation. "I think I would have a hard time living here," I finally said. "I'm used to driving my car and doing what I want and traveling all over. Do any of you ever think you'd want to live anywhere else?"

There was a silence.

"It's too dangerous out there," said one of the girls. "When I have children, they'll be able to go outside without worrying. I just couldn't live out there," said a girl second from the end.

The other girls looked down awkwardly. Silence.

"Is there anyone here who would like to trade lives with me for just one day?" asked Bernie.

A hand shot up from a girl on the end, then down like lightning, and the girls muffled their laughter.

"It's too dangerous out there, I said, and I'll say it again," reaffirmed the girl who said it the first time. "It might be fine for you English but not for us." "English" was how they referred to all of us outsiders. There seemed nothing negative about the label.

"Okay," Bernie pushed on, "if you could change just one thing in the way you live, what would it be?"

"I would have a driver's license," said the girl on the end quickly.

"So," I asked, "you would drive to Great Falls?"

"Oh, not Great Falls, it's too far. I would just like to drive to Belt whenever I felt like it."

"What would you do there?"

"I don't know. I would just drive there and then I would drive back."

Silence.

"Do you worry, as your colony grows, about the scarcity of farmland for new colonies, and the fact that it's getting harder and harder to make a living as farmers?"

There was a snort from the steps and all eyes darted there. It was Mark, a sixteen year old. "What's funny?" I asked.

"Now, what are they going to worry about that for? They're girls, and it isn't their job to worry. That's the men's job."

The girls looked down.

Mark went on to ask if we knew that Ken Griffey Jr. had left the Seattle Mariners. Before we could answer, he asked if we thought he looked like Ricky Martin. We all laughed. Radios and television are strictly forbidden in the colony.

Silence.

Judy took a deep breath and looked directly at Bernie and me. "We *are* worried about our future," she said. She then uttered something to her girl-friends in German.

With that, the girls sat straight up, Judy counted to three, and they began to sing—a capella songs in harmony, delivered in reedy voices so lovely they reminded me of the Bulgarian Women's Choir. I stole a glance at Bernie, whose mouth, like mine, hung open in awe. Nothing could have surprised us more than the subtlety and beauty of this tonal quilt they wove in front of us. We couldn't understand the words, but they felt like laments, pushed out of the mouths of these young, concerned women and delivered together as the integral team they were. They had been together since birth and through school, living across the sidewalks from one other in lives destined to be lived across the side-walks from one another forever. These were the boys who would grow to be elders of their church in middle age and would dictate the chores of these young women while listening to baseball scores on the radios kept hidden, I suspect, underneath their beds.

It was a world that confused me at the time, one I wanted to accept wholeheartedly for its simplicity and for the utter kindness of its residents. Yet it seemed to offer so few choices to its young people, especially the girls. I asked Paul if the girls ever ran away, and the look I received was not unsure or quizzi-cal. *No.*

Theirs seemed a world somehow devoid of the possibilities gifted by the imagination. But was that really true? I still wonder, certain that those har-monic voices heard in that basement one night a few Octobers ago painted nothing short of choral masterpieces in all of our minds.

I remain confused.

The Road Home

JANET THOMAS

It was a road trip paved with good intentions. My foster daughter, Alli, and I were off to Phoenix for Christmas. It was a long way, about three thousand miles round trip, but we were driving on purpose. Both of us were orphans in one way or another and the family-ness of the Christmas season had us running for cover. It's what had bonded us at the beginning and will until the end. And it's what made the phrase "foster mom" sound foreign and fictitious. She was my spiritual daughter the instant we met. And I was the mom she adopted. And so there we were, adopted mom and spiritual daughter, on the road, and on the run, for the holidays.

It was a little car, a 1988 Toyota Tercel, but it had gone only ninety-odd thousand miles, got good mileage, and had fairly new tires. A friend bought us some chains just in case, and a squirt can of instant flat tire fix-it. We shoved in sleeping bags, Trader Joe truffles, too many books, ten pounds of nuts and raisins, too many clothes, our favorite stuffed animals, three flashlights, not enough batteries, too much cash, and a Costco phone card with 450 minutes of talk time. We also took along a boxy tape player to replace the broken one in the car, and a few books on tape—including *A Walk in the Woods* by Bill Bryson, which, it turned out, we would listen to twice. It was all about how disaster comes right on the heels of good, perhaps even glorious, intentions.

■ ■ ■

So Alli and I hit the road. Due south first to San Francisco, then to L.A., then a sharp left to Phoenix, where her brother Davin had moved six months earlier. We planned to arrive two days before Christmas Eve, spill out presents and good cheer through Christmas Day and then head back home the next day. New Year's, we'd decided, must be spent at home, with friends.

I'd first met Alli when she was seven years old. She was curled up on a chair with her brother, who was eight. I knew only bits of their story: an abusive mother, a series of foster homes since they were three and four, and a recent rescue from the system by their long-absent father. I'd gone to their home with their cousin, with whom I was just beginning a relationship. I hardly knew him, but as soon as I met the kids, I wanted to wrap them up and take them home. Within weeks, Davin and Alli had disappeared with their father, and over the next few years they were thought, at times, by the family to be dead, so complete was their disappearance.

It was four years later, after many miracles and misfortunes—often one and the same—that we were finally reunited under the same roof. No more foster homes, I promised Davin and Alli, only to discover all too soon that I had to become an official foster mom if we were to stay together. I remember at the time knowing that being alone and taking on two kids at this time in my life was impossible, unthinkable, and perhaps even unbearable. But there was no choice. Some things in life come our way and we either do them or die.

I had my own theory about it all, never on record until this moment. I am, as often as possible, a Buddhist. I've had in my life two abortions, both in the months before Davin and Alli were respectively born. To say that my abortions were as painful as they were inevitable is to honor the opposing forces of nature. Just like taking on the kids—there was no way I could do it, and I did. In that first moment of meeting Davin and Alli, I felt an instant and complete recognition. They were my spiritual kin. This private bond had stayed my secret throughout all the years we shared. Reincarnation only sounds reasonable. But now Alli and I were off on our big adventure, and I thought that perhaps somewhere on the road through the mountains or the desert, I would tell her that she really was mine all along.

But truth has an agenda of its own. It is impossible to express to another that which is unfathomable—in both depth and understanding. With my biological son, long grown away from home, I'd shared that physical, spiritual bond long before love needed language. But with Davin and Alli, there was no going back, which put the language of love at an unredeemable disadvantage. Trust is a visceral thing. It doesn't start in the head. I knew that from my own life. With Alli and Davin, I had wobbled around all the words but didn't know how to say them. I was neither mother nor father, which is where true love should come from, in the beginning, when words don't count.

For Alli, this road trip was to see her brother. For me, it was a way to tell her that I loved her. In our eight years together, we'd never really had a vacation. I'd gone on road trips my entire adult life—usually alone, often on the run from some ghost or another. Driving was dreamtime, a chance to catch up with my selves. Alli had more than a few selves of her own, and I thought that she, too, would liven to the reassuring rhythms that unfold on the road. We could both do with a little unfolding, I thought, watching her out of the corner of my eye as we set off, first on the ferry and then down the freeway. I recognized her sighs and the deep breath of relief that nothing, for now, needed to be attended to. Not even life.

We snuggled into the car in silence for those first few hours down Interstate 5 heading south to Ashland, Oregon, where we would spend our first night on the road. No music, no books on tape, no talk; we were lost to our own private reveries when suddenly, coming upon Centralia, about sixty miles south of Seattle, I recognized The Farmhouse restaurant, where I knew we could get a real hot turkey and gravy sandwich. It was our first unscheduled stop. We started to talk then, about the Christmas dinners she had never had, the Christmas pleasures never felt.

A few miles later, stuffed full with turkey and cranberry sauce, we made our first unscheduled detour, and it was a big one. We abandoned the Interstate 5 to Ashland plan. *We must start out by going to the Sylvia Beach Hotel on the Oregon coast,* I thought. Alli is a reader. We can't be this close and not go there. At the Sylvia Beach, reading is raised to the exalted state where it belongs. Writers, from Dr. Seuss to Jane Austen, are celebrated in rooms full of their works and their worlds. *We can afford the Oscar Wilde room,* I thought, with its two single beds crammed in between the romance and tragedy of Oscar himself—it's the cheapest room in the hotel. Then we'll wake up in the morning and wander up to the attic library in our pajamas and perch with endless cups of tea and watch the sea and read our first day away. "Well?" I asked Alli. "Yes," she said without blinking.

There is a phrase in the lexicon of travel lore, "companionable silence." It is an elusive state born out of trust and familiarity. It holds common longings and private dreams. It can also speak of shared loss and grief, all that is known and unknown between two people. We drove the road out to the coast in the dark, both watchful of icy pavement and oncoming traffic, both silent, together under the night. It was after seven when we arrived. Oscar's room was ready and waiting.

The Sylvia Beach is a book lover's lair. The halls creak with language; the nooks and crannies breathe prose and poetry, romance and mystery. Alli, whose life had been saved by books, sank into the place as though she had been born there. The next morning we perched and read, serving one another tea. Then we walked on the beach and decided to stay another night. After all, we had a long road ahead of us.

It got longer the next day when we decided to take the coast highway south. We got early morning lattes and drove under a deep blue sky beside the deep blue sea. Alli had never been by the open ocean before, and she loved it. She told me stories of her road trips with her dad, how she always wanted to see the ocean. Their destinations, however, had been to hidden places, in the woods and in the mountains. The ocean was light, expansive, playful, and daring. We played tag on the beach and threw our arms in the air.

We drove that coastal day away, stopping here and there when it was too beautiful not to, crossing into California shortly after dark. We hadn't arranged for a place to stay, but figured that in Crescent City there would be beds for the night; there was also the Redwood Hostel down the road. And after eating cheap but good Mexican food, we decided that the hostel would be best. We'd get to sleep in the dark and wake up by the sea.

Our plan was to spend a few days in San Francisco and then bolt south for a two-day drive to Phoenix. We'd arrive December 23, find a cheap motel close to Davin and his girlfriend, Heather, do Christmas with them, and then head home the day after. Even though we'd already whiled away our schedule, it would simply shorten our time in San Francisco, or so we thought.

San Francisco was home to my first true love. And like all loves that are true, it had stayed so over the years. We were not constantly in touch, but we were constant friends. Richard, a filmmaker, knew we were on our way and had welcomed us to stay at his place in San Francisco. I'd seen him earlier that year, when he and his girlfriend were in the Northwest, but he'd not yet met Alli. When we were about an hour away from the Bay Area, I called his office—which was also where he lived—and discovered that he'd been suddenly called to Seattle because his mother was dying. "But we're expecting you," said his assistant.

We pulled up in the early evening and settled in to sleep in his guest loft. Alli had heard all about Richard and we were both sad. I called him on his cell phone. His mom had died. He was doing what he could and would be back in San Francisco in a couple of days, for Christmas. Then he'd go back to Seattle for the service. Maybe on our way back we could see him.

The next morning I woke up sick. Every muscle and all its relations ached like an impacted tooth. Alli made me tea and breakfast, which I could barely eat. "It's all in my head," I muttered to myself, until my body got in the way. I was good at getting sick at Christmas, but I'd thought that being on the road would cure me of my seasonal ills. It couldn't, however, prevent the flu. For two days I could barely move. Alli curled up quietly and patiently with her books and waited for yet another detour to pass. We called her brother. "We're not there yet," we said. "But we are on our way."

It was the morning of December 22 by the time I was better. Richard would be home later that day, but Phoenix was too far away for us to wait. We packed up the car and were on the road by 8:30. As we were one block from getting on the freeway, the car quit running. We pushed it around a corner out of the way of traffic onto a rundown side street that had a parking space only because the street cleaners would be there that morning. For ten minutes we sat speechless as the engine turned over and over and refused to start. Suddenly Alli said, "Let's ask her for help." She jumped out of the car and before I could see who "her" was, she was in conversation with a woman on the sidewalk. I climbed out, chagrined. The woman was obviously on her way to work at some fancy place downtown. She looked suspiciously at the car, bumper-stickered with support for Ralph Nader, Tibet, Wales, whales, and working families against the WTO.

"Where in Washington?" she asked, noticing our license plates. "Near Seattle," I said. "San Juan Island," said Alli. The woman looked shocked. "I used to live there," she said. "Do you know Lynne Mercer?" "Yes," I said, "We rent our house from her." We were all speechless. Within minutes we were in her living room calling the nearest service station for help and catching up on all the island places and people we had in common.

"You knew," I said to Alli when we were back in the car waiting for the tow truck.

"I had a feeling," she said.

It was noon by the time the car was towed to the station. Six hours and more than six hundred dollars later, the burned-out electrical system was fixed. We were back on the road and on our way once again—back to Richard's place. This time he was there. We ordered Thai food for supper and caught up with all the complexities of life and death in one another's lives.

Alli and I unrolled our sleeping bags once again in his loft. "Now what?" we wondered. To go, or not to go? By this time I knew what I'd known all along. I didn't really want to go to Phoenix at all. I loved Davin, but I was afraid to see him, afraid to face the consequences of the life he had chosen, afraid to face the girlfriend who always spoke for him on the phone and asked for money, who was pregnant with her fifth baby (not his), all of whom had been placed in foster care, afraid to face all the ways in which too-late love had not worked. I was going to Phoenix for Alli, because Davin was all she had. But now circumstances had caught up with us. I felt strange, as though I had willed our dilemma, as though my psyche had short-circuited the car on purpose.

"We could," I said to Alli, "try to get there for a day; or we could turn around and get back in time for Christmas on the Oregon Coast." She burst into tears of dismay and disappointment. The truth was, we were out of money and out of time. The lofty goals of this trip were getting lost along the way; so was my patience. We went to sleep with no answer on the horizon, and in the morning went out for an early breakfast. The car was packed up yet again, but we still didn't know in which direction we would go.

Alli ate her favorite breakfast with sausage, then phoned her brother. No answer. We said good-bye to Richard and went off to buy Christmas presents. Then we called Davin again. No answer. We went into the bakery and got something tasty to eat. Still no answer. I could feel my gift of this trip becoming yet another notch of disappointment in Alli's life. Once again, promises made and not kept. Love's unfolding lie, unfolding me with it. Even though it was a stretch, we could've made it to Phoenix. But I was facing my own truth. I had had enough. I was tired.

By noon we were on our way north. Alli, whose life had taught her that nothing was ever reliable, was resigned to whatever happened next. She was very quiet; so was I. "I love you," I didn't say. "Isn't it enough for us just to be on the road together?" I knew the answer: of course not. It was the other love, the silent knowing kind that was her birthright that she was missing. The kind of love that she should feel without knowing it's there. My theory of reincarnation paled in comparison.

As we pulled away from the dense traffic of Marin County and into the rolling hills of the northern California countryside, Alli breathed out loudly just one word, "Home." And I knew what it meant. Throughout our years together, Alli had spent a lot of her time in her room. It was a room full of her girl-ness, where stuffed animals competed with books, dragons, horses, and crystal balls for attention. Even though she was eighteen, nothing about childhood had she given up. In the safety of a second chance, she had held to innocence most of all. "Home," I knew, was her room. I wanted it to be with me.

We slept that night surrounded by giant redwoods. We woke up to a walk in the woods and ended the day by fixing a Christmas Eve dinner for a lone and grateful traveler at the hostel in Bandon, back on the Oregon Coast. After Alli was asleep, I put her stocking at the end of her bed. When I woke up, there was mine. We giggled at all the silly things.

It was Christmas and the day sang with sun and warmth. We ate pumpkin pie and chocolate mousse cake for breakfast high on the Oregon dunes. We called the Sylvia Beach and there was room at the inn. Still, there was no answer at Davin's. At sunset we walked the beach, then found a local restaurant open for Christmas dinner and had yet another almost home-cooked turkey dinner. In the evening we went to the movies and watched Tom Hanks make friends with his volleyball on a deserted island. It was as unlikely a Christmas as either of us could have imagined.

The next day we finally reached Davin; he and Heather had spent Christmas in the hospital because of a potential complication of pregnancy. Alli and I looked at each other and I knew: we could finally call this trip our own. But still I could say nothing to her about this unidentifiable bond between us, our destiny.

We lingered a long time leaving the Sylvia Beach Hotel. Inside the car, it was like being underneath a teenager's bed. We settled ourselves in for the road home. Christmas was over; the days were getting longer. Light was on its way. As I was starting the car, Alli surprised me with a card and a package. Inside the package were two carved turtles—a big mamma one and a little baby one. Inside the card she had written: *"Dear Janet. This has been great, as well as sad, but I have had a great time spending it with you! We should do this once a year. Just the girls! Lots of love, Alli."* On the cover was a cluster of delicate white flowers growing like miracles out of rough red sandstone. Two circles were carved, coiled together, on the surface of the rock.

When we got home to San Juan Island, Alli came out of her room. Within weeks, she had a busy social life and a future she could name. She was taking scuba diving and flying lessons and finally paying attention to school. It was a stunning transformation.

Then, in early spring, Davin and Heather arrived on the island to await arrival of Heather's baby. They brought with them all the old familiar alienation and despair. Overnight and without a word, Alli gave away her stuffed animals, packed up her things, left home, and moved in with them. Our relationship, eight years in the making, ended as abruptly as it had begun. I became the enemy.

For months I was in mourning. I heard word of Alli only occasionally, and never from her directly. After Heather's baby was born and quickly taken into protective custody, the three of them left the island and headed back to Phoenix. There was no good-bye. It was as though we'd never met, Alli and I. Our Christmas trip, so perfect and important, seemed like a mirage, something that had happened to two other people.

Finally, on my birthday this past October, she called. Her life with Davin and Heather had unraveled, but through the distress she had taken control. She had signed up for Job Corps, gotten a high school diploma and a boyfriend, and had started training to become a healthcare worker. She'd done it alone, on her own.

"I cry all the time," she said. "I miss you."

We made plans for her to come home for Christmas.

Two months later, in the middle of the drive from the airport back to the island, we reminisced over every detail of our road trip the previous year and talked about how much had happened since.

"I don't know what happened to me," she said.

I do, I thought.

We'd taken to the road, and it had led her, finally, home.

The Limitless Road

BHARTI KIRCHNER

"Five... four... three... two... one... go," the race director shouts through a loudspeaker. The prerace jitters dissolve in a surge of adrenaline and I rush forward from the middle of the pack, keenly aware of the thumping of hundreds of feet all around me. The day is overcast and cool, but a brilliant sun is shining through a gap in the trees far down the road. Spectators lining the course yell encouraging words: "Looking good. Way to go, number thirty-five!" Beads of cooling perspiration begin to form on my forehead as my mind sheds the last vestige of prerace anxiety. My legs feel light, as though they can run forever, as though nothing could hold them back. I drink in the crisp, pine-scented air and revel in the melodic twittering of the birds, preternaturally clear over the chaos around me. The adventure of weekend road racing has swept me up again.

'Tis in the human nature to seek adventure. In the classical sense of the term, this would likely refer to a foray into the wilderness or an uncertain voyage toward a distant shore. The path is often uncharted, the destination hazy, the rewards doubtful, and yet we press on, lured by mystery and a desire to conquer. In modern times, however, adventure has assumed an expanded meaning. It needn't take place miles from home or entail mortal danger. The destination might be clearly marked. The reward could simply be self-knowledge or self-mastery. As an urban dweller in America's modern West, I've chosen to undertake one such alternative: distance running. It's a feat that starts right outside my door.

My dream of running began during a two-year stay in Europe. In the picturesque city of Amsterdam, where I was employed as a database specialist in the often pressure-filled world of software engineering, I'd de-stress myself by taking a stroll after work along the wooded trails of Amsterdamse Bos Park.

In this magnificent wooded park on the outskirts of Amsterdam, runners of various sizes, shapes, and ages would glide gracefully past me. I had admired their measured footfalls, relaxed arms, and rhythmic breathing. The experience had spoken to something primeval within me, and ever since I'd carried with me a secret desire to run. The sport seemed to offer fitness and a joyous feeling of liberation.

Yet I wasn't without doubts. I'd grown up in India, where girls were strongly discouraged from engaging in physical activities. My fitness pursuits up to that point had consisted solely of yoga and other traditional conditioning exercises that were by no means strenuous. Would I have the energy and stamina to run?

My quest began the following year, in the early eighties, when I purchased a pair of Nike Daybreaks at an athletic store in San Francisco. Job relocation had brought me there from Europe. A pair of well-fitted running shoes, I was told, was the single most important investment a runner could make. It was on a mild spring day that my new purchase beckoned me. They cushioned my feet superbly and their wide toe box allowed my toes to spread out. Floating in a feeling of comfort, I tied the shoelaces, slipped out of my Richmond District house, and turned left.

Golden Gate Park, a beautiful four-mile-long sanctuary guarded by towering eucalyptus trees and laced with gentle trails, the "urban runner's mecca," was only a block away. The bright California sky, muted by incoming afternoon fog, bathed the row of pastel-colored houses in my neighborhood in a dreamy golden haze. Along the sidewalk, dogwoods blossomed in creamy white profusion, and assertive orange poppies peeked out from fissures in the concrete. A gust of damp wind gently puffed out my windbreaker, reminding me that the Pacific Ocean was but minutes away. As I reached the entrance to the park, crows nesting in a pine tree up ahead cawed raucously, as though protesting my intrusion. My fancy footwear obviously didn't impress them in the slightest. To avoid the uproar, I took a slight detour. As my feet landed on a carpet of benevolent grass and obstinate weeds, I sensed an immediate joyous connection to the earth.

What better place to start training than in scenic San Francisco, referred to by locals simply as "the city," where the weather is near perfect year-round. The timing, I believed, was right, too. The running craze of the seventies hadn't abated in the new decade. If anything, the sport had expanded to include amateur athletes of many different fitness levels. Soon after my arrival in the city, at a neighborhood get-together, I'd overheard a paunchy sixty-five-year-old man rave about the three "Bs": Boston Marathon, Bill Rodgers, and the locally famous Bay-to-Breakers Race. Later that evening I found myself caught up in the enthusiasm of a harried young mother who waxed eloquent about the precious "quality time" she spent running.

On this day, my destination was the Polo Field, an oval dirt track in Golden Gate Park. Once reserved for horses and their riders, it was slightly under a mile in circumference. Though a few horseback riders could be seen cantering along the dusty track, they were vastly outnumbered by runners, whose skimpy shorts flirted with the wind. Scattered throughout the area were spectators who watched with rapt attention as the runners went round and round.

The energy was contagious. Following their lead, I set one foot in front of another and pushed my body forward. Not accustomed to such effort, my untutored legs soon turned to lead. Within a few yards, fancy footwear notwithstanding, I began to gasp. I paused to refill my burning lungs with air, attempted another jog with the same result, then stopped for good. Lamenting my lack of cardiovascular fitness and hoping no one else had noticed it, I strolled the rest of the circular path, trying to make myself as inconspicuous as possible. But I made a decision to try again when there would hopefully be fewer witnesses to my feeble effort.

The next day I returned to the Polo Field and watched as seasoned runners powered with ease and grace through loop after loop of their practice. I resolved to "flow" just like them and set my goal of completing a mile. Once again I zoomed on. This time I managed a few more yards, but soon ground to a halt, chest heaving. Later I would learn that in runner's vocabulary I was in "serious oxygen debt."

Running was obviously not for me. I'd just have to take up some other sport. Or should I try one more time? The debate just raged in my mind when I spotted a man approaching. I had seen him here before. This tanned, athletically built, middle-aged man of average height usually stood against the hedge bordering the track, watching the runners with keen eyes. He didn't merely watch; he checked their form and stride and corrected them. And he kept time with a huge stopwatch. As they finished, he cheered them. Now he halted a few feet away from me, tipped his black cap slightly, and said, "Madame, let me present myself."

I was amused by the formal tone. Had he mistaken me for someone else?

"I am Adnan Haddad. Ah, I see you're wondering about that name—it's Lebanese. You're probably also wondering why I've approached you. I coach runners. I've seen you jogging here."

I blushed. So he had witnessed my futile attempts. Surely he was paying me a compliment when he called my few seconds of sprints "jogging."

"I can't really call myself a 'jogger,' Mr. Haddad. I'd just like to be able to do a loop around this field."

He smiled and nodded knowingly. "I think I can help you do that. And more."

Perhaps noticing the hesitancy in my shuffling feet, Haddad related his background in an effort, I assumed, to put me at ease. Once a wrestler in Lebanon, he had since settled in San Francisco. Recently he'd been chosen to coach the U.S. wrestling team for the next Olympics.

An Olympic coach, no less. I couldn't believe my luck. I kept on listening.

"You start, then you give up. You won't go very far that way."

"I run out of oxygen."

"Ah, this is why I recommend the walk-run strategy to the beginners."

"And what's that?"

Whereupon Haddad explained the method: run, slowing down to walk when you must, then as soon as you can, start running again. Go a bit farther each time. Soon you'll walk less and run more.

"You think you can do that?" he challenged me.

"Of course I can."

"Then show me the next time." A faint smile played on his lips.

We chatted a while longer. Haddad informally coached college athletes, amateur runners, local and national class racers, as well as novices. Running had once been his favorite fitness activity. Now he helped other runners. And he believed that someone like me, bereft of any sports training, could take on this challenge as well. It was as though he had already seen a budding runner in me. My spirit was boosted.

"A woman of the East," he said in conclusion. "I see determination in your eyes. The road is for those who can endure."

He mumbled something about meeting me at the same place in two weeks. Then he waved good-bye, turned past a bed of tiny blue forget-me-nots, and slipped away, while I stood there turning this unusual incident over in my mind.

The next day after work I ironed my tank top and shorts and stretched to limber my muscles. Then I headed for the Polo Field to practice what Haddad had suggested—interspersing my strolls with one to two minutes of running. During those brief periods, as my legs flew through the air and my lungs devoured large amounts of oxygen, I began to feel what running must feel like to the already initiated. It was the giddy experience of extending one's physical capabilities, the contentment of meeting a goal. At the end of the practice session, I noted that I hadn't overly strained my capacity. My legs still felt strong. I left the park exhilarated, hungry for more.

In each of the following days, I made a concrete effort to lengthen the running period and shorten the walks in between. Armed with this new strategy, just before the two weeks was over, I circled the entire length of the Polo Field nonstop, thereby accomplishing my goal of a mile. Savoring my hard-won victory, I walked taller. As I passed some feathery ferns, I caressed the leaves and shed my remaining doubts. Finally, I was ready to become a runner. On my way out of the park, I even waved at the crows. This time they barely cawed at my intrusion.

The appointed day came. I arrived at the park on time, ready to show Coach Haddad my new running prowess and seek more advice from him. My eyes roamed the entire area. My heart pounded in anticipation. As usual, runners bustled and horses snorted, but few spectators were to be seen. The sky was darkening, a storm about to break. But there was no sign of Haddad. His absence took me by surprise. I felt abandoned, without moorings.

Fifteen minutes passed. I queried other runners, but no one had seen him. I waited as long as I could, then did my usual loop and left the park in a somber mood, just as the rain began to pound the earth.

In the following days I continued to inquire about Haddad. Finally, a week later, someone informed me that he had died of a sudden heart attack.

But how could that be? In a moment the day was drained of any color. I didn't want this kind man to die. I found myself unable to move. For the next week or so I couldn't run or even go near the park. I mourned Haddad's loss every bit as much as other, more experienced runners did. In the thrill of an adventure, I had stumbled across heartbreak.

Eventually I returned to the field. In Haddad's honor I resumed my daily loops. My body adapted to the stress; my strides became more fluid. Soon I completed two miles, then three. It didn't take long before I realized that I had exhausted the training possibilities in this relatively small area. The question I asked myself was: Where do I go from here?

One afternoon toward the end of a run, when the exertion had cleared my head, I had a flash of insight: I'd already learned what I needed to know about the sport. Coach Haddad had advised me to endure, the best lesson he could offer. The rest was up to me.

I began to run the roads. Over time, despite a modest beginning, I went on to include a daily training run of several miles through the streets of San Francisco. My days still belonged to my job as a software specialist, but the evenings saw me out on the road, exploring my neighborhood and escaping the rigors of the day. In that hour of solitude, I listened to the rhythm of my heart; I contemplated. Problems that had stymied me during working hours, such as finding a "bug" in a client's malfunctioning database, melted or "debugged" themselves during my evening runs, the time when I trusted my inner knowing more. I could be at the busy corner of 22nd and Geary when a solution would jump out at me; at other times, such mundane workday concerns would remain in check till I arrived at my desk the next day.

The decade that followed saw me competing in innumerable 10k and 15k road races and one half marathon. On Sundays, instead of sleeping late or curling up with a bulky newspaper, I participated in races in the company of hundreds of fellow runners. An urban adventure had begun for me, an adventure that started on a designated mark on a road, went on for many grueling miles, then finished beneath a clock and a banner mounted high on another road. I ranked locally in my age group and even brought home a few medals as a bonus. Soon I was keeping track of the time and distance of each adventure, with the intention of bettering both the next time out.

"Is road running daring enough to be called an adventure?" at one point I asked myself. My territory was paved and lined with orderly rows of evergreens. Traffic lights interrupted my progress; passing vehicles honked. A misguided sense of direction would land me, at worst, in an undesirable locale, rather than in the jaws of a beast. Minutes after a run I could go home, shower, put on clean clothes, and nap. My answer to the question, was, however, affirmative. Road running does offer plenty of mental and physical challenges and it does demand a certain level of fitness. As in an adventure, only through sustained effort was I able to experience the true rewards of road running and discover previously untapped resources of inner strength.

The road, I found, is a great leveler. Runners, regardless of their abilities or their station in life, share the same course, the same joys of competition, and identical challenges. Running with a group whenever I could, I formed unexpected friendships. It's easier to relate when you run the same road. Yet at the same time, running offers the most private of all experiences.

I don't know at what point road running stopped being a mere physical exercise and became a metaphor for freedom and fulfillment. Even in the confines of a city where life has predictable parameters, one can unchain oneself through a mere jog on the sidewalk. The mind becomes lucid; the body loses its inhibition. The fulfillment comes simply from being liberated and achieving the goal of a certain speed or distance. For the urban runner, the road stretches to infinity. Even the asphalted road that carries a sign at every corner seems beyond the map and imbued with a certain mystery.

Eventually a time came when I decided to try my hand at writing. It didn't surprise my family and friends that my very first article was published in a running journal, and it was about a road race. Soon I contributed a number of other articles in various sports magazines about different aspects of running. In due course I progressed to other topics such as food, travel, and fitness, but

I'd come back to focus on running time and again. Through words on the page I'd re-experience the joys and travails of my runs.

Once a runner, always a runner, so goes a motto. In the mid-nineties I attempted my first novel, *Shiva Dancing*. By then I'd relocated to Seattle and had started to explore its roads and trails through daily runs. But I hadn't forgotten my humble beginning in Golden Gate Park. It seemed only natural then that my protagonist, Meena Gossett, would be a runner and that she'd live in "the city," on the edge of Golden Gate Park. Meena, who had been kidnapped from her village in India at the age of seven, was raised in San Francisco by an American couple. In her mid-thirties Meena was a full-fledged runner and racer. Running came much more easily to her than it did to me, I might add, and her 10k times were superior. Yet, in powers that fictional characters often possess, she pushed me to perform better.

The book's focal point was Meena's journey back to India and her discovery of her self there. Running, I assumed, would be merely a way to show yet another aspect of her total existence. After work Meena trained in Golden Gate Park to unwind and to prepare for a race. A few paragraphs about her running were all I'd intended to put in the book. Yet the sport had a way of sneaking into the plot whenever it could. Soon I introduced a male character, who turned out to be a runner as well, and who would naturally notice Meena in the park. In the race, Meena lost first place to another woman, whom she would, at a future time, befriend. The woman would help Meena solve a case of business malpractice, one that'd thrown her life in turmoil.

The novel was, by no means, an autobiography. It was simply a work of imagination in which some of my own life experiences came into play. Yet when it was published in 1998, readers besieged me with questions: Were you married at age seven? Had you been kidnapped? Are you a runner? No, no, and yes, I replied. I was simply sharing with Meena a job expertise in the software field and a penchant for running. Once Meena became a runner, it was easier for me to understand her and portray her. For both of us, what had started out as a fitness activity had opened up the pathway to a wider universe.

And in the end, running, like all adventures, is about exploring possibilities. The road beckons to us and we answer its call. Sometimes we wince from the pain of a blister; at other times we raise our hands in victory. We keep going even when we believe we've exhausted our mental and physical reserves. Only in retrospect do we realize that the road has extended the limits of these reserves. It has dared to show us how far we can travel. This is why we creatures who seek limitlessness crave the road.

Slipping the Knot

SUSAN EWING

Thud. A woman swaddled in a navy blue snowmachine suit knelt on the ground cleaving dents into a forty-pound slab of frozen, ground chicken. *Thud. Thud. Thud.* Before long, the pink slab was reduced to baseball-sized chunks, which she tossed into an old dog food bag for later distribution to the huskies. Enormous oil-black ravens watched from lichen-furred spruce trees.

Before now, I had only seen the Yukon Territory through the windshield of a truck on my way back and forth from Alaska. On most of those trips, the Yukon meant little more than endurance driving on the way to somewhere else. But this time the Yukon was the place and there would be no windshield. The road was a trail with a view largely unchanged from the days of Jack London and Robert Service. And it was February.

Outfitter and chicken chopper Jeninne Cathers was going to guide me and four others on a 300-mile dogsled trip along an old Klondike gold-rush mail route, which is also part of the Yukon Quest race trail. The Quest is a thousand-mile-long dogsled race from Whitehorse (the largest town in the Yukon Territory of Canada) to Fairbanks, Alaska. It's billed as the world's toughest long-distance mushing competition, partly because of the terrain and partly because there are fewer checkpoints than in the Iditarod, so mushers have to carry more dog food and survival gear. The record finish for the Quest is ten days, sixteen hours, twenty minutes. We would take at least twelve days to complete our shorter tour, camping or staying in bush cabins along the way.

At home I had penciled in the route on a 1987 Yukon Territory highway map unearthed from a box in my closet. That was the year I left Fairbanks for good, driving away one last time with one more man and a precious old dog who outloved and outlasted them all.

■ ■ ■

We would take off from the Cathers's family cabin on Lake Laberge, cut across the frozen lake, and travel northwest to where the Pelly River spills into the Yukon River. Along the way we would cross the Dawson Highway three times, allowing Jeninne's younger brother Brad to meet us with dog food and other supplies.

My pencil line looked like a gray snake slithering in three arcs across the red-ink ribbon of road, with its head resting on Lake Laberge and its tail curled around the abandoned mining town of Fort Selkirk. Names on the map rang like a pick on hard rock: Pyroxene Mountain, Miners Range, Silver City, Cofee Creek. Older names echoed too—Aishihik, Hootalinqua, Nanutak, Klukshu. Names even more ancient have been lost on the wind; this part of the Yukon escaped the crushing glaciers of the last ice age, offering refuge and migration routes to ancient people and animals.

Our trail would follow frozen rivers and chains of lakes, and cut through rugged bush country covered by dog-hair forests of black spruce and lodgepole pine. Low mountain ranges humped here and there like giant beavers let loose on the landscape.

Since I was the least experienced member of the group, Jeninne encouraged me to come up a few days early to practice. I liked the idea of spending more time with the dogs. Between them, Jeninne and her father, Ned, have ninety-one Alaskan huskies. Unlike Siberians, an officially recognized breed, Alaskan huskies are a conglomeration of northern breeds mixed with hounds, setters, pointers, and mutts for attitude, athleticism, and tough feet.

Not quite thirty, Jeninne had been mushing dogs more than half her life and had run the Quest six times. I was forty-five and had managed to get my young malamute-mix to pull me around on a plastic-and-aluminum folding dogsled. Nothing about this shuffle of facts struck me as dangerous.

The first practice day went fine, following Jeninne along the shoreline of the icebound lake with my own small team.

"Are you warm enough?" she shouted back to me. I waved a double-insulated mitt and smiled, subarctic wind tapping at my teeth.

The second day we wound up a steep trail behind the cabin. In some places I had to get off the sled, set the edges of my felt-lined boots against the slope, and push the sled with my shoulder while the dogs heaved into their harnesses. Each time I got off to push, the dogs looked around at me as they held the sled from sliding backward. Now I understood dog "team."

Going up was strenuous but simple. Going down would be infinitely more complicated. We would be going fast. I would have to steer.

Sled runners respond to pressure somewhat the way downhill skis do. You can also drag a foot outside the runner to persuade the sled to track a certain way. The catch is that you have to take your foot off the brake to steer. The brake is a spring-loaded, spiked contraption that you stomp on to, theoretically, stop the sled. (For emergency stopping there is also a snow hook: a heavy, evil-looking steel claw that you dig into the snow like a hand-set anchor.)

I worried about the downhill run all afternoon and was good and anxious by the time we circled back and started the descent, a bobsled run of straightaways, curves, and hard turns through the forest. The physics were confusing. The lead dogs could be blasting out of a turn before the sled even entered it. I made the first few bends, but the dogs picked up speed. Careening toward a hard turn, I jumped on the brake with both feet and felt the double spikes scrape futilely along the frozen ground under the thin layer of snow. The dogs dashed cleanly around the turn but the sled didn't, slamming smack into a tree with a great and awful *CRACK* that popped me off like ejected toast. Piled in the middle of the trail, I peered up in time to see the sled rocketing on alone behind the anarchy of grinning dogs.

By the time I caught up a little way down the trail, Jeninne had snagged my wagging team, which, amazingly enough, hadn't wrecked themselves or the sled. Jeninne never raised her voice to her dogs and was equally patient with human travelers. "I've hit that tree a few times, too," she said charitably. Straightening my official beaver-fur musher's hat, I hobbled back onto the sled and off we went.

■ ■ ■

The other members of the party trickled in: two men from Germany, one from Australia, and a woman from Paris.

On the evening before we were to go, Ned started the generator so Jeninne would have good light to write out her final dog-team lists. Sitting straight-shouldered at the family dining table, she contemplated the personality and experience of each dog, listing, erasing, listing, erasing, listing, until she was satisfied with each team. As she created the teams, she also kept the musher in mind. I got the smallest team, only five dogs. The rest would drive eight to ten.

Rosa was to be my lead dog. The slightly fretful six-year-old matriarch had a shiny black coat and cinnamon eyebrow spots that levitated over her concerned, light-brown eyes. Some Native Americans believe such "Four-Eye" dogs have mystery power.

Rosa's four-year-old daughter Savanne, a leader-in-training, would also run at the head of my team. Built like an adolescent gymnast, Savanne had a sleek, coyote-colored coat.

Lion, a good-old-boy of ten with a broad, happy face and light-tan markings, would be my point dog, running behind the leaders.

Rosa's sons-of-different-fathers Bronson and Alabama would run behind Lion in wheel position, directly in front of the sled. The handsome half-brothers were larger versions of their Four-Eyed mother. On the big side for Alaskan huskies at well over sixty pounds each, they would be my power dogs. Three-year-old Alabama was confident and friendly. Two-year-old Bronson was terrified of strangers. When I tried to handle him during our practice days, he pulled me off my feet trying to get away, preferring to choke to death rather than make eye contact or let me touch him. Just as I was worrying whether I should ask Jeninne for a different dog, she said she was putting him with me on purpose.

■ ■ ■

On the morning of our departure, it was a sunny ten degrees. Packing the sleds threw the dog yard into a frenzy of hysterical barking: *Take Me Take Me Take Me OOOOOOO TAKE ME.* Inside the din of ninety-one crazed canines, we loaded the sleds with dog food, extra harnesses and lines, picket cables, chainsaw, ax, personal gear, a wall tent, and boxes of people food that Jeninne's mother, Mar, had organized—frozen French fries, vegetables, and fish sticks; cans of beef stew and ravioli; foil pans of homemade desserts with evocative masking-tape labels: Chocolate Dream, Strawberry Freeze, Summit Cake.

Before we began harnessing dogs, Jeninne and Ned tied each sled to a tree or post with a slip knot that can be yanked loose for takeoff. Finally all the dogs that were going were in place, barking, howling, yapping, desperate to GO. Ned harnessed the acutely agitated Bronson for me and, yelling in my ear, offered to pull my knot so I could hang on with both hands for the ballistic takeoff. Deep under multiple layers of down, fleece, and polypro, my heart flapped like a trapped ptarmigan.

If there was a ready-set-go, I missed it. Jeninne shot off in a blur of paws to the intensified shrieks of the left-behind dogs. The trail out of the dog yard to the lake bent quickly out of sight, and when Jeninne disappeared, Ned yanked the tail end of my slip knot. Rosa, Savanne, Lion, Alabama, and Bronson whiplashed into full speed, ears pinned back, heads and tails low, hell-bent on catching their mates ahead. They weren't barking now.

I hung on for dear life through the dog yard and managed to steer around the first turn into the winter-bare willows. We burst out onto the lakeshore and as the dogs ramped pell-mell toward the ice rink of Lake Laberge, I made a quick visual check: no tangled lines, all dogs pulling, no one choking or limping. When

I looked up I saw Jeninne ahead, splashing up short rooster tails of water from her sled runners. Before I could say "Uh-oh," I heard crunching. My heart sank and then so did I, up to my crotch in frigid water.

In the first second, I caught my breath and thought, *Dry! Stay dry!* In the next, icy water filled my boots as though they were buckets. In the third second, I realized some slick but solid footing supported my weight, so I was not on my way to the bottom of the lake. The fourth second hissed *team.*

"It's okay, dogs," I said through clenched teeth.

Taking a breath, I reoccupied my body, which had been trying to stay tucked up under my collarbone. Plates of inch-thick ice—crust of the overflow Jeninne had broken on her way out—clinked around me.

Rosa and Savanne churned the water, their attention locked on Jeninne stopped on solid ice in the near distance. Lion flailed behind them. The panicked Bronson turned in his harness and clawed up onto the bobbing sled, threatening to pull Alabama underwater in the process. Bronson watched in horror as I splashed aside a plate of ice and pulled myself forward to do the hardest thing I would do on the whole, hard trip: I pushed him off the sled.

"Let's go, Rosa. Okay, Savanne. Good boy, Lion. Good, Alabama. It's okay, Bronson. Good boy." The dogs paddled forward through the dark water.

Lake Laberge sucked at my legs, clutched at my concrete boots. The sled floated heavily. Twice Rosa and Savanne clambered onto a promising ice shelf only to have it crack under their weight. The third time they tried and failed, I panicked. "I can't get out!" I shouted shrilly to whoever was responsible for signing me up for this trip. The dogs hesitated and looked around at me. Right.

"Okay. Let's go. Good, Rosa. Good girl!"

Although it seemed like a week, we were probably in the water only a few minutes. Rosa and Savanne found solid ice and scrambled up with Lion right behind. Alabama and Bronson climbed out and worked together to haul out the sled with me holding on. The dogs sprinted toward Jeninne, shaking themselves as they went, while I hoisted to my feet on the scraping runners. Rosa and Savanne ran straight to Jeninne's outstretched hand.

"You all right?" she asked me, looking at Rosa.

"Yeah." I figured we would go back to the cabin, dry out, and tell Great Overflow Disaster stories over cups of hot coffee.

"Can you wait an hour to change? The lake's not a good place to stop."

She looked from me to the reassembled group struggling to hold their teams on the glare ice, estimating how many seconds we had until the lines of dogs devolved into a Gordian tangle. The others had seen me go through and found another way around.

"With all that water in your boots, at least your feet won't get frostbitten," she said cheerily as we strung out across the lake.

At least I was mostly dry from the butt up. The work of keeping the sled tracking across the checkerboard of ice and crusty snow patches stemmed my shivers and kept my core temperature up, though I couldn't tell whether my feet were in pain or had lost all feeling. Half an hour later, an urgent message arrived from Stumpland: "Save us."

"I have to do something," I called to Jeninne as she and I clawed our snow hooks into a small patch of snow to let the other teams catch up. I had brought a spiffy new thermos on the trip, but no spare boots. Jeninne reached quickly into her sled bag, brought out her own extra pair and tossed them to me. Struggling out of my flooded boots and dead-fish socks, I slipped bare white feet into the felt-lined sanctums. I wore her boots, two sizes bigger than mine, until we arrived after dark at the little cabin where we were to stay the first night. I wore them as we tied our picket lines among the brittle-limbed trees and moved each dog to his or her place by the light of headlamps; I wore them, ga-lumping, until all the dogs were fed.

After a night in front of the stove, my boots were dry and I moved like a woman resurrected through morning chores: haul and heat water to mix with the dry dog food, feed the dogs, feed ourselves, pack our stuff, pack the sleds, harness dogs, retrieve and pack the picket lines, pull the slip knots, and go. Except I had tied my knot wrong. Dietmar, the strapping young German fire-fighter who usually ran his team behind mine, jumped to my aid. He pulled back against the straining, barking dogs while I threw off my clumsy mittens and frantically worked the tight line loose from the tree.

That night after chores, I sat leaning against my sled with my headlamp focused on my cold, bare hands and practiced the slip knot with a stick and a string. Things take on extra significance in the middle of nowhere in the middle of winter. As I worked on the knot, I thought about all the illusions we use to secure our lives, the promises that offer to hold things in place even while their fingers are crossed. These alluring twists have seduced me time after time, and I am still surprised when they come unraveled. Happily, I am reasonably durable, like a husky's foot.

■ ■ ■

In the morning, I was up early to help Jeninne feed dogs. Sitting on her heels, she laid out some tooth-marked bread pans, glanced down the nearest picket line, and scooped a specific amount of kibble for each dog. I followed her scoops with a sprinkling of dried egg mix from a cloudy plastic bag.

Dietmar was up too and came along to fill each pan the rest of the way with warm water. He and I took turns delivering the sloshing pans to each dog in order: Canasta, Vegas, Roulette, El Paso, Saber, Havoc, Prairie, Steele. Next picket line: Algonquin, Belinda, Mustang, Kalika, Lantra, Deerhorn, Gambler, Drumlin, and so on, until all the dogs on all the lines were fed.

When the people had eaten and sleds had been repacked, it was time to harness the dogs. I tied my sled to a tree with what I hoped was the perfect slip knot and stretched out the gang line. The wild takeoffs intimidated me, and my hands trembled as I sorted my team's harnesses—large for Bronson, Alabama, and Lion; small for Rosa and Savanne. As soon as we started messing with lines and sleds, the dogs stood, stretched, and yawned. Some planted their rears carefully, sitting erect as Egyptian dog statuary. As soon as Jeninne fetched her lead dog, Gypsy, off the picket line, the whole extended pack burst into a trilling, yipping, yodeling ululation.

Fetching the first dog is like lighting a fuse; it sets in motion an urgent excitement that defies containment. As much as this part of the morning put my stomach in solid square knots, I also loved wrestling ebullient dogs from the picket line to the gang line, harnessing them while they tried to pee on anything in squirting reach, and refereeing snits over perceived insults. It took me five minutes to get hold of Bronson and another five to wrestle him into his harness, even though he was short-leashed for safe measure to the picket line. I unclipped him and we took turns dragging each other to the sled.

When my team was all hooked up, Rosa raised her nose in the air and howled. Savanne pressed her flank to Rosa's and tossed howling yips over her shoulder like mice. In between howls she leapt against her harness like a springtail, chopping her teeth. Lion spread his toes and scratched and snorted like a cartoon bull. Alabama was seized with a head-shaking sneezing fit. Bronson stood with his legs splayed and planted as if on the deck of a pitching boat, an astonished expression on his Four-Eyed face. This was his first camping trip.

At last all the dogs in all the teams were hooked up and all the mushers on their runners, knot-ends in hand. *Yank,* off went Jeninne. *Yank,* off went Marie France. Me next. My team was jerking the sled hard enough to shake the tree. *Yank!* The knot pulled clean and I was flying free like some latter-day Jacqueline London.

■ ■ ■

For the most part of that day, as every day, the rough trail demanded attention. I had imagined *shooshing* along swiftly and silently with a loose captain-of-the-ship stance on the runners. Instead, I jumped on and off the sled, pushing, pulling, tipping, jogging, and dragging my feet one way and another as we crossed gullies, negotiated steep banks, and finessed the alternate steering and braking of downhill runs. But there were also stretches of easy-going trail with time to look at the scenery and listen to the whiffing draft of ravens' wings as they flew low overhead, *ka-rooking* us through their territory. A wolf pack dodged into the woods as we swept along the edge of a small frozen lake; the dogs pricked their ears and sniffed the air and watched the woods, trotting more smartly until we had put their lupine cousins well behind.

It was a long day and we didn't make it to camp before dark. Northern lights fluxed green and pink. In a closer spellbound sphere, the dogs' eyes reflected in our headlamps—a floating train of green and red orbs, winking on and off as the dogs blinked. Green for brown-eyed dogs, red for blue.

My next immediate concern after the slip knot was Bronson. I had to convince him I was worth knowing. I let him be invisible while I had big, happy visits with the other dogs. *They* thought I was okay. For several mornings, I left him on the picket line long enough to wonder whether he was going to be left behind. Every morning and every night, I delivered his food dish personally.

On the fourth day, he let me harness him without struggle, though he was stiff and we didn't look at each other. On the sixth day, he leaned tentatively toward me when I came to collect him. The next day I fetched him first.

■ ■ ■

Each morning Jeninne sat up in her sleeping bag in the dark, precisely at 7:00 A.M., and set the patient cadence for the first round of never-ending chores to support thirty-nine dogs and six people. To get the gallons of water we needed to feed and water the dogs, we collected snow or chopped ice and melted it over campfires or propane burners in cabins. People and dogs used the same water, and my thermos took on a faint scent of wood smoke and duff. In one cabin we found a gas-powered auger and drilled through two feet of lake ice to make a water hole. That night tiny, translucent invertebrates sculled through our drinking water. Most days it was at least noon before dog chores were finished, camp struck, cabins cleaned, dog poop picked up for disposal down the trail, and the sleds repacked. We traveled five to eight hours a day, covering anywhere from twenty to forty miles.

Traveling by car, it's easy to be overpowered by an rpm-induced momentum. It gets harder and harder to make unplanned stops. One's bladder is brought into conformance with the car's fill and empty cycle. The mind gets fuzzy, the body goes slack. This dog-powered trip was more moment than momentum, with a fluctuating rhythm easily and often interrupted. There was no time to get fuzzy, no chance to go soft.

By the end of the first week, I was so tired and sore it was hard to imagine lasting another. My parka had acquired a patina of soot and powdered-egg fat, with a spot of dog blood on the sleeve, the aftermath of a misunderstanding between Alabama and Bronson. While I leaned on a tree in the starlight gathering the energy to crawl into my sleeping bag, Rosa lifted her muzzle from where she was curled on the picket line and kissed the night with a long, sweet note. The other dogs joined her, some getting up, others remaining tucked into the snow, just raising their heads to fill the air with woodwind howls. Rosa got to her feet and sang louder. After a few minutes she turned three delicate circles, lay back down, and the song evaporated in the dark.

I made my way to the large canvas tent, pushed through the flap, and curled peacefully into my place amid the soft breathings of my companions.

■ ■ ■

Rosa and Savanne were responsive to me, but their hearts belonged to Jeninne, and Lion was everybody's pal. So as we settled into the trip, Alabama, Bronson, and I threw our emotional lot together. I came to feel as though I could get through anything behind the big boys with the black, furry balls.

Jeninne said it was some of the worst trail conditions she'd ever seen. Light snow cover left brakes and snow hooks nearly useless on rivers, lakes, and parts of the trail, forcing us to topple moving sleds onto their sides to drag the dogs to a stop. We slammed over meadow tussocks normally buried under snow. Low-hanging branches promised to sweep away inattentive mushers. Approaching and leaving campsites often required tricky maneuvers behind excited dogs—dodging trees, making sharp turns right out of the chute, staying upright and behind the dogs on the sliding board ride down a pitched bank to pick up the trail on a lake or river. At McCabe Creek, we had to pass a small herd of stamping, heavy-coated homestead cows—"Good dogs! *On by! On by! On by! On by! On by! On by!*"

Traveling through the old Minto Burn, fire-killed deadfall littered the trail, threatening to break legs, and did break a stanchion on Dietmar's sled. Climbing one icy sidehill off the Yukon River to the plateau above, I walked beside my heavy sled, keeping it tipped on the uphill runner and pulling on the side lashings in the worst spots to keep it from crashing off the trail while my team strained toward the top.

On the tenth morning, Bronson kissed me.

A few days before the end of the trip, Jeninne offered to rearrange the teams and give me another dog or two. But I was just beginning to feel competent with my five and was savoring a taste of the full-partnered, joyful, exhausting flow of Robert Service's gold-rush road. *Bid good-bye to sweetheart, bid good-bye to friend; The Lone Trail, the Lone Trail follow to the end.*

I appreciated the offer and declined. The point wasn't how many dogs or how many miles or even where the hell we ended up. The point was the musical *zzzztttt* of my line zipping free from around a tree trunk, and learning how to open frozen snaps without getting my lips stuck to them. The destination was secondary to the satisfaction of shouldering my fair share of chores, not maiming myself with the snow hook, helping the others as I could, and taking my foot off the brake at corners. When we said good-bye, Jeninne thanked me for taking good care of her dogs.

After a couple of weeks at home, my leg muscles quit screaming and my chapped hands were healing. My rib was only bruised, not broken.

Friends ask if I had fun. I don't know how to answer. They want to know if I would do it again. I feel Bronson's shy kiss and see myself reaching for the loose end of a slip knot.

Driving into the Bitterroot

MARLENE BLESSING

It was not death that set us on the road. It was life. Only a week earlier, I had said a public, a ceremonial farewell to my dead husband, Richard Blessing—that, on the heels of our many private farewells. I said only, "He's gone." Meaning I would not see his strong, hulking form swaggering toward us ever again, the sly, broad slit of his smile identifying him as man, not beast. I would not hear his miraculous put-downs of brain cancer, a disease that would take all function in his left side, but that would never still his busy mind. And I would partake of his healing imagination only from the page now, from published poems and stories, never again from a fresh, new sheet filled with startling directions for living.

Now, Constance and I were heading out together on the open road, two friends driving from Seattle to Missoula, Montana. In early April 1983, the closer we came to the Continental Divide, the drier and more subtle the landscape outside us became. Seattle's wet, insistent green gave way to rolling fields still shy of the feathered heads of ripened and waving wheat. All was newly plowed and planted, everything geometric and just beginning. Eventually we would drive across the narrow panhandle of Idaho, over the high, rocky highway that intersects the Bitterroot Range, and down into the Bitterroot Valley of Montana. We were looking for a place where spring had not yet struck. In Missoula, April is the cruelest month, but only because it does not break open in a flourish of new growth as it does on the Northwest coast. The land here is hesitant to yield to life, as was I.

Only a few years before, Constance and I had traveled away from home to get closer to some sense of resolve about our lives. On the back roads of Hawaii, from campground to gecko-filled motel room, to rented trailer with scuttling Japanese beetles and cockroaches, we both decided that, men or no men, we needed careers. Out of the month we spent together, improvising each travel day as it came—today a simple stretch on a sunny beach, tomorrow an authentic Hawaiian meal prepared by a Hawaiian man and his French wife—came plans for improved lives, lives with direction. Maybe we had been foolish to ignore setting goals for so long. Maybe we had been living in the seventies. Maybe it was not a goal we wanted so much as a change. In the years that followed, I would become a book editor, she a graphic designer. And our professional collaborations would be many.

Constance and I had long been in the habit of extended conversations that ranged from the cosmic to the comic. When we first met, we launched into a wandering examination of Fritz Perls's *Gestalt Therapy Verbatim*, she rocking hypnotically in an old chair as her voice jumped up and down, me listening to her excitement about dream interpretations and role-playing, thinking how I hadn't engaged in such satisfying play since I was little. Over the two and a half years of Blessing's illness, our talks shrank to the brief and useful. "Is there anything we can do?" "Yes, just come and see him. He brightens when you're here." Or "Are you coming to workout tonight?" "Yes, I really need to get out and move." Brief and useful, trying to keep it smooth, hard and flat like a skipping stone that can be tossed across calm waters in an unending series of arcs.

As we drove along the silent stretches of Interstate 90, Constance and I now resumed our oceanic conversations. They took us to other countries. We were always in danger of being swept away. My car, a noisy red Subaru, whirred faithfully along, sounding like a tinny mechanical moth. But after the first hundred miles or so, its noise faded and our talk became the engine that moved us forward. Months of time spent together in hospital rooms and living rooms and bedrooms and bathrooms made this space, this airy space of Western landscape an empty, broad comfort to me.

I love to drive. I have always loved to drive. When I was a little girl, my father used to place me in his lap and let me hold the steering wheel with him, believing always that I was in control. But control wasn't what this drive was all about. If escape from a deep grief were possible, I would have driven this interstate until no maps could find me. No, this was really an exhalation after holding my breath for so long. And it was a recognition. I needed Constance my friend, Constance my protector, Constance my memory of the before, during, and after. And I was selfish in my need.

■ ■ ■

Grief pools past and present together, while the future seems as blank and uninspiring as a minimalist canvas. There are many details of our journey

I simply can't recall, in part because even at the time I was in a daze, having a hard time adjusting to the notion that I would live in a present and future. Blessing had had his run of mortality. In his last days, he had told me that he felt he had done everything he wanted to do, had had a full life. Everywhere, I thought, there is life and death happening simultaneously, with most of us living in the unaware spaces in between. Would I ever feel my life had been full enough? Would there be peace?

I was still trying to shake off the memory of the piercing, a cappella strains of "Amazing Grace" from the soloist at Blessing's memorial service. I didn't want the pitch of music at all, only talking or quiet, with the calm sound of tire tread spinning on concrete in the background. Moving in the bubble that is a car through grand landscapes offers something as settling as the pure motion that puts babies to sleep, and something as perfectly unsettling as space exceeding time. And there was one more thing. The solace of conversation between old friends, stitching together then and now, filling and refilling the emptiness.

My own sense of order and ordinariness had fled during the last days of Blessing's battle with cancer. A whimper, a crack in his voice, was call for alarm. By contrast, these views of irrigation equipment in the fields, the crackle of the crisp road map in Constance's hands, road signs with town names like Ritzville revived my contact with the everyday.

■ ■ ■

Constance and I buzzed along, the rotary engine, the talk, all in synch. Sometime after we crossed the border into Idaho, the car began to buck and clink, all motoring power disappearing. Shocked, I edged the car over to the shoulder of the highway. "I don't know what could be wrong," I puzzled. "I had the car checked out before we left."

"My Volkswagen behaved like that one time when it was out of gas," said Constance. And suddenly we knew the problem. For all those miles we'd talked, we had never once stopped for gasoline. It would take a miracle more impressive than turning the Biblical wedding jars of water into wine for a car, even a high-mileage car, to run all the way from Seattle to Missoula without refueling.

We both laughed, a roar, really. The first deep laugh, a way-down-in-my-belly laugh, in months. There was nothing but this moment, a very stupid moment, a great moment with a great friend. The joke was on us. We *were* the joke. Years later, in Mexico, we would find a perfect little memento that would encapsulate it: a small *retablo* with two clay skeleton women, hands flying, and the caption below reading, "*Las Mujeres,* blah, blah, blah..." How right they were.

It was no big adventure to hitch a ride to the nearest service station and back. Our driver told us how lucky we were to fizzle out where we did, since farther on there were no gas stations for at least eighty miles. I suppose we both knew we would have to look at the gas gauge from now on. But we were cradled in this journey, somehow protected from looking too far behind or ahead, from worrying about the *how* of travel.

■ ■ ■

The first time I was introduced to the wife of Montana writer Richard Hugo (Dick, to his friends), I remember that Ripley Schemm had the warmest, most compassionate eyes I had ever felt, and a honeyed, throaty voice. Dick Hugo was surely fortunate to have found such a woman, and his private letters to Blessing, which I would read years later, wondered, in a goofy, childlike way, how he could have lucked into such a great woman. She lost him to cancer only months before Blessing died. At one point in his illness, he confided to my husband that little alien spies were in his body, taking it over bit by bit. The invasion he imagined wasn't too far different from the ogre Blessing visualized who was throwing pebbles into the water and making him hiccup for more than two weeks straight. Both poets were very funny men, as well as being deeply superstitious, sure that bliss had to be paid for with some kind of loss. Who's to say they weren't right?

Our destination was Ripley's house on Wiley Street in Missoula. Once again, my need had triumphed. I needed to be with someone who could grasp the depth of my sorrow, someone who had her own well of it. I thought, *Finally, I can be in the presence of someone who will not, like my thirty-something friends, be awed or discomfited by my recent experience*—Constance excepted. This is no different from the brotherly feelings veterans of wars have toward one another, where there is infinite freedom to say nothing and to say everything, having survived the losses of battle together.

When we pulled up to her house, I felt relief. I hadn't had any destinations, any arrivals in several years. It's clichéd to say so, but I was desperate for a brief home away from home. From the moment we arrived at her doorstep, Ripley swept us into her care.

■ ■ ■

By the time morning came, the smell of bacon was wafting upstairs from the kitchen. Ripley had been up for several hours, an early riser who loved being present for the emergence of light. Even today, I am still in the other camp, someone who luxuriates in dream time, warm bedding, a pillow to confide in. During the time of Blessing's illness, there were few continuous hours of sleep and little dreaming. Both of us, together and apart, seemed to be keeping a watch. The long drive, this arrival in the Bitterroot Valley, the night of long sleep all signaled a changing time, full of emptiness and promise.

Dick Hugo loved waffles. And bacon. And a good cup of coffee. Thanks to him, this is what we woke up to. I remember Ripley watching us kindly. I don't think she ate with us. In fact, I don't think she ate at all. Her grief seemed to move her toward the unworldly and disembodied, while mine pushed me deep into the body. I was hungry for food, for a good long walk by the river, for every sensation I could now register.

Constance is no fan of early morning food. The orange juice, bacon, and waffles looked like a kind of hard labor to her. I, on the other hand, wanted an all-you-can-eat buffet experience. I craved the sound of a butter knife rasping along the toasted surface of the waffles laden with butter, then warm maple syrup. And then, yes, a splash of tangy orange juice and a kind offer to refill, and refill. My thirst was unquenchable. I'm not sure why we sometimes have an unerring instinct for the things that will begin to heal us, whether a burning bundle of sage, cherry-flavored cough syrup, or the company of friends. But this breakfast with women friends held powerful medicine for me.

The days in Montana flowed like the Clark Fork River near Ripley's home, even though we visited for only a short time. The beautiful country around us was a fourth friend, never silent in the way we think of landscape as quiet background. In such a place, a person can see the way sky or open space occupies more of our imagination than the land below it. To someone who's never felt this amazing proportion of air to land, this will sound other-worldly. But those who have experienced the magic of Big Sky understand in their bones the way being physically insignificant next to such space is healing.

Had someone, even we, recorded our visit, it would have been a play-by-play of simple, ordinary events: *took walk... ate sandwiches... talked about dead husbands, then drank bourbon... went to bed.* And like ordinary ingredients mixed together, with the alchemy of proper timing, preparation, and heat, an extraordinary result was born.

■ ■ ■

Just as a dried wishbone is a poor reminder of a banquet with intimates, my flawed memory of those distant events seems like a good luck charm, but no substitute for the actual. Constance and I have had many travels together since that time, and we've talked on and on without ever again running out of fuel. One particularly offbeat experience from the drive into the Bitterroots added poignancy to everything.

We walked along the river one day, talking about what a lark it would be to write a romance novel. If we could co-write a potato cookbook, as we had just done, surely we could switch gears and gin up a torrid love story. Of course, neither one of us had ever read such a book, at least not anything other than *Gone with the Wind*. This could be a diversion (more fun than testing three potato recipes a day for six months), a way for us to play a little make-believe. We'd change our names into one lacy, purple pseudonym, so that no one could trace our folly. Now the freedom began.

I pictured our heroine as looking a little like Constance—petite, curly red hair, spunky yet not abrasive. As I recall, she was a Jessica and would have adventures that would transform her into a Jessy. She would begin as the daughter of a Boston shipping magnate, lose both parents to a storm at sea, inherit money that her brother and would-be suitor would wrest from her, and be left with no choice but to hit the road. Naturally, by the end of the novel, she would be a successful bank robber, live in a canyon with a dark-haired lover, wear leather chaps and wonderful boots, and be richer on all fronts than had she submitted to her New England fate.

Ripley was amused by our fantasy and offered to introduce us to a man, a local writer, who had many writing identities and who made a good living writing potboiler adventure novels, Westerns, spy thrillers, etc. So one night, she scooped us into her car, drove us to what I remember as a motel apartment, and led us into an almost-empty living room with only an old La-Z-Boy recliner and a man in his thirties, who looked at us with tolerance.

I think now it's a good thing that we never shared our story-line with Mr. X. That wouldn't have interested him anyway. He led us cautiously into his writing temple, a room outfitted with what, for those times, was a magnificent, technologically state-of-the-art writer's office. Against two walls stood bookshelves filled with hundreds of mass-market books, all his. We stood at attention as he explained what serious work this was, how one couldn't succeed without respecting and knowing the genre (whether mystery, romance, adventure, or Western). He told us that he had once almost completed a Ph.D. in English literature, but found that this work of writing formula fiction was more satisfying and challenging. An art, even.

By the time we shook Mr. X's hand, after an evening of standing and listening to him, we were grateful to climb back into Ripley's car and head for Wylie Street. She had once again proven to us that, like a good fairy godmother, she was out to make our wishes come true. But it looked like Jessica, aka Jessy, would have to wait for release from her bottle. Constance and I agreed that we hadn't cleansed ourselves sufficiently to be acolytes to Mr. X's code of seriousness.

■ ■ ■

The final memory that holds from our trip is the day Ripley, Constance, and I visited Annick Smith at her place outside of Missoula. I can't help thinking of this as my "three widows" time, since she, too, had lost her husband, David Smith, when she was about my age. As we sat in Annick's warm kitchen, watching this handsome, thoughtful woman toss a generous salad, she said some reassuring things about how time helps, how we remember the love and put the pain in storage. She drew a long pull from her cigarette, then exhaled, and for a moment I found myself wishing I still smoked, could still feel that pleasant burning in the lungs, could have a grown-up thing to do with my hands and smoky, drifting clouds of my own making to watch.

Sitting among us, Constance, I realized, had lost someone too. Not a husband, but a dear friend. How different was that kind of absolute farewell from any other? And beyond that, I would one day learn that she carried secret instructions from Richard Blessing. She was to look after me. Being the caretaker in her boisterous, mistake-making, hard-loving family, Constance took on this charge quite naturally. Only later, a year later, on a Greek island, would she finally explode. My need, my insatiability, my recovered life were too heavy for her. She was up to her eyebrows in taking care. As we argued, then cried, then laughed and howled, then quieted, an old time ended.

More than thirty years into our friendship, we are still discovering new roads together. Both of us acknowledge that our Bitterroot time was an important piece of our foundation, and also a practice for the life to come, one of receiving and letting go. Even now that I am living in Denver, with a mountain of geography between us, I can hear her teasing, sassy assessments of my behavior. We are the same friends, talking as ever and constantly reuniting in rainy places, desert places, even tropical and Mediterranean places. When I picture her daily life, as I often do to feel close, I see her standing in her vegetable garden, hands on hips, cat next to her switching its tail. Heavy clouds brood overhead, only threatening to rain. She bends over to thin some tender lettuce, stands again in her perfect-posture way, and loses herself in dreams of spring.

■ ■ ■

A SHOW OF MAGIC
for Constance

I'm not talking about stagestruck rabbits, paper
flowers pulled from the armpit, even tricks
up the sleeve. It's been too long since I believed
a woman could be sawed in half cheerfully, her dainty
toes waving good-bye to an audience divided.
There's magic enough for me in the fact that today
arrived openly, looking safe and transportable as a child's
red wagon. No chicanery there. No chance to misunderstand that
a loaf of bread, a toy, a life can be set within and moved
with some purpose from one place to the next.
                                   I don't expect
delight or amazement as I do these ordinary
things. Think of the habit we have of swallowing the daily
whole. Reflexive as anything, I find less
reason to applaud the magnificent, more desire
to revive the plainest truths.
                                   The single woman
depends upon friends. And there is no doing it
by halves.
              We all wait for something primary as
the red of the wagon I outgrew. So waiting
together, talking simply about the day as it passed,
we pull nothing but love from our hats.

The Lightning Field

MARY BRUNO

There are two ways to drive from Albuquerque to Quemado. You can take Interstate 25 south, turn right at Socorro, and follow Highway 60 straight there. Or you can head west on Interstate 40 and wind down into Quemado along Highway 117, a serpentine descent through ancient lava fields and high desert plains. For reasons having to do with birds and astronomy, I choose the former.

I'm on the road by 9:00 A.M. At 9:05 I cross the wide, flat Rio Grande. I'll follow its floodplain all the way to Socorro. The sky is a big blue bowl overhead. How, I wonder, can Montana be Big Sky country? How much bigger can a sky get?

I speed south on Interstate 25 through a pancake-flat landscape of desert scrub. Vertical relief comes in the form of the craggy blue peaks of Sandia and Manzano Mountains to the east and tepee-shaped volcanic mounds scattered across the plain. These perfectly symmetrical cones remind me I'm driving through the most seismically active part of New Mexico.

When Spanish settlers first arrived here, this whole basin was a grassland, but grazing herds and the creosote bush have taken their toll. Creosote poisons its neighbors. Based on the lack of botanical diversity, I'd say it's a pretty potent strategy.

The Cole Porter tune "Don't Fence Me In" is playing in my head. It's an unPorterlike western ditty that my dad used to sing to us when we were kids. David Byrne covered it. But I like my dad's version better. Slow and kind of dreamy.

My response to the West has a lot to do with my relationship to the East, where I grew up. I'm from North Arlington, New Jersey. It's a tiny town—one mile square—just seven miles north of Newark and, depending on traffic, about fifteen minutes west of Manhattan. A third of the town is the Holy Cross Cemetery, a shady tract on a ridge overlooking New York City, where my father and his parents are buried and where I once spotted a Canada warbler. The rest of the town is a jigsaw of modest single-family homes and garden apartments, seven elementary schools, two high schools, two churches, the Little League baseball field, the high school football field, and a public library.

I lived down near the Passaic River. My maternal grandmother used to tell stories about swimming and ice-skating on the river in her youth, and crew teams from the local high schools still practice there. But the lower stretch of the Passaic, our end of the river, flows through the most crowded and industrialized part of the United States. To me, it was always a menacing swirl, slinking its way down to Newark Bay.

A high concrete bulkhead contained the far bank and supported the stretch of Route 21 known locally as Mac Carter Highway. The bulkhead had huge round drains; giant mouths that spewed who knew what into the already murky waters. People said there were larger intake drains beneath the water's surface, and I lived in fear of falling into the river and getting sucked into one of them.

Above us was Ridge Road, the town's main street, named for the ridgeline it followed. From there, you could look east across the Meadowlands—final resting place of mob victims and the fine marble remains of New York's old Pennsylvania Station—and see the Manhattan skyline, glistening or twinkling depending on the time of day. If you drew a straight line from my childhood home due east, it would connect with Manhattan Island at West Thirty-third Street, six miles as the crow flies.

None of these topographic details were apparent to me as a child. I remember standing on the ridge one clear December morning and taking in Manhattan. I was twenty-four years old, a graduate student in ecology, home for the holidays. That was the first time I realized that "the Meadowlands" was a vast salt marsh.

In New Jersey, in much of the East, the handiwork of man usurps all natural features of the landscape. Towns, cities, houses, superstores, highways, high-rises, shopping malls, office parks, garbage dumps, bridges, bulkheads, billboards, refineries, tunnels, overpasses, parking lots, stadiums, people, progress. Discerning actual contours is like eyeing a woman swathed in loose-fitting layers. Lean sinew or flubber underneath? Impossible to tell.

Here along New Mexico's Interstate 25, the landscape is naked and unfamiliar and vaguely unnerving: mesas, mountains, plains, volcanic cones, collapsed calderas, dry creek beds that rip through the parched earth like scars. As I close in on Socorro, mountain ranges pinch the Rio Grande; as the river slows and pools, the desert turns to marshland, and I arrive at the Bosque del Apache National Wildlife Refuge.

It's early October and I'm in time for the biannual gathering of snow geese. These seagull-size birds stream south from their summer breeding grounds in the Alaskan tundra to winter in Central America. They've stopped at Bosque to rest and feed. Hundreds of miles to go. Hundreds of thousands of birds. Snow white with jet black wing tips, they mass on the marshy pools until acres of blue water become a feathered white sea.

I'm tempted to linger at Bosque long enough to see the sandhill cranes. An elderly woman at the visitors center assures me that a whole flock has just been spotted in a nearby field. But I'm scheduled to meet Robert, *The Lightning Field* caretaker, in Quemado at 3:00 P.M. The cranes will have to wait.

I'm back on the road by 11:00, traveling west on Highway 60 now. After I pass Magdalena, an old silver mining town, the road climbs through a dwarf juniper forest. The trees are round and deep, deep green, and they pop against the blond grassy hillsides. The groves are densest on the hills to the north, gradually thinning into a few lone trees on the south side of the road. It's as though a small child with an armload of marbles stumbled and his spilled treasure rolled out across the floor, each marble escaping as far as friction would allow.

Just before Datil I take a detour, veering south across the grassy Plains of San Augustin. This was once a vast inland sea. In fact, the whole center of New Mexico, referred to by geologists as the Rio Grande Rift, is gradually widening east to west as the two slabs of continental crust that flank it pull slowly apart. Their estrangement might allow a new inland sea to inundate this plain one day, epochs hence.

Until then, the Plains of San Augustin are home to the Very Large Array. I can just make out the cluster of white humps rising up from the plain. Twenty-seven satellite dishes, 94 feet tall, 235 tons apiece, blindingly white, mounted on railroad tracks, trained upward, staring intently at the sky, tirelessly gathering data on distant galaxies and quasars and listening, always listening for signs of extraterrestrial life. As I walk beneath the towering telescopes, I follow their gaze upward and ponder those big questions they've been built to answer: How old is the universe? Where does it end? Are we alone?

Just past Datil I cross the Continental Divide and enter true west. The divide is an imaginary line that separates the country by drainage. To the east are the streams and rivers that empty into the Rio Grande, the Gulf of Mexico, and eventually the Atlantic Ocean; to the west are those that find their way to the Pacific courtesy of the Colorado River.

I've always been drawn to water. I love the Western words for waterways: canyon, gully, gulch, ravine, wash, draw, and, my favorite, arroyo. As far as I can tell, the distinctions have to do with size and depth—a gully being a small gulch, for instance—and the presence or absence of water. But for me, the names conjure up cowboys and horses and canteens and dust and the strange arithmetic of water: too much or too little is deadly.

No danger of dehydration or flash flooding today, though. I stocked up on bottled water at Pie Town's Pie-O-Neer grocery a few miles back, and there's not a cloud in sight as I approach Quemado.

Quemado is a speck of a town just east of the Arizona border. When I pull in to the local cafe at 2:45, Robert is already there. He could have come from central casting. Blue jeans, cowboy boots, compact wiry build, sandy hair, taciturn. (Now there's a word you don't get to use much back East.) He heaves my bag into the back of his pickup and off we go.

Where I come from, people chat. And chat and chat. When you grow up in a crowd, you either retreat into shyness or you develop a personality. In New Jersey, personality is the preferred survival strategy—a weapon, really. But it doesn't work on Robert. He relays the essentials: when he'll come back to get me, how to operate the shortwave radio in case of an emergency, where to find the food, to be on the lookout for rattlesnakes. Beyond that he just drives, forty-five minutes along dusty gravel roads, through a locked barbed-wire gate to a homesteader's pine cabin on the edge of *The Lightning Field*.

Robert stays long enough to show me around the cabin. It was built in the 1930s and came with the property. The Dia Center for the Arts, which financed and manages the installation, renovated the place for the 1978 opening of *The Lightning Field*. It's still spare, but it's comfortable with three bedrooms, two baths, a kitchen, and living room. The cabin sleeps six, but I'm the only guest so I have the place to myself.

That night I dine on lasagna from Robert's wife, Karen, and kick myself for forgetting to bring wine. I turn in shortly after dinner, curling up in a wrought-iron bed, half expecting Lorne Greene to come tuck me in. The bedroom has one long, narrow window that, come daybreak, will afford a splendid view of *The Lightning Field*, but it's as dark as pitch now so I crack open my copy of *Riders of the Purple Sage* and try to ignore all the strange creaking sounds.

I bought this Zane Grey classic for the trip, along with *Desert Solitaire* by Edward Abbey and Wallace Stegner's Pulitzer Prize–winning *Angle of Repose*. For reasons decidedly unliterary, *Riders* is my favorite. The story is set in southern Utah, not too far from *The Lightning Field*. Zane Grey's romantic descriptions of the landscape synch my interior life with my day-to-day experience, and sections of the book are better than *Sex and the City*. I'm at the part where a monster thunderstorm pounds the hidden valley where Venters and Bess have set up camp and, well, here:

Then the storm burst with a succession of ropes and streaks and shafts of lightning.... She clung to him. He felt the softness of her, and the warmth.... No more did he listen to the rush and roar of the thunderstorm.... He grew conscious of an inward storm.... A storm in his breast.... A storm of real love.

YOWZA!

I had never heard silence until the next morning when I wander outside the cabin. The air is clear and chill, the sun not quite up. The grid begins about 200 feet from the cabin door. I walk halfway there and stop. The silence is so complete, so utterly complete that before long it begins to let in sound. The faint hum and creak of human machinery. Skeletal sound, muscular sound, circular, cellular, molecular sound. The sound of me. Then the sun scales the horizon and the first rays of light strike the poles.

For five years, sculptor Walter de Maria wandered around New Mexico, Arizona, California, and Nevada in search of a site for his work. He wanted a place that was flat and isolated and frequented by lightning, and he found it on this empty plain north of Quemado, 7,200 feet above sea level and eleven and a half miles east of the Continental Divide.

De Maria has created other large installations. For *The New York Earth Room,* he filled a 3,600-square-foot loft on Wooster Street, wheelbarrowful by wheelbarrowful, with 280,000 pounds of rich, loamy dirt.

De Maria was born in 1935 in Albany, California. He lives in New York City now. He declines requests for interviews, but he did contribute a 1980 piece about *The Lightning Field* to *Art Forum* magazine. The article is titled "Some Facts, Notes, Data, Information and Statements." The four italicized statements offer the best, maybe the only insights:

The land is not the setting for the work but a part of the work.
The invisible is real.
Isolation is the essence of land art.
The sum of the facts does not constitute the work or determine its esthetics.

The Lightning Field is a rectangular grid of 400 stainless-steel poles. The grid measures one mile by one kilometer, roughly the size of my hometown. Each pole has a sharp, spearlike tip. There are 25 poles in each mile-long row, 16 per kilometer-long row. The poles are spaced 220 feet apart (plus or minus $1/25$ inch). Their height varies—from 15 feet to 26 feet 9 inches—to compensate for the gentle swell of the terrain so that, according to de Maria, "the plane of the tips would evenly support an imaginary sheet of glass." The poles are perfectly parallel, and subterranean concrete foundations secure their vertical position in winds as strong as 110 miles per hour.

Like a mirage, the poles disappear in the middle of the day. Looking out from the porch of the cabin I see nothing but cracked dry earth, a blue bell-jar sky, sagebrush forever, and the occasional jackrabbit. At dawn and dusk, however, when the sun sits low, its long rays find the poles. They glint yellow and gold and pink, and their whittled tips ignite like birthday candles. Then the sun creeps a few more degrees along its daily arc and the party is over, the candles snuffed.

It takes about two hours to walk around the grid. The ground is crusty and dotted with anthills. My hiking boots make crunching sounds. When I enter the grid, I remember de Maria's imaginary glass ceiling and feel sheltered.

If I look down a row or column head on, the poles line up like a well-drilled regiment and all but the pole closest to me disappear. If I glance off to either side, the regiment is a forest of spears thrust willy-nilly into the earth by members of some warrior tribe between battles.

At the time of my visit, the poles have been in place for eleven years. They've been exposed to desert wind and weather, sandblasted and sunbaked, frozen, drenched, and zinged by lightning. But they show no trace of wear. They remain polished and unblemished, no rust or corrosion, not a stain or a scratch. Invincible.

De Maria hasn't disguised or usurped or in any way defiled the landscape with his work. He hasn't really enhanced it either. The grid is simply there. Its creator visited this place and left behind a kind of reference point. Its relentless precision is eerie. Some future civilization may stumble upon the grid and spend centuries pondering its point. I hear *The Lightning Field* creeps out the locals. They call it "the planet" and stay away. To me, de Maria's steel garden is oddly welcoming, a familiar industrial touch in an empty, silent natural place.

I missed lightning season, which is May through early September. I've seen photographs of jagged streaks kissing poles and turning their polished tips into electrodes. But even when Zane Grey–size killer storms punish the plain, actual lightning strikes are rare. In the *Art Forum* piece, de Maria explains that lightning has to get within 200 feet of the field before it can "sense the poles." Not many storms come that close. But every now and then, writes the sculptor, the electric current in the air sizzles so intently that it creates a Saint-Elmo's-fire glow around the grid.

True to his word, Robert retrieves me at the appointed hour. *The Lightning Field* disappears in a cloud of dust, and in no time I'm back in Quemado.

In the years since my visit to *The Lightning Field*, I've occasionally run into other people who've been there. They're almost always cultural types, artists, arts administrators, arts reporters. I was an arts reporter when I made the pilgrimage. They tend to talk or write about hearing the grid's "music," or how the grid establishes "a sort of equivalence between the age of the work and the age of the earth," or how being in its "midst…we lose our sense of hierarchical importance in nature." It makes me appreciate de Maria's straightforward accounting of his work, a feat of engineering as much as art.

What I love about de Maria's work is its unfailing order. Four hundred poles stand clean and shiny in straight, precise lines in what my Jersey City cousins would call "the middle of fucking nowhere." That's something you can count on in this Land of Enchantment where the sun wants to evaporate you, the rain to sweep you away, and the earth's crust is fickle underfoot. Walter de Maria enchanted me with tidiness.

I take Highway 117 and Interstate 40 back to Albuquerque. It's a glorious drive. Patches of snow hide in the lee of roadside rocks and trees, and the late afternoon sun bathes it all in sharp gold light. The trip offers one final wonder. As I crest a long grade and head downhill toward the lights of Albuquerque, the biggest, roundest, orangest harvest moon I have ever seen rises in the north. A Jersey girl to the end, I mistake it, at first, for a billboard.

 **Beulah Land**

LINDA HASSELSTROM

Oh, Beulah Land, sweet Beulah Land. Heat waves shimmered as I sang and squinted down the line of speeding trucks on Interstate 80. My feet stuck to hot tar. I'd jerked my hat off, thinking I might get a ride faster if drivers saw the long blond hair, but now it stuck to my neck.

Trucks whistled past at seventy-five. As each car approached, I'd close my eyes, willing it to stop. My shoulders and arms, white from working in an office, were turning pink, and my sunscreen was in Beulah, the 1954 Chevy behind me. During traffic lulls, I'd prop one hip against her fender and try to remember where I was.

Humming, I scanned the flat Nebraska horizon and could almost see those pioneers trudging beside the muddy Platte River, singing the old hymn about the land of heavenly joy somewhere ahead. My grandmother's cracked voice rang in my ears, left over from the rare occasions when we'd gone to church together. *Here shines undimmed one blissful day.* Yeah, the usual heavenly day, 100 degrees with 99 percent humidity. If I looked over my shoulder, I'd probably see Lincoln, 150 miles of cornfields behind me.

As soon as I'd opened Beulah's hood, I'd seen the broken fan belt. Smiling, I'd gotten a couple of old nylons out of the trunk, then twisted and tied them tightly. But when the engine turned over, shreds of taupe nylon flew like autumn leaves; my improvised replacements were too old.

Still, I wasn't discouraged; in 1976, Nebraskans were all friendly. My old Chevy was the most reliable vehicle I'd had since I'd sold the green one I'd driven in high school. Beulah was the kind of car I'd choose to be sturdy and durable, with wide hips and a big chrome grin, wearing genuine leather seats shiny with neat's-foot oil. The original floor mats were a little worn in spots, and I'd installed a hood ornament from an old Dodge: a silver ram with full-curl horns.

Altogether, Beulah symbolized the way I saw myself. At thirty-three, I was beginning to accept the well-known statistic that I was more likely to be killed by a terrorist than to marry for the second time. As a self-employed writer, I conducted workshops all over the plains, driving alone and adept at roadside repairs. I avoided bars and dark alleys, but I'd been raped by a co-worker who was seeing me safely home. A pacifist, I carried emergency gear instead of weapons—tools, tire chains, flares—counting on quick thinking and glibness to keep me out of trouble. Salt of the earth, my plains neighbors; I knew them.

But apparently I didn't know how to get them to pick me up on this hot day. A farm couple went by in a rickety truck. I could tell by the way she looked at me that the woman wanted to stop. Her husband refused to look at either of us. Next was a small blue sedan. I smoothed my hair, smiled; the car slowed as the man driving looked me over. His passenger raised the brim of her blue hat with a red-tipped finger. I could read her tight little lips saying, "Hippie bitch." Looking embarrassed, the man accelerated. Then came a fat red van with fins like a luxury car, children looking out the windows. The bus stopped ahead of me, and a woman with a bread-dough face opened the rear door. "What's the problem?" she said.

"Fan belt broke. I just need a ride to Grand Island, about ten miles." She watched my eyes, then spoke over her shoulder. "Fan belt broke, Harry."

She motioned me inside. Stepping past her, I squinted in the dark aisle. I stopped when one of the kids squawked. "What?"

"Don't step on the *baby*." I looked down. A red-faced infant lay on the floor in front of my foot. I lurched sideways and fell into a seat by the window, inhaling odors of stale bread and warm urine.

"The floor's the coolest place," the woman said, facing me from the seat ahead. "Where in South Dakota are you from?" asked the man behind the wheel.

"Near Rapid City, in the western part. I'm on my way home from a job in Lincoln."

"That's near Mount Rushmore, ain't it?" he said, shifting and wheeling back into traffic. "We went there on vacation once; them hills are just beautiful."

"In fact, that's why we picked you up," said the woman. "People were so nice out there. When we saw your South Dakota plates, we decided to pay it back." Her arms jiggled and dripped sweat as she brushed curls back from her forehead.

"Took off from Detroit yesterday." The man eyed me in the rearview mirror. "Headed for Colorado, up in the mountains. I got a brother there."

"Then we're going home through South Dakota."

"Was it this hot in Detroit?"

"Yeah." He shook his head. "All that pavement makes it hotter. Can't wait to get into the mountains. How do ya like the bus? I built it. I work for Chrysler."

I nodded appreciatively, hearing in my skull the country song about the guy who took his car from the assembly line "one piece at a time." I counted kids with big eyes staring at me from the bunks suspended along both sides: seven without the baby.

"Where could we camp in the Black Hills that doesn't cost much?" asked the woman, pulling a map out of a pocket on the seat in front of her.

In gratitude, I would have told them all my secret spots, but we got to a truck stop in Grand Island first. They took the kids to the bathroom while I found a mechanic who said he had a fan belt. As the family pulled away, the kids were whining for lunch and the woman was saying, "I'll make sandwiches."

I spent an hour sitting on a tire nursing a soda before one of the mechanics came to take me to my car. As he pulled onto the interstate, he tossed a lock of blond hair back, widened his blue eyes and said, "So, honey, what are you doing driving around out here by yourself?" He stretched his arm along the seat back so his hand landed casually on my shoulder.

"Heading home to my four babies," I said, leaning away to roll down the window. Nothing deters lechery like children.

Blondie slapped both hands on the steering wheel and speeded up. He set a new speed record for installing a fan belt and drove off while I was fastening my seat belt. Beulah started on the first try and I eased into traffic, thinking how lucky I was to have gotten out of my marriage without a child to support.

The sky was flat blue, shimmering with heat. I paused at the truck stop to wash my face and buy a soda and sandwich. As I finished the sandwich, I crossed the 100th meridian, the line beyond which less than twenty inches of moisture falls a year. At our place, more like sixteen. I whooped with joy, happy to be back in the West, home country. Three-thirty. I wouldn't make it home in daylight, but I was determined to keep driving.

"I've reached the land of corn and wine," I bawled, "and all its treasures freely mine." What came next? Those pioneers had seen the tan grass outside my windows as the lobby of paradise, where they would tarry until summoned to the Celestial City. "For this is heaven's borderland," I sang, and was still holding the last note as Beulah slowed and drifted off the highway.

"Now what?" I got out and pulled the hood release, snatching my hand away from the hot metal. Smelling gas, I removed the gas cap and rocked the car until I heard sloshing. Around me, pavement rippled as if it were melting. Aha! A rest area just up the interstate. I raised the hood, sprayed the houseplants on the back seat with warm water and left the windows open an inch.

Then I hung my purse on my shoulder, squared my shoulders, and marched down the road, reasoning that in the West, the Code of Chivalry wouldn't allow a real man to ignore a reasonably attractive blond afoot in a heat wave.

By the time I staggered into the rest area, still on my own two feet, I'd decided Western chivalry doesn't begin in the middle of Nebraska. I lurched to the fountain and sucked water until I gathered enough strength to ask at the information desk about service stations. A smiling farm girl pointed out the pay phone and said the closest station was about three miles east, behind me. Yep, this was the West.

Walking fast, I reached Beulah as the tow truck pulled up. The driver peered under the hood, then tried the starter, shaking his head. Then he said, "Sure you're not out of gas?"

I ground my teeth. "Filled up in Grand Island. I can see gas in the tank." He took the gas cap off and peered in, then rocked the car. While he hooked up the wrecker, I got emergency money out of the glove box, slipping some bills in the coin pocket of my jeans.

I hadn't even noticed Brady, Nebraska, as I had shot past it singing hymns, but when the tow truck pulled in front of a concrete block building with two Standard Oil pumps in front, I estimated the population at sixty, counting kids and dogs.

"I've been meanin' to fix up the shop," the driver said. "Got to do it now—just got married. That there's my brand-new trailer, eighty feet long." He nodded toward a pink double-wide behind the building. Beside the trailer stood a new yellow Olds. Cottonwoods planted by a homesick pioneer bent and whispered like old ladies over a wedding cake.

He sighed, strolling into the shop as I trotted behind. "Yep. Inside that trailer is a brand-new wife moving new furniture around. Those things don't come cheap, and I got to be making money." He shook his head. "We just got married Monday, so I don't want to spend the whole damn night working on some old '54 Chevy." He winked and punched me on the arm. "She's a feisty blond, but packed a whole lot fuller than you are, sweetie. My name's Bob."

"I don't want to waste any time either, Bob. I've been away from my four babies for six months." I'd planned to leave the little snivelers in Grand Island, but the situation called for instant reproduction. "But Bob, I been sending money home, so I have just enough to get home on. What do you think is wrong?" ·

"I don't have the foggiest notion," he said placidly. "And I've got a motorcycle tore down, so I can't do nothing for you." While I was drawing breath, he wiped sweat off his forehead with a greasy arm and bellowed, "Hey, Leonard, I brought you a pretty lady in distress."

A scrawny geezer crawled out from under a Harley, dug a toothpick out of a pocket, and stuck it between his teeth as he wandered over.

"What seems to be the trouble, honey?" he said, looking at my breasts.

"It choked a couple times and quit. I can smell gas, though."

He nodded, shoving back his cap to scratch his forehead. "You're just out of gas." He groped in his pants pocket, found a match, scratched it on his zipper, and lit a cigarette, grinning at me.

I squared my jaw and bit my tongue. He grunted and limped over to the car. With the gas cap off, he pushed on the fender, leaving two black handprints. Then he picked up a cottonwood branch and shoved it into the tank, pulled it out, and sniffed the end. "Dry, all right. You're just out of gas."

"A half hour ago, when Bob rocked it, gas sloshed up the pipe."

Leonard shook his head. "When'd you fill up last?" he asked, taking down the gas nozzle. When he squeezed the handle, the bell on the old pump cheeped and numbers started wheezing past.

"Grand Island. Fan belt busted and I got it fixed there." I looked under the hood.

"Well, you're out of gas anyway."

"Wait a minute, Leonard. I smell gas up here. Why would that be?" I knew exactly what it was, but telling me would make Leonard happy.

He came around in front and looked down in the neighborhood of the battery. "Oh, hell. I wonder if that's your fuel pump." He started the motor, then came to lean over the fender beside me. We stared as gas squirted everywhere. Nodding, he muttered, "Damn, damn, damn."

Feet shuffled behind me and I turned around. Three greasy-haired boys wearing jean jackets with the sleeves torn off stood, their thumbs hooked in their belts, smirking. "Sheeeeit, Frankie—a fuel pump," said one.

"You know, Panch, I bet there ain't a fuel pump for that old wreck in miles." Since their lips didn't move, I couldn't tell which one was speaking. The third one put his hand up to his eyes and peered around the horizon, grinning. Leonard was bent over Beulah's interior, banging a wrench.

"Hell, no," said one. "Why, I bet he'll have to go clean to Lincoln to get a fuel pump for that thing."

"You know what that means, don't you, Frankie?"

"Yep. That little honey's going to be looking for a place to spend the weekend in Brady, Nebraska."

"You see any motels?" They all turned in unison. I squinted at the horizon myself, hoping for a motel, or South Dakota.

"Why, no, I don't." They all rubbed their hands down the front of their black jeans. "Nothing but our little tent over there under the tree."

"The Green Canvas *Ho*-tel."

"The *No-tell Mo-tel.*"

"Open all night, entertainment and generous hospitality all free." They laughed together and sauntered in lockstep back inside the garage.

"Goddamned bitching piece of iron, excuse me," Leonard yelled, holding up my fuel pump, blood running down his arm. "Cut my finger on the son of a bitch. I'll go in and see if I can find one anything like this." He looked at me, eyes bright, then found his cap on the carburetor and yanked it down. "You stay here." Maybe he'd been listening.

I rolled down the windows and sprayed the houseplants again, but I knew they were goners. Then I sat on a tire in the shade of the building, breathing deep and reminding myself that most foul-mouthed men are harmless. Should I spit defiance at them, swear worse than they did? Maybe innocence and an appeal to Leonard would work better. I hummed a little. *A sweet perfume upon the breeze/ Is borne from ever vernal trees.* When the bikers came into the sun, blinking, I ducked inside and saw Leonard talking on a phone in the corner beside an old pop machine. I got a warm Coke for a nickel and sat on an antifreeze box.

The three goons walked around Beulah, looking in the windows at my books and suitcases. One kicked a front tire. Another leaned against a rear fender, puffing a joint. Then Bob unlocked the Coke machine and opened a free one.

"Are those your guard dogs?" I asked.

"What say, sweetheart? Oh, no, they're just traveling through, soon as I fix that Harley."

"I hope you hurry."

"Sure thing, honey. We don't like them California boys harassing our women." He smirked.

Leonard hung up. "Bob, I can get a fuel pump over in Gothenburg. I called the fella in the Chevy garage there; he'll go down and open up for me."

Bob said, "I got to finish up these motorcycle boys; you just do this job for her and you can have the money, OK?" He stepped behind the counter and opened the cash register with a bong. "That's twenty-five dollars for the tow, sweetie. Why don't you pay me now in case I finish before you get back and wanta head home to that pink trailer?" He winked.

"That's a lot of money for a three-mile tow," I said. My father taught me to haggle.

"I can tow it back out there and not even charge you nothing extra," Bob said without a breath.

I handed over five dollars and a traveler's check. "Last one," I said, tossing the folder into a wastebasket beside Leonard.

"You wanta stay here in the shade," he said, glancing into the waste bin, "or ride to Gothenburg with me, honey?"

"I'll ride with you, Leonard." I followed as he strutted around the corner to a blue 1949 Ford pickup, sun blazing off it like cold fire.

"This here's Henry. A little old, but he still has a lot of pep." He giggled. "Just like me." He popped the clutch as we left the parking lot.

"Are those plastic Hell's Angels friends of yours, Leonard?"

"Them? No, they're just passing through."

"They have dirty mouths and they're trying to scare me." And succeeding. Time to establish my character. "How would you feel if they talked to your daughter like that?"

"Oh, they're just men, honey, talking to a pretty girl all alone. What *are* you doing out here by yourself?"

"You know, Leonard, I'm a grown woman, and we're allowed to have jobs and cars these days." I sighed heavily. "I've got four children to provide for; their daddy ran off. I've been working in Lincoln and I'm headed home, minding my own business."

"Oh hell, they don't mean no harm. Here, have a Camel." I hadn't smoked since an interminable night involving Camels and whiskey in college, but I took it and inhaled.

"Hell, we'll get that fuel pump in and you'll be on your way in no time. Here." He held his lighter out. The truck was bouncing so hard I finally had to grab his hand to light the cigarette. He looked sideways at me and smiled, "Where'd you say you're from?"

"Hermosa; about the size of Brady, only we don't have a garage anymore."

"Where's that from Sturgis?"

"About seventy miles south. Why?"

"Oh, I go to Sturgis every year for the motorcycle rally. Got me a hog and I race up there, last ten years. I don't win any races, but I enjoy the beer and the girls. All them cycles really gets those girls' motors purrin'." He threw out his bony chest.

I stared, reassessing his age. His face was wrinkled and the strands of hair hanging out from under the greasy cap were gray. Suddenly the pickup cab seemed very small.

"Since I been retired, I ain't had as much money, but I've got time. I do a little work for Bob and use his tools. Ma, she thinks I'm crazy. Wants to buy a boat and move to Florida. It'd be too far to ride to Sturgis, and that's the only place she can't keep an eye on me. What'd you say your name was?"

"Marie," I said, then remembered I'd written my real name on the traveler's check.

"No, I mean your last name. When I get to Sturgis this fall, I want to come down and give you a ride on my Harley."

"Johnson." Leonard didn't handle the money; he'd never see that check. Bob was probably tucking it into his new wife's size-40D bra right now. "You just ask for the Johnson place when you get to Hermosa." If Leonard came looking for Marie Johnson, he'd get action: her six brothers are jealous of competition. They all have big muscles and little eyes set close together.

"I worked construction for years, so I'm in good shape. Then I took one of them correspondence courses and become a mechanic. But I had to quit when I got hurt." He looked at me expectantly.

"How'd that happen?" I said, on cue.

"I was fixing a dump truck, underneath it, you know? Well I heard this noise and I knew she was dropping, and I threw myself forward 'cause if I'd a throwed myself back I'd a got my head stuck between the box and the frame." He looked at me to be sure I understood.

"As it was, the box dropped on my back. I yelled once before I passed out and my partner heard me. When he raised that truck box, I tell you I slid out of there onto the floor just like a snake." He illustrated with a sinuous movement of his arm in the air between us, dropping his hand onto my knee as he went on with the story.

"My partner dragged me out and called the ambulance." He squeezed my knee. "I was in the hospital about a year and they said I'd probably never walk again."

I lurched closer to the door, leaving his hand behind as I rolled the window down. "But I just kept working at it until I could walk again. I never give up." He winked. "I'd been ridin' a cycle, so I figured I might still get around on two wheels. Strong arms." He held up an arm, brown and shining like a mahogany sculpture. This time, his hand landed on the steering wheel.

Sweat trickled, rolling down the inside of my arm. The old pickup bucked along, swaying in the backwash of big trucks snorting past. Smoking, Leonard said nothing for a mile while I slid my right hand down inside my pants pocket. My jackknife was still only three inches long.

"There's Gothenburg; old Swede town. A bunch of them damn Swedes got this far on the Oregon Trail and said, 'Ay ben not going no furder; dis country gets vorse and vorse.' You know what a Swede is, don't you? It's a…"

"A Norwegian with his brains knocked out? You must be Norwegian, Leonard."

"Yeah—and I bet you're a Swede, ain't you?" He pounded the steering wheel. "Johnson and that blond hair. I usually stick my foot in my mouth."

We were both laughing when we got to the Chevy garage. Leonard banged on the door, and a portly fellow in a lavender leisure suit unlocked it, beaming. "Hel-*lo*, Leonard. How are you?"

"I'm finer'n bird sweat, George. How's yourself?"

George nodded. "Fine. Fine. This is the damsel in distress? What's a little girl like you doing out here all by yourself?" He put his arm across my shoulders and squeezed.

"Car trouble makes this damsel damn grouchy, George."

"Awful nice of you to come down here like this, George," Leonard said. "Save this little gal from being stranded in Brady." I dropped my purse and bent to grab it, ducking away.

"Hell, Leonard, I wouldn't do it for anybody but you." He looked at me, no longer smiling. "We go way back, Leonard and me—way back." He winked and patted Leonard on the shoulder and the two of them went through a door labeled "Parts."

Wondering what the old grease monkey had on George, I found a water-cooler and drank deep. When I straightened up, George grabbed my shoulder again. "I found one, little gal. Only about, oh, $24.95 ought to do it."

When I opened my billfold, Leonard's eyes pivoted toward it. I didn't know what he was going to charge me, so I riffled the five ten-dollar bills that were left after I'd paid, so he could count them. He grunted and went outside. When I got in his truck, he turned left out of the lot instead of right toward the interstate.

"Where are you headed, Leonard?" I said, my hand on the door handle. The thought of escaping Leonard with George as my only acquaintance was not comforting.

"Oh, I thought we'd go down to the Lucky Strike and have a cool one. Must be a hundred and ten in the shade." His hand started crawling across the seat. His palm stuck to the vinyl and he pulled it loose with a *slurp,* like a sound from a horror movie.

Ah, I thought; the secret of his romantic success. "You're a dangerous devil, Leonard and I'd love a drink, but I don't dare. If I drink one, I'll drink eight and then where will I be?"

He chuckled. Exactly.

"I told my dad I'd be home by seven tonight and what with that fan belt, I'm three hours behind already. It'll be past midnight and if I know my dad, he'll send my brothers out if I don't show up on time. Those boys will back-track every stretch of road all the way to Lincoln."

I shook my head. Leonard stared at the bar.

"Then he'll worry about them being too slow, so he'll call the sheriff, which is ridiculous. He hasn't held a state office for ten years. In fact, I'd better call when we get back to the garage." Babbling, I pictured Leonard drunk twenty miles from my broken-down car, and tried to figure out what I'd do if this didn't work. I wanted to cry. Instead, I visualized pulling a snub-nosed pistol out of a shoulder holster and jamming it between a couple of Leonard's bony little ribs.

Across the street, tinny music howled out the open door of the Lucky Strike. The pickup idled down the street. Then he shifted into second.

"Yeah, you're right." He pulled a stick of gum out of his pocket and popped it in his mouth. "It's gonna take awhile to get that fuel pump in that old wreck if I remember right." He threw the gum wrapper out the window. I breathed. He said, "Do you mind if I take the old road back? I hate that damn interstate."

I leaned back. "No, Leonard. I like old roads." The sun flashed in our faces and then dropped behind the everlasting cornfields. *As on thy highest mount I stand, I look away across the sea.* The air smelled like silage and pigs.

After awhile, Leonard said, "What's you say you did in Lincoln?"

"Edited a university history course for TV. You ever see those?"

"Yeah, I watch them once in awhile." He turned the radio off. "Both my boys went to college. That's why I worked them two jobs for twenty years. I'd have let them work their own way through, but my old lady said I had to help them. I paid for the books, but they had to work theirselves for money to live on. They done good, though. One of them teaches sociology out on the coast. The other one, he went in the service his third year in school and got into computers. God, he could have made a bundle when he got out. You know what he's doing?"

He faced me, twisting the gear shift knob furiously. "You *know* what he's doing? He's driving a dump truck for the county." He snorted. "Lot of god-damn good a college education did him. He could have done that right out of eighth grade. I done better than that and I never went further than fifth."

"Maybe he'll change his mind when he gets married. You know, responsibility."

"Last time we seen him, he brought a woman home one Saturday night and took her to church with us the next morning. That's been a coupla years. Haven't seen my other boy since he moved to the coast."

"They must be proud of you, working so hard so they could go to school. When I was in college, some of my friends wouldn't bring friends home. They were embarrassed if the folks didn't talk right or had grease under their fingernails."

"Hmmm." He frowned and chomped gum.

I leaned out the window and tried to feel cool while sweat pasted my shirt to my skin. Was today's mess a metaphor for my life? Logic told me I could learn from my mistakes, but I felt like a failure. I'd failed at marriage, been raped. Maybe I'd never feel safe again. *Where mansions are prepared for me/My heaven, my home forever more.*

Zillions of June bugs buzzed around the forty-watt bulb over the shop door. Country music bubbled out the open door of the pink trailer, a neon prairie schooner marooned among cottonwoods, a carnival ship on the black horizon. Leonard clamped a trouble light on Beulah's hood while I got the fuel pump out of the box. The price tag read $19.95. Maybe the extra five bucks was Lavender George's Sunday-opening tariff.

Leonard rolled under the car on a dolly, grunted, and said, "You up there? I need a hand." I leaned over the bumper and saw his face under a tangle of hoses. "I'll turn this wrench as far as I can from under here, then you grab it and turn it as far as you can, take it off, and hand it back to me. I'd like to get my hands on the bastard who thought this was a good way to install a fuel pump," Leonard wheezed. "Don't drop that wrench in my teeth." Sweat ran out of my hair and dripped, along with leftover gas, into Leonard's face.

We'd traded the wrench back and forth a few times before he muttered, "How come a college woman don't have a better car than this old bitch? Christ, she's older than you are."

"Watch your language, Leonard. This car is named after my great-aunt, a Mormon lady of great virtue."

"Well, if she's so damn virtuous, she could afford to buy you a better car."

"I had a new car. My ex-husband took it when he ran off with his little girlfriend. Now I'm older, wiser, and poorer."

We were twisting in the last bolt when the hair stood up on the back of my neck. The three bikers were right behind me.

"Yer suite is ready, honey."

"The finest accommodations Brady has to offer." They guffawed. "The *only* accommodations Brady has to offer."

"Got a few six packs too. Hell, it's Saturday night." The nearest one, who might have been speaking, clamped a hand on my butt and squeezed.

I yelped before realizing it was my turn with the wrench. I whacked his wrist with it and said, "Back off, boys," but my voice shook. I took a deep breath and bellowed, "Back off! Go play with yourselves!"

The one I'd hit doubled a fist, then howled and grabbed his wrist, as if the pain signal had finally reached his brain.

Yelling, "What the hell's going on up there? Give me that wrench!" Leonard rolled the dolly out, smacking into one guy's ankle. Swearing, the guy bent over and hit his head on the bumper. "Ouch! Bitch," he screeched. The other two giggled and they drifted back into the garage.

"Thanks, Leonard. What happens next?"

"Right now all I want to do is get this goddamn thing fixed." He shoved the last bolt home. When he tried to hand me the wrench I was looking over my shoulder, so the wrench clanged on the concrete beside his head. "Goddammit!" he yelled. "Pay attention. A little grab-ass didn't hurt you, and anyway, I can see their feet if they walk up here again."

My watch said 6:30 when the dolly squealed and Leonard slid out from under the car. "You gas up," he said, and walked into shadows beside the garage. After filling the tank, I started the car. Leonard came back and leaned into the engine, looking and listening. "No gas spraying out. I'd say we got 'er in there just right. That's it, honey." He slammed the hood and said, "Come on inside and pay me." His smile looked broad and wet.

I slipped my nine-inch brass tire gauge into my back pocket before I followed him. The three bikers were sitting on a stack of tires drinking beer and shoving each other.

"How long is this going to take, Bob?" one asked. "We got us a date here with the little lady. I'm first."

Bob, kneeling by a Harley, looked at me thoughtfully when I said, "If I were you, Bob, I'd keep an eye on this slime with a new wife all alone in that trailer."

Leonard said, "About fifty dollars I guess, honey. Leave you enough to get home on."

"Come on, Leonard. You saw how much money I have. I can't get that old crate home on this tank of gas." Noticing the greasy cut on his hand, I remembered how hard he'd worked in the heat. "I could write you a check. It wouldn't bounce." But he'd have my name and address.

"Make it forty, then. You should have let me buy you that beer. Might have talked me down a little." His eyes glittered under his sweaty forehead. The three boys stirred behind me. I handed Leonard four tens and turned to face them.

Leonard said, "I'll see you when I come to Sturgis for the races this fall, Marie." He led me outside, whistling softly while I tightened the straps holding the bicycle on its rack over the trunk. Bob came out, wiping his hands. "No charge for the tank of gas, honey."

"Thanks, Bob. Thanks, Leonard. I really do appreciate your help."

"Wait a minute," yelled one of the bikers, running out of the garage. Bob stepped in front of him and put a big greasy hand on his chest. "She's going right down that road, kid, minding her business. You mind yours."

The other two headed for the two bikes beside the garage. One yelled, "They can't stop us; there ain't no law in this town."

I shut my eyes, hoping to conjure up a woman who made herself a legend in our community. One night when the social whirl didn't meet her expectations, she threw everybody she could catch—men, women, children, and a couple of dogs—off the dance-hall balcony.

Leonard patted my shoulder. "Take care, little girl."

"Thanks, Leonard. Can I outrun those two?"

He leaned close. "That's OK, honey. It's a little-known mechanical fact that heat loosens oil plugs. They fell outta both those bikes awhile back. They won't go far." He waved his grease rag at me as I roared out of the lot. I waved back, wishing I'd hugged him, and drove seventy with the windows down and the radio up. I watched the rearview mirror, knowing I couldn't tell two motorcycles from a car's headlights anyway.

On the outskirts of Sidney, I tucked Beulah into a slot between two eighteen-wheelers parked broadside to the highway. No one passing could see the car's distinctive shape. In the truck-stop rest room, I washed my hands and scrubbed grease off my forehead, then realized my arms, jeans, and shirt were streaked with oil.

I flopped into the nearest booth, almost colliding with a waitress wearing a skirt that barely covered her hips. "Thisboothisreserved," she said. When I gaped, not hearing her, she shook her head, jiggling the two fuzzy dice dangling from her ponytail. "This booth is reserved," she said slowly.

"Reserved? This is a goddamn truck stop. What are you talking about?"

She pointed to a sign: "Reserved for Truck Drivers." Over her shoulder she said sociably, "Touch my ass again, Sam, and they'll find pieces of you in *Dee*-troit." My opinion of her rose fifty points.

"Don't I look like a truck driver?" I said, spreading my filthy, sunburned arms. A couple of truckers laughed and applauded.

"Well, whyn't ya just say so?" she griped, slapping a menu and a glass of water in front of me. "I don't have time for guessing games."

Eyes under Cat and Texaco caps measured me as I gulped water. My hands were shaking so hard most of it splashed on the table. Before the waitress came back, I dug my keys out of my pocket and ran to the car. Beulah wouldn't start until I pumped the gas, shaking and cursing; then I whizzed out of the lot.

Next time I saw a highway sign, I was doing sixty on a narrow strip of rutted asphalt, Highway 385 north. My left arm hanging out the window felt fried. I inspected each little town: no gas station.

Chugging along in the sticky dark, I was thinking how farmers' yard lights looked like fireflies when I saw headlights on a side road. The car swung in close behind me as I passed, headlights glaring in my rearview mirror.

Each time I slowed down or speeded up, the car stayed with me. At forty miles an hour, I topped a rise and saw the lights of Dalton, Nebraska, one empty street lined with dark buildings. Light flared around a tall sign at the far end.

Halfway through town was a stop sign. I braked gently, because the other car was still on my bumper. Beulah lurched ahead, the car behind so close all I could see in the mirror was the silhouette of a man's head. When I braked again, the car hit my bumper so hard my flashlight fell off the seat and I heard metal snap on the bicycle rack. In the rearview mirror, the man's face, red in my taillights' reflection, was young and clean-shaven. I pulled ahead a little, looked both ways. *Bang!* The car hit my bumper. And again.

Leaning out the window, I shrieked, "Cut it out, you dumb son of a bitch." His door opened as I bent over to grope on the floor for the flashlight, two feet long and heavy with batteries. As he reached for my door handle, I sat up and stomped the gas. Gravel shot back from my tires. He yelped and swore. I raced toward the light and swerved into a gas station as the other car left the stop sign.

As I slammed on the brakes and honked the horn, a heavy man inside looked up from the cash register. I ran toward the door he held open a crack. "What the hell's all the racket about, sister?" he said. "I'm closing up."

"I'm sorry. That guy was running into me back at the stop sign." I pointed at the other car, cruising slowly up the street toward us.

"Huh?" The man's eyes narrowed at me.

"That guy—he was hitting my car! Have you got a phone? A sheriff?" The last streetlight stood in a weedy lot a block beyond the station. The other car pulled over beside it and turned, engine idling.

"Have a little fight with the boyfriend, did you, honey? Just take it on back home. This is a gas station."

I took a deep breath and pushed my hair back from my face. "Listen to me. I'm from South Dakota. I've never seen that guy before. When I stopped at the stop sign, he ran into me, and then backed up and hit me a couple more times."

"Oh, he's just playing around." Engine roaring, the other car raced back the way we'd come, turning sharply at the stop sign. "Just having a good time on Saturday night."

"He wasn't playing when he hit me. Look at my car." The rim of the front bicycle wheel was bent, and a support on the rack dangled loose. "He wrecked the rack and the bike both."

"We don't ride bicycles out here, sister. You want some gas or you just going to complain all night?"

"Gas, please. Do you know that guy?" With my pocketknife, I cut the canvas straps on the bike rack until I could tie it to the bumper. The man moved to the regular pump and stuck the nozzle in my tank. "Don't you know him?" he said, grinning.

"Hell, no." An engine rumbled and the same car zipped up the street without stopping, headed north, the way I'd be going.

"What are you doing out here by yourself in the middle of the night, anyway?"

"Trying to get home. I had car trouble. You got any law around here?"

"There's a county sheriff but I think he's out of town. That boy probably won't bother you again. Where you headed?"

"South Dakota, if I ever get out of this damn state."

He hung up the gas hose and stuck his hand out. "That'll be ten dollars, missy. Didn't your daddy ever tell you it ain't ladylike to swear? You got no business bein' out at night. Women who stay home don't get in trouble."

I laid a bill in his hand. He stalked inside and closed the door. I heard the lock click.

I eased onto the road. Cars slumped like cold slag in front of dark houses. Beulah's graceful three-thousand-pound shadow leaped across the brome grass in the ditch. At the edge of the dark behind the streetlight, I floored it.

An hour later, I cruised to the tune of my rattling bicycle through Bridgeport, black as a cornfield. On the bridge over the North Platte River, I stopped and stumbled to the railing. Was that a breeze? My eyes fell into the flow of water. My mind drifted; I seemed to see piles of household goods abandoned by pioneers following their dreams west. *Where streams of life forever flow,* I sang softly, feeling discarded. Leaning on the railing, I cast curses on all the men I'd met that day.

After awhile, I opened the rear doors to roll the windows down and noticed my dead houseplants. I picked up the biggest one, a jade plant with a trunk thick as my wrist, and staggered to the railing. Where was she now, the friend who'd begged me to take it when she moved? When I pushed the plant over, it struck the muddy water and a geyser exploded, splashing me with drops that looked silver in the faint light. One by one, I pitched them all. When the last one hit the water, I was drenched, laughing and cool for the first time that day.

On the outskirts of Alliance, I decided I could drive two more hours home if I could find gas, but both stations on main street were closed until 7:00 A.M. "Vacancy" flashed a motel's red neon sign. When I turned the key off, I sagged like a bag of wet sand.

Cold air swallowed me as I opened the glass door. I felt in the coin pocket of my jeans, checking to be sure the bills I'd stashed earlier were still there, and hoping they were twenties. A bald man in coveralls filled an overstuffed chair, watching a late show and smoking a huge green cigar. He didn't look at me.

"Got a single?" My voice was coarse as gravel.

"Yeah." Looking at me, he exhaled a billow of smoke that veiled his face.

"How much is it?" I pulled two bills out of my pocket, holding them below the counter, out of his sight; both tens.

"You alone?" Chewing the cigar, he leaned forward in his chair, trying to see around me to the car.

"Yeah."

He peered at me through the cigar smoke while he stuffed his hand inside the coveralls and scratched his belly. "You ain't got somebody else in the car?"

"Go look if you want to."

"What's a girl doing running around motels at this time of night for?"

"Car trouble. Trying to get home," I said. "Haven't you heard? They passed a law that women can drive cars." I tried to smile and felt my upper lip lift in a snarl.

"We don't have that commie pinko liberation shit in Nebraska." He exhaled another cloud of green smoke and leaned back in the chair.

I straightened, smiled carefully, and said, "Sir, I'd appreciate it if you'd watch your language. I've left Lincoln today heading home to my four children. I live two hours north, but I'm out of gas and there are no stations open. I've had car trouble twice and I'm exhausted. I'd like a single motel room, and I plan to occupy it by myself."

He grunted. "Eighteen dollars." He tapped a long ash in a metal ashtray balanced on the arm of the chair.

Two dollars left, unless I found another cash stash. Maybe I could write a check in Hot Springs, forty miles from home. "Thank you, I'll take it."

He didn't get up. "Register's there on the desk." I turned it around and signed my name while he put his fat hands on the arms of the chair and lunged forward. On the third try, he stood, turned the book around and said, "That your name?"

I bit my lip and flipped open my driver's license. When he pulled on it, I tightened my grip. He looked me, little eyes hard, and wrote the number in his book. Then he lifted a key off a nearly full rack behind him. "Here ya go, honey."

I snatched the key. "Eighteen dollars doesn't buy you the right to call me honey, buster." While I started the car, he copied my license number.

Since I'd planned to be home, I didn't have an overnight bag, but I dragged a clean shirt out of a suitcase, found my bottle of gin in a wastebasket and a twenty in the plastic tampon case under the seat. I collected the flashlight and tire gauge, locked the car, found a pop machine in a walkway and some quarters in my pocket. I bought three cans of Squirt. As I unlocked the door to the room, I saw the man at the office window, staring.

I locked the door. The TV was bolted to a battered bureau. I turned on the bathroom light and yanked the moldy shower curtain aside. There was no glass, so I drank half a Squirt, filled the pop bottle with gin and drained it. Then I sat on the bed and started to shake.

Why had the day been so terrifying? Experts say a woman's best protection is acting confident and staying alert. I'd done both. I tried to keep my vehicle in good condition, planned trips to allow extra time. No weapon would change the way some men talked and thought. Yet I hadn't been physically harmed. Maybe I'd have to develop instincts, learn to tell which men were dangerous and which weren't. Either that or lock myself in the house at dark.

Finishing the second gin and Squirt, I noticed a wide gap in the window curtains and thought I heard a shoe scrape on concrete outside. I snapped off the light and checked the lock. Then put a chair under the doorknob and shoved the chest of drawers, TV and all, against it. With two safety pins from my purse, I pinned the curtain together. Then I locked the bathroom door and showered until my fingers turned blue. I dabbed myself with a dusty towel, put on the clean shirt and filthy jeans. With a good grip on the flashlight, I turned off the bathroom light, waited until my eyes adjusted and opened the door.

I was sitting on the bed in the dark, toasting the family in the clunky bus, when I noticed a red glow beyond the curtains. I tiptoed to the window and opened a two-finger slit. Across the street, flames leapt from the roof of a building labeled "Auto Parts." I unpinned the curtains, plumped up the thin pillows, and leaned back. When the fire died to bright embers at 3:00 A.M., I slid down in the bed and slept.

■ ■ ■

In 1991, sixteen years later, I pulled off Interstate 80 at the Brady exit. I was headed to eastern Nebraska to do a series of readings from my books. After rewriting the story of that day a dozen times, I'd resolved to revisit the scene. Had Bob graduated to more sophisticated larceny after the newness wore off the trailer and the wife? Maybe I'd pull in and ask him to diagnose the clatter in the Bronco—test his honesty, since I knew the sound came from my dead catalytic converter.

Queasy, I thought how much I'd learned doing the jobs that support my writing habit, driving across the plains to give workshops and speeches. My preparations for bad weather and bad people have become second nature, but I travel cheerfully as well as alertly.

Cardboard flapped in broken windows of the gas station, still the only major building in Brady. The old yellow Olds was jacked up in front of the double doors, one rear wheel missing. The cottonwoods behind the shop were dead. Canted over, the faded pink trailer was streaked with black streaks, like flames. A dirty curtain blew out a broken window.

A wizened old man stood in the shop doorway, his belly dragging his pants down, suspenders stretched and puckered. Squinting against the sun, he pushed his cap back on his head. I recognized Bob and suddenly felt short of breath. I gunned the motor and spun out of the station, throwing gravel. I sang loudly as I merged into traffic, *Oh, Beulah Land, sweet Beulah Land.*

■ ■ ■

Five years later, in November 1996, I totaled the Bronco in a rollover on black ice, my first accident in 163,000 miles. Witnesses said I did everything right; the investigating highway patrol officer absolved me of error. A friendly tow-truck driver helped me load my possessions into a rental car so I could continue my speaking tour. He apparently didn't notice me collecting cash from old tampon containers, ashtrays, collapsible cups, and other hiding places. Surveying the scatter of jumper cables, flares, a tow chain, coveralls, a pistol, knives, wrenches, and spare parts among my boxes of books, he said, "You were ready for anything, weren't you? Except rolling your car."

The Clearwater

KIM BARNES

I take the river a step at a time. My feet slide from the shoulders of rock; my toes wedge between boulders. I am timid about this, moving out toward center where the water is deepest, where the big fish might lie.

Here, at Lenore, the Clearwater is not easy. Too wide to cast from shore, too swift, too pocked with hidden currents and sudden holes. I go at it anyway, still without waders, determined to find my place of stability, the water at my belly, my thighs numbing with cold.

My husband fishes below me. On shore, our daughter and son dig pools in the sand, and I feel a rush of gratitude, the joy of living only minutes from water, the same water I and my brother played in as children. It is as though I am reliving my own young life, there on the banks of the Clearwater, as though I exist in two dimensions and know the pleasure of each—the child's pure delight in the moment; the woman's recognition of continuance, of nostalgia, of the water around her and the sun on her face.

I choose a fly I think the fish might favor, its color the color of the day's light and leaves and wings. I praise its tufts and feathers, its hackle and tail. I load the line, thinking not of the S I must make through air but of the place above sand where the water eddies, the V above whitecaps, the purl below stone.

I do not think of the line or the fly or the fish as much as I think about the water moving against and around me, how the sky fills my eyes and the noise-that-isn't-noise fills my ears—the movement of everything around me like the hum of just-waking or sleep, blood-rush, dream-rush, the darkness coming on, the air.

I forget to watch for the fish to strike, forget to note the catch, the spin, the sinking. I pull the line in, let it loop at my waist, sing it out again, and again. The trout will rise, or they won't. The nubbin of fur and thread will turn to caddis, black ant, stone fly, bee, or it will simply settle on the water and remain a human's fancy. Either way, it's magic to me, and so I stay until my feet are no longer my own but part of the river's bed. How can I move them? How can I feel my way back to shore, where my family is calling that it's time to go home? They are hungry, and the shadows have taken the canyon. They are cold.

From my place in the water, they seem distant to me. I must seem like a fool, numb to my ribcage, no fish to show. But I am here in the river, half-in, half-out, a wader of two worlds. I smile. I wave. I am where nothing can reach me.

■ ■ ■

North Fork, Middle Fork, South Fork, Main: see how the flow of the sounds is smooth, so lovely. The rivers themselves flow together this way, spilling down from the mountains. They drain the north Idaho land my father and others like him logged and loved so easily in the years before their doing so seemed to matter.

Now, as sales are staked and trees are spiked, the land slumps from beneath its covering of burned slash and razored stumps, slides off the hills and down the draws, sloughs off its dying skin like an animal readying itself for another season. Always, the runoff of rain, the soil it carries, the ash and cinder, the dry bones of trees.

Here, where I live with my husband and children above the Main Clear-water at Lenore, twelve miles from where the forks have all come together, we see the movement of land in the water's flow. Spring thaw, and the trees come fully rooted, ungrounded by the wash of high current. Old log jams from previous floods break loose; new ones pile against the bridge footings and small islands. Each becomes a nest of lost things: fishing lures, loops of rope, men's undershirts, women's shoes.

I wonder, sometimes, if my own life's mementos are contained in those tangles, perhaps a barrette I lost while fishing Reeds Creek, or one of my mother's pie tins with which my brother and I panned for gold. Or the trees themselves fallen from the riverbank I sat on as a child, searching for the mussel shells we called angel's wings, though they were mahogany brown and often broken.

What the river takes, the river gives, and so it is with my life here. Each hour I spend with my feet near water, I feel more deeply rooted; the farther away I get, the less sure I am of my place in the world. For each of us, there must be this one thing, and for me it is the river. Not just the river, but the composition that begins as the North Fork and flows into the Main. I have known this river from its feeding waters to its mouth where it meets and becomes one with the Snake. I have known it before the dams, and after. I have known it as a child knows water, have known it as a lover knows water, and now as a mother knows and recognizes water as she watches her own children who are bent at the waist, leaning forward to bring up the sandy wings.

■ ■ ■

I am closest to the Clearwater when I am closest to its origins, and to my own. Reeds Creek, Orofino Creek, Weitas Creek, Deer Creek, the Musselshell—they feed the river as the river feeds me. It has taken me longer to feel intimate with the stretch of river that curves into *omega* below our house. I watch it each day, uneasy with its width and deep holes. I realize, too, that I distrust this length of the river because it no longer moves of its own volition: Dworshak Dam controls a great part of it now. The North Fork, the river I once knew as a tree-lined stream the color of turquoise, now ends in a man-made reservoir covering more than fifty miles of land that was first logged for its timber before being flooded. The river bulges at its base, its narrower neck seemingly unaffected by the distant concrete obstruction. People drive northeast for hours to reach the Bungalow, Aquarius—places where the water remains swift and the fish are often native.

But I know better. The river's betrayal sometimes shames me, the way it carries on as though what it travels toward is not a state of near stasis, depositing sludge along miles of riprap dikes, piling its dross against the pylons and locks and turbines. It cannot rid itself of what it is given, cannot carry its silt and timber and ash to the mouth of the ocean where it can be broken down, taken to great depths, washed and sifted into sand and dirt. Instead, the silt falls from the slow current, depositing itself in great layers, narrowing the river's channel. The river becomes murky, the flat color of pewter. The trout are replaced by bottom-feeders, lovers of warm water. Every year, the Corps of Engineers sponsors a trash-fish derby, paying the fishermen to catch and kill what their dams have spawned.

Like so many others who love this land, it has taken me some time to understand that this place—its rivers and streams, forests, mountains, and high meadows—does not absorb but reflects what we bring to it. Perhaps, then, what I see in the river is some mirror of the contradictions that make up my own life—the calm surface, the seeming freedom. Certainly, the river is a metaphor for memory. "I am everything I ever was," Stegner said, and so it is with the river—water and rock, metal and mineral, stick and bone, trout-flash and deer-lick. Perpetual, even in the face of destruction, I think, even as I read the sad stories of pollution and poisoning, fish-kill, and disease. Perpetual because the rain must fall and the mountains must accept and the water must run toward ocean. A comfort, knowing that the amount of water in our world never changes, that there is never any more nor any less, only the same and in various forms: ice, liquid, vapor. I trust that water will withstand, given its basic demands—to fall, to move, to rise, to fall again.

This, then, may be my final recognition: the inevitability of movement. We slow, we go forward. We age. We rise to greet each morning. We fall into sleep each night. Constant as rain, perpetuated in death and birth and rebirth.

It has taken me time to understand the need I feel to be consumed by the river. Raised a stoic, I am seldom given to need. Need is a weakness, a loss of control, the Achilles' heel of human existence. My connection to the river is complicated by its pull; I resent the power it possesses to draw me. Yet I want its sound in my ears, its smell, its taste. I want to be immersed—my hands, my feet, my hips. Like all seductions, it necessitates surrender.

I am learning to let go.

■ ■ ■

I bring to the river my love and those that I choose to love. I bring to it my child's memories and my woman's life. I bring to it hunger but always joy, for whatever it is that weighs on me dissipates in those few miles between our house in the canyon and the water's edge.

I understand how water can become something grim, how it can rise and take and swirl and drown. How it can become something to fight against, something to resist. The dam on the North Fork, the largest of its kind, was not built for electricity or simple recreation, they say, but for flood control in Portland, 400 miles west.

There's less flooding now, although three springs ago, in 1996, not even the dams could keep pace when the temperatures rose and the snowmelt came down with rain. We watched from our house above the river, stranded between washed-out roads, watched the roofs and porches, the dead cows and refrigerators and lawn chairs, the still-intact trailer house that slammed against the Lenore Bridge.

How can I cheer such destruction? For that is what I felt, an overwhelming sense of boosterism. I wanted the river to win in some essential way, wanted to see it rise up and lash out, pull down the dams and drain the reservoirs, ferry away the docks and cleanse itself of silt. I wanted it to show a god's righteous anger, a larger reflection of my own frustration and resentment.

I didn't mind, then, that we couldn't get out. My husband had made a last, grand effort to snatch our children from their school in Orofino twenty miles east, hauling them back over bench roads not yet torn away by the massive runoff, roads that crumbled and disappeared behind them. Other rural parents with children in school were not so lucky: it would be a week before any travel was allowed in or out, except by helicopter. Our family was together, protected by our place high on the canyon wall. We had food, water, wood. We had days ahead of us without school or teaching, weeks before the roads would be cleared, and now the sun that had started the ruin was back out and warming the air into spring.

We packed sandwiches and cookies, cheese and crackers, and a bottle of fine red wine. We hiked to where we could watch Big Eddy, the place where the river curled against itself and created an enormous back current that caught and held the debris. While the river ran thick with trees and fence posts, goat huts, and wall-papered sheetrock, we ate and drank and gathered ladybugs for our garden. Certain logs were red with their hatching, their coming out of hibernation. We scooped them up in handfuls and carried them in bundles made of paper towels and candy wrappers. Their odor was strong, dry, astringent—a promise of summer.

We watched a jet boat make its way down the river. Foolish, we thought, to risk such danger. The river was running at a near-record high; the water was choked with flotsam, some larger than the boat itself. The two men inside were not wearing lifejackets, and I shook my head. What were they thinking?

The boat pulled in at a smaller eddy downstream, and there we saw what they followed: a large raft of finished lumber, floated loose from the mill at Orofino. Scavengers' rights. If they were willing to risk it, the lumber was theirs.

One man kept the helm while the other bent over the gunnels to grab the wood. They pulled it onto the boat's bow one plank at a time until the craft sat low in the already threatening water. We held our breath, knowing that if they were to fall overboard or if the boat capsized, we could do nothing but watch.

They loaded the wood. They let the current swing them about, turn them upstream. They made their way slowly, navigating through tangles of barbed wire still stapled to barn doors, past trees three times the length of their boat. They had their booty. They were gone.

I couldn't imagine such nonsense, such greed. What desperation could bring on the willingness to risk so much for so little? I felt content, driven by nothing other than the warmth on my shoulders and the love I felt for this land and my husband and daughter and son, who gathered around me to show what they had found: a mantid's egg case, triangular and strangely textured, like meringue hardened and fired to a ceramic glaze. We would take it home as well and put it in the garden, where it would hatch its eaters of grasshoppers and aphids.

I must have believed, then, that it was love that would see me through the long hours of darkness, that would keep me grounded during the wild summer heat. I must have believed that, like the river, what we love may surge and wane but remains nonetheless constant, giving, taking, carrying on.

And doesn't it? Perhaps it is we who fail love, refusing to allow its seduction, its pull and sway. Love is a river we step into, like the waters of baptismal rebirth. We close our eyes. We bow our heads. We allow ourselves to be taken as the water closes over our heads. For that moment, we must believe.

■ ■ ■

"I don't think we can make it." I looked at what was left of the road, stretching down before me into a dusk of low trees.

My daughter and son moaned. After a day of writing, I had picked them up from the sitter's in Orofino, promising a late afternoon along the river. My husband was in the mountains near McCall, hiking the upper lakes, safe with the friends he'd known since high school. There was a place I'd heard of, just down some side road, where Ford's Creek met the river, a place with sand and stiller water, where Jordan and Jace could swim and I could spread my blanket and think. The stretch of river we were after mattered to me: it was a section of the last few miles of the Main Clearwater, the last free-flowing water between the headwaters and the ocean.

I needed the river in a way I had not only hours before. It wasn't fishing I was after. I was sour with bad news, begrudging even the rod, line, and fly their pacification. That afternoon, I'd gotten a phone call from across the country and learned that our close friends' marriage was in sudden and serious peril, rocked by confession of a particularly insidious spate of infidelity. The levels of betrayal had shocked me, and the narrative of contentment and ongoing friendship that I had trusted was suddenly gone.

The anger that I felt surprised me. I am not comfortable with anger, having been taught from the cradle that anger, like other unmanageable emotions, is best kept under lock and key, somewhere in the heart's deepest chamber. The river would help, sweep away the confusion of emotions with its own ordered chaos. The river would help me find my footing, my point of rest.

But now this: I'd chosen the wrong road. Even after having made the decision to put the car into reverse and back our way out of the ravine, we were going nowhere. The tires of the front-wheel drive Toyota spun and chattered in the gravel, unable to push the weight of the car up such a steep incline. The dirt and basalt-studded bank rose close on my left; the road crumbled away on my right, slumping into a gully of black locust, poison ivy, and blackberry brambles thick with thorns.

"*Now* what." I said it in the way my mother always had. Fatalism. Tired resignation.

I eased the clutch, tried again. Nothing but smoke and the bitter smell of burning rubber.

"I think we'd better get out of the car," Jace said. At seven, he's the cautious one, always sensing the adult's boundless capacity for error.

"No," I said. "It's okay. Let's just go on down. We can turn around at the bottom." I had no idea if this were true, but my choice was to keep going or for us all to begin the long walk back to town for a tow truck. I also felt a kind of apathy: What was the worst that could happen? The river was only 500 yards away. We'd find our way out.

What we found instead was an increasingly narrow once-road. I saw that, for years, the rain had washed down the path scraped from the hillside, taking what dirt remained with it to the river. What was left was a deep schism that forked and meandered its way around rocks too large to be moved. I concentrated on riding the ruts' shoulders until there was no rut to straddle but only a series of woven ditches. I kept thinking it would get better, that the road would even out, that *someone* had made it down here because the vegetation was scraped from the center. I kept wishing for the Suburban with its high clearance and granny gear, but I doubted that the path we traveled would have allowed its girth.

We bounced over boulders the size of basketballs. The skidplate caught and dragged. Jordan and Jace whimpered in the backseat. I tried to act as though this were nearly normal, to be expected. If I stayed calm, in control, they would feel safe.

"Mom, please." Jordan had her hand on the door handle, as though she meant to jump.

"We're almost there," I said. "We'll get to the river and be glad." We were far into the darkness of trees now, the yellow pine and locust, the dense undergrowth of vine maple. I jostled the car around a corner, then stopped. I could see ahead to where the road leveled off, where sunlight broke through. Between us and that point of flat ground was a final pitch downward, where the road hooked a ninety-degree right angle. The bigger problem was that the trail became narrower still, hedged in by the bank on the left and, on the right, an old tanker truck settled into a bog of brambles.

I examined my passage. A boulder twice the size of our car protruded like a tumor from the eight-foot dirt bank. The abandoned tanker, its red paint faded to rust, was just as intractable; steel and stone, and only the space of a small car between them.

If I stop here, I thought, *the tow truck might still be able to reach us.* But I had begun to doubt the plausibility of such a rescue, given the tight turns and narrow corridor down which we had traveled. I thought *cable, winch,* but could not imagine the logistics of being dragged backward from the ravine without damaging the car beyond repair.

"Mom?" My son's voice quavered.

"What?" I was snappish, weighing our chances, calculating the risk.

"Can't we just walk from here?"

I thought of the brambles, the probability of rattlesnakes, what unseen dangers might wait around the corner.

"Just hang on." I inched the car toward the passage, like Odysseus steering his ship through the straits. I sucked in and held my breath, giving the air what room I could. One scrape and we were through and bumping into the clearing.

Whoops and hollers from the backseat. "We made it!" Jace shouted. Jordan crowed. I stopped the car, got out, and circled it twice, looking for damage. Nothing but a few shallow scratches. No dripping oil. The muffler remained miraculously intact.

"Watch for snakes. Wait for me." I gathered our water bottles and bag of sandwiches, taking in the lay of the land. Between us and the river was the railroad track, built high on its ridge of rock. To the left I saw the remnants of a gold mine, its entryway framed in old timbers. To my right was a settling pond, green with algae. As we began our short walk, two blue herons rose from the still water, awkward on their wings.

There was a game trail, which we followed to the tracks and over. What we found was a long beach of rocks and a smaller one of sand. The children had all but forgotten the trauma of our trip and stripped themselves of shoes and socks before wading in. I felt the heat, then, the sweat gone sticky at my collar and waist.

I walked a few yards upstream, found a rock close to water, where I could dangle my feet and keep an eye on my son and daughter. I tried not to think of the sun's low slant, the hard way out. I tried not to hear what I was thinking: there *is* no way out of here except to leave the car and walk. No way I could make that first climb and twist between the rock and truck.

I closed my eyes. The river filled my ears, and I began to float with the sound. I needed to find something to dislodge the fear—not only of the trek ahead of us, but the fear that had come while listening to my friend's grieving. It could happen, anytime, anyplace, to anyone. One minute you're on solid ground, the next moment the earth has cracked open beneath you. You get up in the morning and look in the mirror and tell yourself what the day will consist of, and then the light jerks sideways and you are left falling through the dark.

Behind me a dog barked. I turned to see a large yellow Lab, and then an older man walking the tracks. He stopped and raised his hand in acknowledgment of our presence. I hesitated, suddenly aware of another danger: a woman, two children, alone.

He could help us, I thought. He might live close by, have a tractor or winch. I thought, *I can't let him know we're stuck here, can't let him see how vulnerable we are.*

"How's it going?" he yelled.

I nodded and gave him a thumb's up. He stood for a long time, and I thought he might decide to walk toward us. And then what? For all I knew he was one of my father's old logging friends. For all I knew, he was a transient bent on some evil.

He stayed on the track, and I watched him disappear around the bend. There was too much to be afraid of, too much to fear. I rose and waded the rocks toward my children, suddenly distrusting even the river, its currents here strange and unpredictable.

They were making a catch basin for the small minnows they caught in the net of their hands. They hardly noticed my presence. *I should have them gather their things,* I thought, hustle them toward the car, or herd them in front of me up the rag of road, where we could walk the asphalt into town. It would take hours, I knew, hours into dusk, a woman and two children on a rural road where few cars traveled after dinner. I could hear my mother's scolding voice, the one I have known all my life, consistent through all my unwomanly adventures and forays: "What in the world were you thinking? What could have made you take such a risk?"

Risk. I looked across the river, where Highway 12 tied east to west. Cars flicked through the trees, distant and quick. I knew the benefits of being where I was: The water comforted me, the sand and rock and cottonwood leaves turning golden in the last rays of sun. I needed this, often and sometimes desperately. I believed, too, that my children were made better by such a landscape, that every handful of water they dipped from the river was an hour they would later remember as good.

But why here? Why hadn't I been content to take the easy way, pull off the road and find the familiar beaches and banks, Pink House Hole or Big Eddy, Myrtle or Home Beach?

I looked up, then down the far bank. This part of the Clearwater was different than farther downriver. Not so big. The rocks on the other side seemed still part of the canyon wall, huge and jagged from the blasts of road-making. Maybe it was good to be in a place I had not memorized, to be surprised by stone and current. I ran my hand through the water, patted the back of my neck. I needed to remember what I believed in, remember that things might just as easily go good as bad.

I called my children in. They refused to be hurried, reluctant as I to face the trip out, though it would be much easier, I had cozily assured them, going up than down.

Mosquitoes clouded around us as we walked from the river toward the pond. My daughter swatted frantically: They are drawn to her especially, and their bites leave her swollen and miserable.

"Hurry," I said. "It's getting dark. We need to get out while there's still light."

We crowded in, full of sand and river smells. I made a last check of the ground beneath the car: no oil or other inappropriate leakage. We made a tight turn, and I sighed as we faced the hill. What was it worth to attempt the ascent, lose the muffler, bash in the doors? We wouldn't be killed. What were my choices? It seemed an impossible decision.

I thought of the mosquitoes, the long walk out with two tired children, our feet rubbed raw by wet shoes and sand. I said, "Buckle your seat belts and lock your doors." I gave the engine more gas than usual.

The first pitch was not dirt and rock but a slick of muddy clay beneath a thick layer of pine needles. We spun, then began sliding backward, back into the long thorns of locust, over boulders and humps because the car could not be steered in such muck.

When we came to a stop, I leaned forward, rested my forehead against the wheel. I thought I might cry.

"Mom?" My son's voice was high, nearly shrill.

"Yes, Jace."

"I'm out of here."

He opened his door before I could stop him, slammed it shut, and ran for the railroad tracks. Jordan was fast behind.

I rolled down my window. "Okay," I said. "You stay right there, this side of the tracks. Don't you move. If I can get past this first pitch, we'll make it. When you hear me honk, come running." They nodded, miserable among the mosquitoes, shaking in the suddenly cool air.

I backed up as far as I could, put the car in first, gunned the engine and popped the clutch. I hit the hill with my tires screaming, went up, careened side- ways, bounced off the boulder, lost traction, and stalled, then slid all the way back down, cringing with the screech of metal against rock, wood against metal.

I need to focus on the initial few yards instead of the dogleg corner at its summit, I thought—the boulder bulging from the hillside, the tanker truck with its sharp edges. If things went well, we could get out with minimal damage. If things went bad, I might slide down into the gully with the truck, be swallowed by blackberries, have to fight my way out of thorns, and lord knew what else.

I got out of the car, tried to pull some of the larger rocks off the road, broke off what branches I could. I scuffed at the pine needles, realizing the uselessness of it: The ground underneath was saturated with moisture. I backed up, got a stronger run. Black smoke clouded around me. I got a foot farther before sliding back down.

I went at it hard then, again and again, as the sun settled lower in the west and the sky darkened. I was still afraid, still fearing too much power, too much speed. It was best to keep control, stay steady. But I got no farther. Always, almost to the top, and then the sudden spin and slide.

How many times? Twenty? Thirty? I didn't care about the car anymore, hardly heard the worried cries of my children. I was feeling something building inside of me, something I hadn't felt for a long time. It was hard and headlong, heedless in a way that might be brave. I'd felt it often before, when I was younger and wildly free. No husband. No children. Only my own life in my hands. I'd felt little fear of anything then, and it was a comfort. Now, with so much to love and lose, I'd come to cherish the expected, the easy ways. Risk came in larger increments: sickness, infidelity, divorce, death. I'd begun to live my life as though, by giving up the smaller risks, I could somehow balance out the larger, keep the big ones at bay with a juju bargain—the sacrifice of whatever independence and strength such risks brought me.

Sitting there, the car smelling of rubber and smoke, the heat and the mosquitoes and darkness coming on, I felt something else, and it was anger. Anger at what I feared and must fear, anger that I was where I was and in possible danger.

I felt suddenly and awfully alone, not because of the isolation, but because I was a woman where I should not be, having risked too much for the river.

The car idled. I hit the dash with the heel of my hand. I let all of it come into me, then—the anger I felt at love and death, at men who might hurt me and the men who would never, at the car and the land in its obstinacy. I felt the quiver in my belly and the rush of heat that filled my ears. I needed speed, momentum to carry me through.

I revved the engine, popped the clutch. I made the turn and didn't slow down. I kept it floored. I hit the boulder, jerked the wheel hard to the left, hit the truck. The tires spun. I didn't know what was behind me now, what I might slide into. I turned the wheel this way, then that, seeking purchase. I yelled at the top of my lungs, "You son of a bitch, go!" And then I was up that first pitch and breathing.

The kids came running, screaming, shouting. They piled gleefully into the car. We were going to make it. Everything was okay.

But it wasn't, because now there was another pitch, and then another. We spun. We stalled.

They got out. They ran all the way back to the railroad tracks.

I rocked the car back against the tanker. Bounce, spin, back. Bounce, spin, back. Each time a little farther, and when I found my ground and started careening up, I didn't stop. I bounced the car out of the canyon, figuring the exhaust system was already gone, figuring it had all been decided hours ago and this was the final scene.

When I got to the highway, I set the emergency brake and jogged back down. Jace and Jordan were coming to meet me, exhausted and still frightened. I batted at the mosquitoes and hurried us all up the hill. I was laughing, giddy with adrenalin. They were weepy, a little confused by my gaiety. They never wanted to do it again.

"It was an adventure," I told them. "And see? We're fine."

As we drove the highway home, I felt vibrant, exhilarated. The moon rising was the most beautiful thing, the wind through the windows a gift. I'd check the car for damage tomorrow, but for now nothing could touch us.

My children would sleep well, and I knew that in years to come, they would tell this story and the story would change and remain the same. Always, there would be the road we traveled, the rocks, the ruts, the mine to the east, the tanker to the west. There would be the night and mosquitoes, the smoke as they watched the car beat its way out of the canyon. There would be their mother's foolishness or her bravery, her stubborn refusals. The words might change, and maybe their fear. But always, there would be the river. It would run cold and loud beside them, the water they cupped in their hands and held above the sand to be sieved and drained and cupped again.

It will keep them near me. It will carry them away.

All My Relations

LINDA HOGAN

It is a sunny, clear day outside, almost hot, and a slight breeze comes through the room from the front door. We sit at the table and talk. As is usual in an Indian household, food preparation had begun as soon as we arrived, and now there is the snap of potatoes frying in the black skillet, the sweet smell of white bread overwhelming even the grease, and the welcome black coffee. A ringer washer stands against the wall of the kitchen, and the counter space is taken up with dishes, pans, and boxes of food.

I am asked if I still read books and I admit that I do. Reading is not "traditional," and education has long been suspect in communities that were broken, in part, by that system, but we laugh at my confession because a television set plays in the next room.

In the living room there are two single beds. People from reservations, travelers needing help, are frequent guests here. The man who will put together the ceremony I have come to request sits on one, dozing. A girl takes him a plate of food. He eats. He is a man I have respected for many years, for his commitment to the people, for his intelligence, for his spiritual and political involvement in concerns vital to Indian people and nations. Next to him sits a girl eating potato chips, and from this room we hear the sounds of the freeway.

After eating and sitting, it is time for me to talk to him, to tell him why we have come here. I have brought him tobacco and he nods and listens as I tell him about the help we need.

I know this telling is the first part of the ceremony, my part in it. It is story, really, that finds its way into language, and story is at the very crux of healing, at the heart of every ceremony and ritual in the older America.

The ceremony itself includes not just our own prayers and stories of what brought us to it, but also includes the unspoken records of history, the mythic past, and all the other lives connected to ours, our families, nations, and all other creatures.

I am sent home to prepare. I tie fifty tobacco ties, green. This I do with Bull Durham tobacco, squares of cotton that are tied with twine and left strung together. These are called prayer ties. I spend the time preparing alone and in silence. Each tie has a prayer in it. I will also need wood for the fire, meat and bread for food.

On the day of the ceremony, we meet in the next town and leave my car in public parking. My daughters and I climb into the backseat. The man who will help us is drumming and singing in front of us. His wife drives and chats. He doesn't speak. He is moving between the worlds, beginning already to step over the boundaries of what we think, in daily and ordinary terms, is real and present. He is already feeling, hearing, knowing what else is there, that which is around us daily but too often unacknowledged, a larger life than our own. We pass billboards and little towns and gas stations. An eagle flies overhead. It is "a good sign," we all agree. We stop to watch it.

We stop again, later, at a convenience store to fill the gas tank and to buy soda. The leader still drums and is silent. He is going into the drum, going into the center, even as we drive west on the highway, even with our conversations about other people, family, work.

It is a hot, balmy day, and by the time we reach the site where the ceremony is to take place, we are slow and sleepy with the brightness and warmth of the sun. Others are already there. The children are cooling off in the creek. A woman stirs the fire that lives inside a circle of black rocks, pots beside her, a jar of oil, a kettle, a can of coffee. The leaves of the trees are thick and green.

In the background, the sweat lodge structure stands. Birds are on it. It is still skeletal. A woman and man are beginning to place old rugs and blankets over the bent cottonwood frame. A great fire is already burning, and the lava stones that will be the source of heat for the sweat are being fired in it.

A few people sit outside on lawn chairs and cast-off couches that have the stuffing coming out. We sip coffee and talk about the food, about recent events. A man tells us that a friend gave him money for a new car. The creek sounds restful. Another man falls asleep. My young daughter splashes in the water. Heat waves rise up behind us from the fire that is preparing the stones. My tobacco ties are placed inside, on the framework of the lodge.

By late afternoon we are ready, one at a time, to enter the enclosure. The hot lava stones are placed inside. They remind us of earth's red and fiery core, and of the spark inside all life. After the flap, which serves as a door, is closed, water is poured over the stones and the hot steam rises around us. In a sweat lodge ceremony, the entire world is brought inside the enclosure. The soft odor of smoking cedar accompanies this arrival. It is all called in. The animals come from the warm and sunny distances. Water from dark lakes is there. Wind. Young, lithe willow branches bent overhead remember their lives rooted in ground, the sun their leaves took in. They remember that minerals and water rose up their trunks, and birds nested in their leaves, and that planets turned above their brief, slender lives. The thunderclouds travel in from far regions of earth. Wind arrives from the four directions. It has moved through caves and breathed through our bodies. It is the same air elk have inhaled, air that passed through the lungs of a grizzly bear. The sky is there, with all the stars whose lights we see long after the stars themselves have gone back to nothing. It is a place grown intense and holy. It is a place of immense community and of humbled solitude; we sit together in our aloneness and speak, one at a time, our deepest language of need, hope, loss, and survival. We remember that all things are connected.

Remembering this is the purpose of the ceremony. It is part of a healing and restoration. It is the mending of a broken connection between us and the rest. The participants in a ceremony say the words "All my relations" before and after we pray; those words create a relationship with other people, with animals, with the land. To have health it is necessary to keep all these relations in mind. The intention of a ceremony is to put a person back together by restructuring the human mind. This reorganization is accomplished by a kind of inner map, a geography of the human spirit and the rest of the world. We make whole our broken-off pieces of self and world. Within ourselves, we bring together the fragments of our lives in a sacred act of renewal, and we reestablish our connections with others. The ceremony is a point of return. It takes us toward the place of balance, our place in the community of all things. It is an event that sets us back upright. But it is not a finished thing. The real ceremony begins where the formal one ends, when we take up a new way, our minds and hearts filled with the vision of earth that hold us within it, in compassionate relationship to and with our world.

We speak. We sing. We swallow water and breathe smoke. By the end of the ceremony, it is as if skin contains land and birds. The places within us have become filled. As inside the enclosure of the lodge, the animals and ancestors move into the human body, into skin and blood. The land merges with us. The stones come to dwell inside the person. Gold rolling hills take up residence, their tall grasses blowing. The red light of canyons is there. The black skies of night that wheel above our heads come to live inside the skull. We who easily grow apart from the world are returned to the great store of life all around us, and there is the deepest sense of being at home here in this intimate kinship. There is no real aloneness. There is solitude and the nurturing silence that is relationship with ourselves, but even then we are part of something larger.

After a sweat lodge ceremony, the enclosure is abandoned. Quieter now, we prepare to drive home. We pack up the kettles, the coffeepot. The prayer ties are placed in nearby trees. Some of the other people prepare to go to work, go home, or cook a dinner. We drive. Everything returns to ordinary use. A spider weaves a web from one of the cottonwood poles to another. Crows sit inside the framework. It's evening. The crickets are singing. All my relations.

 **Walking Home**

SUSAN TWEIT

One sunny morning in August two decades ago, I stood at the Eagle Creek trailhead in northwest Wyoming's Absaroka Mountains. A green backpack towered over my head, stuffed with food, clothing, compact stove, sleeping bag, tent, and other essentials. Sadie, a German short-haired pointer, sat next to me, her dog packs strapped on, quivering with excitement. A shutter clicked. David, my friend Joan's teenage son, handed my camera back to me.

"Well," he said, eyeing my bulging backpack, "I hope you've got everything."

"If I don't," I replied with a small smile, "it doesn't matter, because I can't carry another ounce."

I handed him the keys to my compact pickup. "The truck's yours until I get back. And there better not be a scratch on it!"

David took the keys, grinned, got into the truck, and started the engine. "Be careful," he said. "See you in a week or so."

I waved good-bye as he turned the truck, and pulled it onto the highway. The pickup grew smaller and smaller, then disappeared around a bend in the valley. The noise of the engine died away and all was quiet except for the wind in the trees and the river rushing under the footbridge. I shivered, a wave of goose bumps marching across my skin, then shook myself. It was too late for doubts or fear. I was on my own now, and I'd better get used to it. A dipper warbled as it flew upstream.

"Okay, Sadie," I said to the quivering dog, "let's go."

By the time I turned, swaying a little under the weight of my heavy pack, she had dashed across the footbridge and was waiting on the other side, tail waving.

I was twenty-five years old and running away from my life. Two years before, I had been diagnosed with the early stages of an illness in the group including multiple sclerosis, rheumatoid arthritis, and lupus. In these so-called autoimmune diseases, the immune system turns on the sufferer's own body, producing antibodies that destroy our connective tissue, the stuff that cushions joints and links muscle to bone, nerve fiber to muscle, and cell to cell, allowing us to feel, to think, to walk, to talk, to make love. As Norman Cousins wrote in *Anatomy of an Illness*, "I was coming unstuck." I lived with a near-perpetual chill that turned my skin yellow and jaundiced-looking, my toes, lips and fingertips numb. Most mornings, my joints ached fiercely and creaked audibly, snapping and popping like Rice Crispies in a bowl of milk. Some days, my hips were unreliable; I dropped things without knowing why. From time to time, my teeth shed small chips of enamel and my finger and toe joints swelled, flushing red and hot to the touch. Now and then, I would wake at night, drenched with sweat, wracked by fevers and muscle pains. My energy went in spurts: I'd go full-tilt boogie for days, then suddenly hit exhaustion, my brain fogged, my limbs leaden. There was no cure for my illness; doctors didn't even understand what caused it. I was told I'd live two to five years, or perhaps, on the outside, ten.

As my connective tissue disintegrated, my life came unglued as well: My marriage fell apart, I left my career in field ecology, and I moved away from my home, both leaving northwest Wyoming and detaching myself from nature. Finally, lonely, sick, and confused, I decided to return on foot to the mountains I love.

I borrowed Sadie, a friend's dog, and planned to hike from the North Fork of the Shoshone River to Jackson Hole, a distance of more than 100 miles through some of the wildest country in the Lower 48. The trek would take around seven days, depending on my walking speed and stamina. Sadie and I would climb two passes, cross the Continental Divide, wade numerous streams, and navigate a major river. There'd be no roads, no phones, no flush toilets, no grocery stores, no 911. We'd traverse the heart of a region wild enough that it belongs more to the resident grizzly bears than to humans.

When I am stuck and cannot dig myself out of my problems, I go home to nature. I head for wild country, for someplace where I will be alone and can hear myself think, where the noise and busyness of humanity can't drown out the "small, still voice" of my inner wisdom.

Silence is an undervalued resource, a rarity in landscapes where the myriad human-generated sounds—voices, car engines, thumping stereos, jackhammers, cellular phones, televisions, computers—overwhelm mind and spirit. Silence, restful quiet, is critical to our inner lives. "True silence…" wrote William Penn in 1699 in *Fruits of a Father's Love*, a book of advice for his children, "is to the spirit what sleep is to the body, nourishment and refreshment." Silence is where we go to meet our inner selves without distraction, where we tune out the trivial and focus on what is at the core of our lives.

I needed that kind of silence in order to hear my inner voice, so I headed home, making a beeline for the mountains I knew intimately from my years as a field ecologist. Walking across them, I thought, I might find the wisdom I needed to live with my illness.

The night before I began the trek, I stayed with my friend Joan.

"What brings you home at this time of year?" she asked, swirling the red wine in her glass absently as we sat in her comfortable living room.

I took a sip from my own glass before I answered, then said carefully, "I'm taking a few weeks off to think about things." I told her about my planned walk.

Her cheerful smile turned into a frown. She shook her head with a bouncy motion, like a disturbed chickadee. "Who's going with you?"

Reluctant to meet her eyes, I looked away. "Well..." I paused, trying to avoid answering, but I was stuck. "Everybody is busy or away, and—" rushing now, eager to get it over with—"I really need to go by myself. I'm taking Sadie for company."

Her anger hit me like a slap in the face.

"You're foolish to go out alone!" she exclaimed. "You of all people know your limitations!" Mouth set, she continued. "A week on foot and alone in that country with your health—that's just stupid!" Her eyes flashed. "Not just stupid, it's dangerous!"

She paused, as if expecting me to defend myself, but I couldn't.

"You won't listen to me, or anyone else. You'll go anyway, won't you?"

I tried to joke away her concern, but we both knew she was right. I could fall, break a leg and be unable to walk; I could unintentionally provoke an attack by a grizzly bear, drown fording a creek, be struck by lightning on a ridge, trigger a flare-up of my illness—the list of dangers was long. I'd be on my own, miles from anywhere in a maze of roadless mountains and steep-walled valleys, with no way to let anyone know I needed help, much less how to find me. I could die out there and no one would ever know or even find my body before the flesh-eaters devoured it. Thinking about it put knots in my stomach, so I forced my mind away. There was no point in scaring myself. I had to go, and I had to go alone. And if I was going to survive the trip, I had to be tough. I had only myself to depend on.

We turned the conversation to other subjects, and eventually we each went to bed. I didn't sleep much, besieged by fears. The next morning, Joan agreed to let her son David drive me to the trailhead. She hugged me before she went to work, but she didn't say anything. She didn't have to. I knew I was wrong. But I had to go.

Sadie set out up the trail in front of me. Her dog packs jiggled and her feet raised small puffs of dust as she trotted along. As she passed a boulder that stuck out into the trail, her nearside pack hit it with a *thunk*. She staggered for a moment, then looked back over her shoulder as if to say, "What happened?"

I chuckled, and the knots in my stomach loosened. "You're wider now, Sadie," I said as I caught up with her and patted her head. "You've got to allow more room to go around."

She scraped past the rock and headed on. The sun was warm on my face, the air perfumed by pine sap. A red-tailed hawk circled high overhead, then screamed: *Ki-yeer*!

"We'll be okay," I said out loud in the quiet and followed Sadie up the trail.

That afternoon, Sadie and I came to our first creek crossing, a ford on a tributary of Eagle Creek. High runoff from the previous winter's unusually abundant snowpack had swollen the normally small creek to a silty torrent. I eyed the water doubtfully, then lowered myself carefully to the gravel bank to change from my hiking boots to the old running shoes I'd brought for creek fording. We had miles yet to hike before nightfall. I sighed.

Sadie whined.

"It's okay, girl. It's running high, but we can make it."

Shoes on, hiking boots and socks slung around my neck to keep them dry, I hauled myself upright.

"Ready?" I asked Sadie. She wagged her tail.

"Okay," I said, "in we go."

The water temperature was a shock. Bone-chilling cold. The cobbles of the stream bed were slippery, the current stronger than I expected. Sadie, pacing the bank behind me, whined again.

"Come on, girl!" I said impatiently, struggling to keep my balance as I inched forward against the current. I heard her splash in, but couldn't turn to look. I was in past my knees. The bones of my feet and legs ached with the cold. Up to my thighs, and I figured I was halfway across. I couldn't see Sadie, and it took all I had to keep going. I'd worry about her when I was safely out on the opposite bank. Inching forward, my legs and feet numb, rubbery, I was nearly there.

Less than an arm's length from the bank, I slipped into a hole in the stream bottom, invisible in the opaque water. My legs flew out from under me. My pack pulled me down. I grabbed a tree root protruding from the bank. For a long moment, I hung on the balance, the water tugging at me, my pack weighing me down, my arms clinging tight to the rough bark. Finally I pulled myself out, soaked to the waist, shaking and cold.

I remembered Sadie and willed my numb lips to purse and my tongue to whistle. To my immense relief, she appeared a ways downstream. She scrambled up the bank and galloped over, packs flapping, water streaming off her skinny body, tail wagging.

I hugged her close, and she licked my face enthusiastically.

"We made it!" I said, and realized that even my voice was shaking.

Not just the chill: Raynaud's Phenomenon. "Damn!"

Raynaud's Phenomenon, a frequent companion of some connective tissue diseases, is a circulatory ailment in which the blood vessels in one's extremities—fingers, toes and, less commonly, nose, lips, and ear lobes—constrict spasmodically, restricting or eliminating blood flow to these areas. A Raynaud's attack can last from minutes to hours, and changes the sufferer's skin color from healthy pink to pale yellow to sickly blue as the capillaries collapse and the tissues go into crisis without oxygen. In a severe Raynaud's attack, the sufferer moves clumsily, extremities numb, and is likely to injure herself, since the nerve connections to the extremities are essentially shut down by the circulatory freeze. The chill of Raynaud's is as dangerous as hypothermia, making thinking difficult and logic fuzzy.

I couldn't let myself be weak now. My brain clicked on and I began what would become an automatic routine after every stream we forded. Take off my cumbersome pack. Peel off my wet fording shoes. Dry and massage my numb feet and legs. Check for injuries. Put on my socks and force my hiking boots on. Eat a handful of trail mix. Stand up—ignore the wobbling!—and move around. Swing my arms vigorously. Examine Sadie. Haul on my pack and get back on the trail—quickly, no time to feel—before the chill of Raynaud's shuts me down.

One noontime several days later, our first pass and its vertiginous snow-fields safely behind us, Sadie and I sprawled on the grassy banks of the Thorofare River, dogged by clouds of whining mosquitoes. It was lunchtime, and I was starving. I munched my crackers and cheese, trying not to inhale mosquitoes, and scanned the lush green expanse of meadow across the river. Not far away, a sandhill crane nearly as tall as I was probed the wet soil for food. A large, furry animal crept along behind it, belly low to the ground, the way a dog stalks a magpie. When it was just a few feet away, the stalker launched itself into the air, leaping for the bird. At the last possible moment, the crane lifted off on wide wings and flew away. The stalker thudded to earth. The crane circled, bugling its resonant call, then landed and resumed feeding. The furry one resumed its creeping approach. I sat motionless, fascinated, until my brain belatedly registered the stalker as a grizzly bear.

I rose quietly, lunch in hand, heaved on my pack, and motioned Sadie to follow. I tiptoed backward, silent, eyes on the bear, all the way to the trail. It was all I could do to keep myself from breaking into a run. The bear raised its shaggy head and looked across the river. Sadie and I froze. Sweat trickled between my shoulder blades. After a minute, it looked away. We reached the trail and walked oh-so-casually into the cover of a grove of spruces before I thought to breathe. Once we were safely out of sight, I couldn't stop shaking. I forced my legs to hike on, cursing myself steadily under my breath. I was guilty of relaxing my alertness, of forgetting the reality of this very wild outside, including the fact that I am just the right size to constitute prey for some of our larger kin. I was out of touch.

In the language of astrology, I am a Virgo: I was born during the thirty-one days in August and September when the sun "resides" in the constellation Virgo, that is, when the sun and the constellation appear to travel together across the sky as Earth rotates. Virgo rules the zodiac at that time of year, since, in astrology, the constellation housing the sun is the one in power. I am, in fact, doubly Virgo, because not only was the sun traveling in Virgo at the time of year I was born, the constellation was also rising above the eastern horizon at the hour of my birth.

In ancient myth, Virgo is the original earth-mother, the bringer of life's fertility. It is she who is responsible for the seasons, the annual cycle of life and death. To the Greeks, she was the goddess Demeter, whose desperate search for her lost daughter Persephone plunged Earth into winter. Only when grieving Demeter rescued her daughter from the Underworld did life-giving spring return.

I walked into the wilderness to grieve, mourning my losses: my marriage, my home, my place in science, and my intimate bond with nature. I was alone, ill, facing my own personal winter. I knew I had choices, but I couldn't see what they were. Anger at the fate that had struck me with an autoimmune disease kept me frozen in the past, like the wintery earth during Demeter's sorrow. I was searching for a way to return spring to my life, to thaw my heart, to see if I knew how to live.

That evening we came to our last major creek crossing. I followed the trail to the ford shown on the topographic map, arriving just as the sun's slanting light gilded the landscape. The shadows of the lodgepole pines lay like logs across the trail. I walked up to the creek bank—and there the trail ended. At the base of a steep, newly eroded bluff, the creek roared by, high and deep. We'd never make it across. I put my pack down, whistled to Sadie, and hiked upstream for perhaps a mile, looking futilely for a likely crossing. I hiked back downstream, tired now, still searching. No luck. There was no place to ford. If we couldn't cross this creek, we had to turn back. Blue with Raynaud's, shaking, I pulled myself together. I pitched the tiny tent, lit the stove, fed Sadie, and boiled water for my own dinner. As I ate my bowl of noodles, I pulled out the map. Upstream were impassible cliffs, downstream was the uncrossable Thorofare River. In front, the creek we could not ford.

I studied the map, searching for a solution, until darkness erased its fine, undulating lines. Then I crawled into my sleeping bag, near tears. Sadie curled up next to me. I was exhausted but could not sleep. The creek roared in my ears. Large animals—I hoped they were only moose—crashed through the forest nearby. My mind circled and fretted. Sometime in the night, I unzipped the tent door and poked my head out to scan the sky for stars. The night was overcast. I peered intently, searching for a glimpse, however faint, of the constellations. The heavens were blank, unreadable.

Looking to the night sky for enlightenment is an ancient human tradition. Astrology, the study of coincidences between human lives and the movements of the stars and planets, began with the cultures that inhabited the fertile crescent bounded by the Tigris and Euphrates Rivers around 1400 to 1000 B.C., in what is now Iraq. Picked up and modified by the Persians and Egyptians and later synthesized by Greek, Chinese, and Indian cultures, the body of knowledge grew and changed with each succeeding contact. Astrology and astronomy were one discipline until the European Age of Enlightenment separated the two, embracing the study of the observable movements and features of the stars and planets and condemning the unexplainable concurrences of astrology to the realm of myth and speculation.

Psychologist Carl Jung delved into astrology early in his career. It was, he felt, a powerful part of the human myth, the stories we create to understand who we are. Jung saw universal symbols or archetypes—from the Greek *arche*, meaning "primal," and *typos*, "imprint or pattern"—in the stories assigned to the constellations and planets. These tales, he believed, helped us to know ourselves. Later, Jung turned away from astrology, perhaps under pressure from the scientific establishment, which couldn't swallow wisdom so dependent on intuition, so difficult to prove, so contrary to logic.

The conventional understanding of autoimmune diseases posits that the immune system protects us by recognizing and ejecting foreign bodies, defined as anything we are not born with; thus, autoimmune diseases occur when the immune system mistakes our own tissues for foreigners and attacks them, destroying us from within.

Immunologist Polly Matzinger of the National Institutes of Health challenges this theory. Her Danger Model proposes that our immune systems protect us by responding to signals of danger emitted by our cells, rather than by focusing on destroying foreign bodies. Matzinger explains the Danger Model with an analogy to her border collie Annie. When guarding a herd of sheep, Matzinger says, Annie doesn't waste her energy searching for invaders. Instead, she watches for the sheep to show signs of unease and then leaps to defend them. Dendritic cells in our bodies, says Matzinger, act like border collies. These cells' fingerlike projections touch from 50 to 500 neighboring cells. As long as the neighboring cells act normally, the dendritic cells "snooze," but when one of the cells does something abnormal, such as spewing its contents after being infected by a virus or leaking cell fluids after sustaining a physical injury, the dendritic cells leap into action like so many border collies, triggering the chain of events we call the immune response.

Matzinger's model explains many important exceptions to the conventional search-and-destroy immune system model, including why the immune systems of pregnant women do not attack and eject the "foreign tissue" of normal fetuses. But the scientific establishment has not embraced the Danger Model. It is too radical, too intuitive, too contrary to accepted wisdom.

Perhaps our definition of science is simply too narrow. If we define *science* as "a body of knowledge used to understand the world," not solely as *Science*, "the Western system of classifying and comprehending our universe," we allow other types of wisdom—including the intuitive and non-rational—a place in the traditions of learning. As ethnobotanist Gary Paul Nabhan has said, every culture has its science; only Westerners are arrogant enough to think that ours is the sole truth.

The next morning, I rose early in a golden dawn, the forest around me sparkling with crystalline frost. Too miserable to admire any beauty, I ate a quick breakfast while pacing the bank above the creek. I looked at the map again, and then admitted defeat. Sadie and I started off down the trail, headed back to where we'd begun.

About half a mile along, we met a backcountry ranger. I stopped to chat, my voice rusty with disuse. He asked where we were going and I poured out my frustration.

"Yeah, that crossing washed out this spring," he said. "Last winter we had so much snow that all the creeks are still running wild. Bad luck for you." He thought a moment and then said, "You know, there's a place down the creek where you might be able to cross, just above the confluence with the river. Even though it's downstream from where you were, the creek is shallower there. I've done it on horseback."

I pulled out my map, and he pointed to the spot. "Good luck!" he called as we walked away.

My spirits rose as Sadie and I headed off cross-country. Soon we were threading through head-high willow thickets. I sang loudly to warn bears of our approach.

We came out of the willows onto a broad gravel bar, and there was our creek, rushing past in a channel nearly twenty yards across, far wider than any stream we'd attempted so far. I paced up and down beside the flow, scanning the current and reading the creek bottom.

Sadie sat, waiting.

Finally I decided: We could do it. I plopped down on the gravel, took off my boots and socks, and slipped on my fording shoes. Then I looped a piece of nylon cord around the straps on Sadie's dog packs and tied the end to my waist. I didn't want the current to sweep her downstream and into the river.

In we waded. The icy water had already reached my mid-thighs when Sadie, afloat and paddling frantically, hit the end of her cord. I willed my legs to hold and kept going, leaning upstream to counter Sadie's weight. The water reached my waist. I hitched up my pack and kept going. My legs and feet were numb, but I made myself inch along, step by step. Finally, soaking wet and shivering, we made it across.

Two noontimes later, we sat in the shade of a fat Douglas-fir tree near the trail junction above the Snake River. The path behind me led into the wilderness we'd hiked through. Walking the days alone but for Sadie, fording the icy creeks, experiencing the terrors of night creatures and the benediction of golden dawns had renewed my intimacy with the wild that lives deep inside all of us. The trail ahead led to the world we'd left behind more than a week before, with the noise and distractions, comforts and confusion, the separation from that very wildness.

"We made it!" I said to Sadie. I groped in my dusty pack and celebrated by sharing my last food with her. I carefully smeared four crackers with peanut butter, crumbled the end of the cheese over them and dotted the whole with a handful of hard raisins. I set two crackers in front of Sadie. She gulped them immediately, and then delicately licked her lips. I ate one cracker slowly, savoring this final backcountry meal, leaving the other balanced on my knee. The air smelled like sun-warmed evergreen sap and dust from the dry soil underfoot. A breeze whooshed through the branches overhead, the river tumbled by far below. A white-breasted nuthatch called *Yank! Yank! Yank!* then fell silent.

I had gone to the wilderness in the hopes that I would hear a voice speaking from the silence. I had imagined receiving a revelation that would lift me out of my misery and banish my illness. Instead, what filled my head were my own tangled feelings, a jumble of anxiety, loneliness, confusion, anger. Where was the light of revelation in these dark emotions?

Sadie whined, breaking into my thoughts. I leaned over to pet her. The breeze pushed a small cumulus cloud over the sun, its shadow sweeping the ridge like a giant hand. It passed, and the sun's warmth returned.

Perhaps, I thought, the voices of my emotions were just what I needed to hear. Since my diagnosis with an illness explained to be the result of my immune system going awry and attacking my own tissues, I had believed I could not trust my body. I had tried to be tough and self-sufficient, running my life with logic and objective detachment. Perhaps the chill of Raynaud's, the physical shutting down of my blood flow, reflected the metaphorical freeze I had imposed on my body's voice, the intuitions I couldn't prove and the emotions I was afraid to feel. Perhaps I had forgotten how to listen.

The sense that we call "hearing" involves both the physical ability to receive sounds and the discernment necessary to focus on and interpret a particular sound from the welter of signals that bombard us. I think of listening as the latter, the attentive part of hearing. Listening only to the logical, rational side of myself, I had been hearing only some of the signals, receiving only part of the message. No wonder I was lost and confused.

Immunologist Polly Matzinger asserts that the immune systems of sufferers of autoimmune illnesses aren't dysfunctional. Instead, Matzinger believes, our immune systems are like coal miner's canaries, responding sensitively to danger signals we cannot yet discern. Her Danger Model suggests sufferers of autoimmune diseases should attempt to recognize and understand the responses of our immune systems, rather than to suppress their signals.

Perhaps if I listened more carefully, I would be able to discern what I needed to comprehend my illness. First, I needed to know myself better. Nobel Prize–winning geneticist Barbara McClintock claimed that the key to her successful research was a deep connection to the corn plants she used to parse the workings of genes: "I don't feel I really know the story if I don't watch the plant all the way along. So I know every plant in the field. I know them intimately.…" After the solitude and hardships of my trek, I wondered if I knew myself at all. It was time to start listening.

Sadie whined again. Then, with an audible *gulp!* she reached forward and ate my remaining cracker—so much for contemplation.

I laughed and ruffled her ears. "You're right. It's time to go."

I picked up my pack, lighter now than it had been a week ago, and settled it one last time on my shoulders. I stood up and turned for a final view of the trail we'd come on. Then I headed in the opposite direction. Sadie pranced in front of me, her feet raising small puffs of dust as we walked on home.

Nothin' Left to Lose

DIANE JOSEPHY PEAVEY

"What has happened here is but the sound before the fury of those who
are oppressed."
                                        —Inmates of Attica Prison, 1971

Perhaps it was the oppressive heat and humidity. Perhaps it was my own reluctance to leave San Francisco for Washington, D.C., to save a marriage I sensed was beyond help. Perhaps it was my unlikely traveling companion, Glorie, and the way we seemed thrown together by events to ride out our histories in the confines of my small Volkswagen Beetle. Perhaps it was the astonishing backdrop of this trip, the landscapes of the West and the national September events that gripped the nation and us as we drove through heartland America. Perhaps it was the night in the Grand Canyon or that one spin of the late Janis Joplin wailing about freedom that left me wondering if it really meant nothing left to lose.

Whatever the reason, many years later, that cross-country trip still weighs heavily on my mind. I know now I should never have left San Francisco. My marriage was over. But at the time I was heavy with responsibility that if it were to be saved it was up to me. So in 1971, I drove east across the United States to join my husband in Washington, D.C., a town I had left happily two years earlier but where my husband's new newspaper job was returning him, us.

Events were further complicated by my affection for San Francisco. It was as if my life had started when we moved to that city in 1969. There, for the first time, I discovered wild country. A city girl and Easterner born and raised, here I began hiking, first up Mount Tamalpais outside of the city, then more ambitious outings farther east in the Sierras. I discovered the out-of-doors, live oak hillsides and farm country in Mendocino County, national parks of redwoods, the rugged coast of Big Sur, the headlands of Point Reyes, and the grapevine-covered rolling hills of Napa. I traveled back roads each weekend on what I called my freedom trips that changed me forever.

During the week, my urban persona flourished in this city of madcap residents and multicultural neighborhoods that offered a whiff of faraway countries and endless creative energy.

San Francisco is still much of this today. But in the late '60s and early '70s, it offered more. It was the happening place to be. There were flower children, festivals, rock concerts, waves of energy that translated into political power and protest over a war gone awry in Southeast Asia. This brave new world extended east into Oakland and Berkeley in the form of black power that gave new purpose to communities of impoverished poor.

Suddenly the people were in charge, and we felt our power. We were aware, on the edge, ready, if not already involved.

Unable to resist this exuberance, I took a job with the Bay Area Urban League, which, during those years, was blistering with outrage and activity. Those were the years of Angela Davis, Huey Newton, Bobby Seale, the Black Panthers, and I was in the middle of it, one of only four pasty whites out of sixty employees. I loved and anguished over the job, as we struggled for better education and less dangerous schools, job opportunities and prison reform for forgotten people in rotting inner cities. We worked in ghetto storefront offices and were swept up by the anger and the hope we nursed every day.

So I traveled the Bay Area, fund-raising at white corporate headquarters and strategizing at black inner city meetings and rallies during the week. On weekends, I roamed backcountry California.

Still, the trouble began in San Francisco. I rarely saw my husband over the two years we lived there. His newspaper job became his obsession as he struggled to convince Bay Area newspaper readers there was more to a good paper than local humorist Herb Caen. He never succeeded, despite long days and many all-night sessions at his desk. I filled my life without him. We grew apart.

For him, the offer from the *Washington Star* newspaper came not a moment too soon. He packed his own things into his Porsche and left me behind to handle the movers and my own painful parting with this city. At first I wandered familiar streets in a kind of numbness that comes with deep loss, looking forlornly at familiar streets, neighborhoods, and parks, each made fragrant by eucalyptus and flowering blooms, made lovely by elaborate design and architecture, made lively by its funny and unorthodox array of people. The Washington I remembered seemed inert, unoriginal, confining, a government town.

I packed slowly, holding out hope for improbable reprieves. When these did not come, I explored delay tactics. And there I found success in the person of Glorie, a secretary at work. Her parents wanted her to return to Indiana for a family reunion. She was not much interested. But I was.

Perhaps we should share the trip, drag it out, see the West, postpone our respective unpleasant obligations, I suggested. Glorie was intrigued.

Ah, Glorie. A true product of the times and one of the other four whites committed to black power at the Urban League. But she was *really* committed. I mean, her blond Afro would have brought tears of envy to the eyes of Angela Davis. It sat atop her cherubic face that rested on the shoulders of her short, pudgy body, which was usually clad in the miniskirts and boots of the time. Glorie's rap was as street as you could get. But her heart was pure Haight-Ashbury love. By evenings she was an authentic groupie. She hung out at jazz clubs, rock theaters, and even the ballpark to watch and later throw herself in the path of musicians and athletes. And she rarely went home alone.

I was fascinated and listened to her tales of sexual freedom with a mixture of incredulity, horror, and envy. I believed her stories because Glorie was so unabashed in the retelling.

She was thrilled at the idea of a road trip. She had never driven across the United States, probably because Glorie didn't drive at all, a detail I forgot when I extended my invitation. Still, a curious passenger could be as useful as another driver if I worked it right.

We began poring over road maps to plan our route. I was inspired by her inexperience. "What?" I cried aghast. "You've never been to the Grand Canyon, Canyonlands, Mesa Verde? Of course, you must." And instantly I had arranged a trip that would take at least a week longer to cross the country than I had originally planned.

Glorie and I set out just after Labor Day in sweltering heat. I drove in tears across town to pick her up. I had just closed the door of my flat for the last time. I barely remember stuffing her small suitcase into the backseat of my already jammed green Volkswagen Beetle. What I do remember was that I had never seen Glorie's plump, little, very white body in shorts, shorter and tighter than her miniskirts. So tiny were her pants, in fact, and so white was she that she wore sheer blue stockings, the top band of which showed several inches below the hem of her shorts. I had never seen anyone wear stockings under shorts before and I thought it looked quite ridiculous, but I was so deep in my own self-pity I said nothing. Several days later, I realized, it was too late to discreetly raise the issue, although her appearance would continue to embarrass me throughout the trip.

But that scorching day, with memories leaping out from every crosswalk, I simply opened the windows and the sunroof and drove heartbroken through this town I knew would never be home again. Glorie was quite speechless as

I sobbed. But she too knew that my life was over. After all, there was no place like San Francisco in 1971.

The heat only got worse as we drove south through central California. By the time we finally reached Barstow at dusk, I was worn out from crying and sweating and almost drove off the road. Glorie, who I'm sure had been reevaluating this road trip, urgently suggested we might stop for the night.

The next day the heat bore down on us even more mercilessly as we sped through the Mojave Desert. The local radio station set the temperature at 115. Until that day I didn't know my Volkswagen could go ninety miles an hour—top of the dial—and I prayed it wouldn't explode as I pushed hard on the gas to get through the heat. We were amazed at the muted, thirsty landscape. Dried desert scrub brush gasped from miles of gravel floor until the flatness ran headlong into iron-gray and rust-striped mountains. The cloudless sky quivered in the heat.

That may have been the hottest day I've ever lived through. Glorie and I couldn't buy or consume enough liquids. We were too miserable to talk. We drove in silence.

Finally, as the sun was losing its power, we turned off the interstate at Williams, Arizona, and recklessly extended the drive another hour to reach our first goal, the Grand Canyon's south rim, almost fifty miles north. After the sweltering, monotonous drive, we were ready for a little cool grandeur.

And that's just what we got. The view from horizon to horizon was breathtaking. We raced from one lookout point to another trying to see it all, stunned by the beauty around us. Finally we slowed, each step a new sight, each moment a new arrangement of life. We sat on a rock ledge and watched the orange evening light wash across the imposing yellow cliffs, then counted the first pale stars above us.

"I've never heard this kind of quiet," Glorie whispered. I stared at this magnificent sight, only one of so many I had discovered over the last few years that would be lost to me in the months ahead.

A hawk swooped low, its suspended whistle the only sound around us. The smells of cedar and pine filled the air, the stillness as complete as the vast space. Canyon walls led into canyon walls, gnarled limbs of cedar and desert brush, muted green, filled in crevices cut deep into steep cliffs. Thick slabs of rock balanced against the sky; thin, sleek pieces danced on flat ledges.

There was nowhere to look that wasn't breathtaking and, at the same time, calming. I was suddenly aware that for the first time in months, I felt safe, as if this place were a kind of sanctuary. And with the stillness that settled over me came a surprising new lightness, a release from melancholy. And I wondered for the first time what would happen if I just stayed here or turned the car south, north, anywhere but east. Who would know or, ultimately, care? If I had to give up my life in San Francisco, then what else really mattered? I could do anything now, and I thrilled to the spontaneity of this idea. It would change the trip for me.

We followed stars and moonlight back to the car and drove through the early fall silence to our small motel room.

The next day we were up early, two adventurers, hiking longer and farther around the southern loop of the park, amazed that despite the pictures we'd seen of this place, the experience still seemed new and uniquely personal.

I left Glorie and walked on my own, slowing to feel the rhythms of the landscape. I tried to memorize each scene. The smell of wildness and cedar, the touch of soft winds brushing the skin, the smooth sandstone under hand, the exhilaration of cliffs tumbling one into another, blue-red, honey-mustard, across unhurried canyons and down into the river deep and narrow below. I wanted it etched it into memory, stored somewhere private and deep so I could call up these images in moments of despair. And the thought that I could stay here if I chose suddenly became enough to allow me to leave, knowing I would return on my own time and of my own choosing.

Midday we left the park and its cooling landscape to drive through the stark, dry, red earth country to the east. There we passed the string of battered roadside stands with Indians selling heavy woven Navajo rugs and turquoise jewelry. In only several miles, life had again become parched, breathless, forlorn.

We traveled across reservation lands and through Monument Valley, stopping for the night in the southern Utah Mormon community of Monticello, by design. I had been there years earlier on a cross-country trip with my family. We had stayed with a prominent local family who took us on a death-defying back-country jeep ride into areas without roads, over boulders and across creeks to the site of Natural Bridges, then a proposed national monument. I told these stories to Glorie as we settled into a deeply fried chicken dinner at the local cafe, but even though she stared out the window across the little town into the darkness, she could only shake her head at what might lie beyond. And in this alcohol-free Mormon town, because we couldn't have one, both of us intensely wanted a beer. We went to bed early instead.

The next morning, I donned my usual travel clothes: shorts, brown leather sandals, and a tank top sans bra, both because it was already searingly hot at 7:30 A.M. and because it was still the time when women were flaunting a new independence that started from the inside out. In those days, I aspired to look like Ali McGraw in *Good-bye Columbus*.

Glorie was in her standard outfit. Under her white shorts were dark brown stockings that led to sandals studded with red, green, and yellow stones. Her toes, painted a piercing red, were visible through the brown nylons. Her tank top was trimmed unexpectedly by edges of a lacy black bra. I was surprised she wore a bra at all and wrote it off to pudginess.

As we slid into a booth at the cafe, it was clear we were the show in town for the farmers and ranchers gathered at the counter and tables around us. I was convinced the attention was due to the exquisite bad fashion taste of my traveling companion. She had other ideas and as we stood at the cash register to pay for our eggs over easy, sausage patties, and hash browns, she whispered to me, "Diane, I think you ought to wear a bra in these Mormon towns. They're not used to your look."

Today I still hear these words clearly. As then, my mouth again drops open in amazement at this suggestion from the woman who, at that very moment, I thought looked every bit a dead ringer for a Las Vegas hooker. But how could I tell her that? I was left mute.

We drove out of Monticello in my Volkswagen with its brash California license plates, leaving the local citizenry to buzz over "those weird hippies." We headed east into Colorado and Mesa Verde, and I was only able to let go of Glorie's criticism when we pulled into the park and her excitement spilled over me.

Despite her worldly appearance, Glorie was like a child savoring each new site we visited. This early Indian civilization with its homes and villages buried in cliff walls was no exception. She was an eager student and a grateful traveler, and her enthusiasm made my return to many of these stops a new adventure and lightened the heaviness I dragged with me from day to day.

From southern Colorado, we drove through the San Juan National Forest, north through mountains and mining country to Ouray, where we stopped overnight. I planned to start the next morning with a "miner's breakfast" of steak, eggs, and pancakes served in extravagant amounts, as I had done with my family many years earlier. My father had thought it the highlight of our trip at the time, and I was not about to miss the experience on this journey laced with self-indulgences. But as I stuffed myself at breakfast, I was sadly aware that the food was not as I remembered. Neither was I the girl of sixteen anymore.

We drove east from Montrose and north to ski country through cool green mountains. In Vail, we walked around, imagining the place covered in snow and full of skiers in après-ski finery. We liked feeling the chill of approaching winter.

But I knew what lay ahead from there, and I shrank from the experience. Eastern Colorado was the beginning of a new phase of our trip, a huge geographic step closer to the East.

As we drove that day, the mountains of the West disappeared, replaced first by rolling, then flat livestock and farm country of eastern Colorado and Kansas. The hours seemed to lengthen unbearably as the landscape slipped into sameness. We tried to remember anything we knew about Eisenhower, Dorothy before she was swept away to Oz, anything to give meaning to the miles around us.

But the day gave meaning to us instead. Suddenly a radio program was interrupted by the urgent news of prison riots in Attica, New York. Glorie and I looked at each other in alarm. We realized instantly the import of this event. We had both followed the controversies and turmoil in Folsom and San Quentin Prisons in the Bay Area. We knew about abuse and tragic endings. At the Urban League, we had heard the stories firsthand.

In the small Volkswagen, we turned from station to station, trying to find news updates on the prison crisis. It was September 9, and Attica was in a state of siege. Inmates had taken over cell block D. They had taken fifty hostages and seriously wounded a guard. The rest of the prison staff and inmates alike watched with the world.

The prisoners presented a list of "Five Demands to the People of America" that included amnesty and the protection of the federal government. They invited "all the people to come here and witness" the conditions. Among those invited was the governor of New York and presidential-aspirant Nelson Rockefeller. He refused.

These events filled in the Kansas prairie. September 10, we pulled out of Salina after watching the morning news. Prison fires were smoldering. Neither side trusted the other. Injunctions were torn up. Amnesty was denied.

We could have been in Oklahoma or Ohio. We were mindless of our surroundings. All we knew was that we were no longer in the West. We were miserably aware that the air had changed from a clear, dry heat to a stifling, sucking humidity. Then, as if to test our conviction, we encountered our first toll road. It was too much for Glorie, who was already on edge. She glared at the attendant.

"Where do you get off charging us to go through here?" she challenged the woman. "After all the country we've seen for nothing, *you* want money? There ain't even nothin' here." She was slipping into rap but I understood her frustration. Our environment was suddenly too crowded.

September 11, the trip and the news from the prison dragged on. No one was able to make gains for the hostages or inmates. Again Rockefeller refused all appeals to meet with the prisoners face to face. The world waited for resolution.

As we drove, we waited for breaking news and hourly updates, but there seemed little more than Rod Stewart wailing on poor Maggie May. There was one interlude when the voice of the late Janis Joplin filled the car singing "Me and Bobby McGee." It hushed us both and my thoughts turned to the men in cell block D.

It made sense. This moment in the national limelight was their best chance, their only chance. They had rolled the dice. Bet their futures on this brash move. For these few days, they had control of their own miserable lives. This was as good as it would get. There was nothing left to lose. They were free, if only momentarily.

It was the same truth I had stumbled on in the Grand Canyon, the moment I chose my own direction. Although I hadn't fully realized it at the time, from then on, my trip to the East was a temporary move to settle up, say good-bye, close the door gently. That courage had come to me in the silence of sandstone cliffs and deep canyon gorges.

Attica still crowded the news when I left Glorie at the bus station in Indianapolis. She insisted she wanted to make the last seventy-five miles to her home alone. We hugged, reluctant to leave each other with our lives still suspended.

We had seen the Grand Canyon, red rock mesas, Anasazi villages, cowboy and mining country, ski resorts, the desert, the mountains, the plains. We had lived the drama and ordinariness of America, and we had spent days listening to its family being ripped apart. We were now best of friends.

That night, alone at a motel on the Pennsylvania border, I missed Glorie. She understood better than most my fears for the men in New York and for my own life.

The next day on the radio I listened to the news that Rockefeller had again refused his commissioner's request to talk to the Attica inmates. I felt a kind of panic for the men as I turned south off the Pennsylvania Turnpike. Washington, D.C., was just ahead. At the same time, my resolve was weakening. I was frightened to return to Washington, afraid the life, the marriage might swallow me forever. Disgust and fear crowded each other.

At 9:43 A.M. the news broke. The power circuit at Attica prison was turned off. A helicopter circled overhead, dropping tear gas over the yard. Troopers—marksmen—appeared on the roofs and third-floor corridors, firing on the prisoners and hostages below in a deafening blast of ammunition and anger.

At 9:52 Attica was silent. Troopers' bullets had killed ten hostages and twenty-nine inmates, deaths they tried at first to blame on the prisoners. The desperation and the hope of Attica were covered with the stench of death. It was over.

I turned off the radio and off the road in my small car and pulled under a huge chestnut tree, its large leaves sucked limp by heat and humidity. I sobbed, exhausted.

Briefly the world gasped at the reckless conclusion to the crisis. Punishment was swift and prisoners' pleas ignored as if they had never been voiced. But the events have stayed with me all these years.

For the first time, I began to question whether social justice was possible in this country. "How could I have been so naïve in San Francisco?" I asked myself.

A year later, political leaders betrayed us at Watergate and a war fraught with lies and blame finally ended in Vietnam. As a nation, we were left to wonder who we were and whom we could trust. I withdrew further.

I never saw Glorie again, although she called me once, identifying herself by another name, her real name, she told me. She had moved to New Jersey. She didn't like it much. There were silences on the phone.

My husband and I separated within the year. I moved to Alaska, the ultimate West, the widest of open spaces, and I began to feel I could breathe deeply once more.

I never again lived in San Francisco, never returned to the innocent I was then, the foolish girl who thought everything could be fixed—marriages, poverty, hopelessness. Although I visit the city occasionally, now I am an outsider.

Instead, I am at home in the mountains of Idaho, where from my ranch cabin I think back on my trip east so many years ago. I remember Glorie and my despair at losing the landscapes of the West, scenes familiar to me now. But even here, from time to time I find myself haunted by memories of Attica, of its victims and survivors, myself included, and who we used to be.

The Last Cowwoman
of the Escalante

SUSAN ZWINGER

I'm driving out to the middle of nowhere again where I could get in big trouble. I long for an enormous topography where glances are measured in hundreds of miles and human lifetimes in seconds.

Alongside Highway 89 east of Kanab, Utah, the sun is just now coming up, elongating the purple shadows of juniper. Mountain bluebirds zap by, electric pieces of sky. Clouds are scrolling off of the fresh blue, a cool, gorgeous day in southern Utah. I'm going to look for fossils, petroglyphs, and California Condors along the Vermilion Cliffs. In a hissing wind outside, I punch in phone numbers on a naked wall phone and howl over the din to an editor at *Audubon* magazine. He has suggested an essay on wind and water-carved stone. "Wind I've got plenty of!" I shout over the bad connection.

■ ■ ■

Leaving the highway, I drive east along Sit Down Bench to the Grand Bench, a 1,000-foot-high stair step up a giant staircase from Lake Powell to the Kaiparowits Plateau. Two days ago, I drove seventy miles out the Hole-in-the-Rock Road, then walked sixteen miles to a rock slot where the Mormon pioneers roped their heavy wagons down to the Colorado River. Choked, stymied, and dammed, that river is now Lake Powell. This rock slot lies eight hundred feet below the eastern end of Grand Bench, and I long to see it from above.

Above me, the brilliant red cliffs of the Moenkopi Formation, the Vermilion Cliffs, shoot vertically up from the desert floor, eventually rising to three thousand feet at the top of the Kaiparowits Plateau. The Vermilion Cliffs are the southernmost edge of a tilted wedding cake-shaped plateau.

A golden eagle officiates over a fence post, gold flashing on his dark brown head feathers—this is grandiose raptor country. The predawn threads of clouds are gone. That's important because where I'm going out on the slick, red clay roads rain means instant-quagmire for two-wheel-drives.

No cell phone, no radio, no GPS, no other connection to civilization. I hate 'em. Just a diminutive, two-wheel-drive pickup, two kitchen baskets, a small butane stove, and grub. I use a compass and a topographical map to find my way, much cheaper and more practical than the cumbersome GPS and its voracious appetite for batteries.

As I plunge farther and farther from safety, the colors on the Kaiparowits Plateau intensify. Big blue sage against bright red clay earth. High above, the fresh snow is so bright against black piñon forests and the deep red Wingate sandstone, it hurts my eyes. Rapidly the plateau drops from 5,500 feet toward the surface of Lake Powell and below that, the Grand Canyon of the Colorado.

Loaded with fresh grocery store food, I pass by the hole-in-the-road town of Big Water. Trying to be responsible, I saunter into the Kane County Bureau of Land Management office. An old-school BLM bureaucrat who makes no attempt to disguise his disdain for fancy-footed ecotourists and environmentalists glares at me. I want to file an estimated date of return for safety.

"The Kane County crew keeps those roads closed up here because they don't want to be liable for search and rescue for stupid tourists," he says looking pointedly at me. I decide to say nothing: He would have forbidden it. I go back to Big Water where the country store clerk gives me the same road advice.

"Turns to shit out there soon as it rains."

I've checked five or six different weather channels and stations, and all say it will be high and dry for the next five days.

I then dial a friend's phone to let her know where I'm going, but the fax machine squeals in my ear. Time to get the hell out of Dodge.

At 7.7 miles out along the rough dirt road, the dirt track promises strangeness tinged with danger. Soon, the road turns to slick, black shale. Fearful but stubborn, I slosh the truck through three more miles to the last turn-around possible. Yet I do not turn around.

Instead I clamber up a short bluff shaped like a stack of cowboy flapjacks, each cake a different shade of black and gold. I snatch up a piece of this gold and discover what has been glinting like shards of glass: thin sheets of gypsum, sea sediment formed of zillions of tiny shells and organisms.

The road now pumps up and down the steep relief through many small drainages carving down from the 2,000-foot cliffs. To the east and south, far below a precipitous red cliff edge, shines the sudden expanse of Lake Powell. Filling the once-magnificent Glen Canyon, the flat turquoise water is incongruent within the bright red slickrock, appearing sinister and wrong. Out here in red rock, evaporation country, a lake is not supposed to be. The white steam rising from the immense Navajo Power Plant is repeated by a thousand tiny white specks dragging wakes across the blue: power boats. Glen Canyon Dam's concrete smile blocks the mighty Colorado River, blurting out power bolts like the silver-tongued devil.

I'm alone in 70,000 square miles of slickrock. The road grows rougher; the dry chop of mud is hard on the tires. My truck clings to the narrow rims of a canyon whose headlands are eating rapidly to the northwest from the Colorado. They're buying their ticket to the ocean.

I pay keen attention. As I round each blind corner to discover yet another plunge into a water channel, I steal furtive glances down these steep canyons. Chaos fractals at work, each side canyon appears as a miniature of the Grand Canyon. Periodically the dirt track dips down to bare bedrock decorated with stony pillows the size of Volkswagens.

Snow-rimmed side canyons reach straight up to the lofty cliff of the Kaiparowits Plateau. Above those rims, clouds form. I can tell by their black-fringed edges that it is raining high above. Just localized moisture condensation due to orographic uplift, I pray and dismiss the danger. Below me, Lake Powell. Forty miles east, my destination, the cliff above Hole-in-the-Wall.

Virga, or rain that does not reach the ground, sweeps up behind me, as if to erase my very existence. I get out and stick a wet finger into the wind. A weather system plunging down from the northwest would bring the storm with it. I am delighted to find it blowing in instead from the southeast, the dry side.

Out in huge sky country, one becomes keenly aware of the immense invisible topography in the sky, air structures more grandiose than the earth. I love that a life depends on weather-reading. I could easily hike out the forty miles with backpack and food, now that I know I can replenish my water along the way. Still I drive on, worried about the dozens of odd things that may go wrong with an old truck. Beyond an ominously named creek, Last Chance, a slim track leads to the Burning Hills. Turned bright red by the smoldering seams of coal within, they have burned and smoked for eons. I also saw this bizarre phenomenon around Kachemak Bay in Alaska. Kachemak translates as "smoking sands."

Cactus wrens trill their downward waterfalls, and rock wrens rattle their intrepid rattles. The Indian paintbrush smacks the eye with orange-red, and the Mormon's ephedra offers up a heart-fluttering tea. Darkling beetles weave the sand under blackbush and shadscale. With so many gifts, I must keep going. Each new side canyon grows wetter and more beautiful. The road plunges down into a draw. This is the end of the road. I will have to push the rest of the way to Grand Bench on foot.

This is camp!

It is so beautiful and so far out from any other human being in the whole wide world that I weep! The pickup made it out 38.1 miles along Sit Down Bench. High above Lake Powell, I gaze out over thousands of square miles of slickrock. I am wary out here alone, but I won't die. I've got all I need to survive for three weeks.

To protect the fragile desert soil from damage, I rebuild an existing fire ring. I create a fresh salad with diverse salad greens, orange nasturtiums, and lavender pansies (oh, would those cowboys have a laugh now). Thick, green olive oil and balsamic vinegar squirt out of little plastic bottles. Fresh croutons from left-over bread have been baked in the hot desert sun, then tossed with garlic. A cool zephyr up from Lake Powell drops the temperature fifteen degrees. All is right with my world.

Until... a dog barks.

I freeze. This is not a coyote yip. This is a tame dog. That means cowboys or outlaws or four-wheelers. I feel vulnerable, miserable.

I follow the other fork in the road, which drops precipitously into a draw. As I reach the rim of the draw, my heart sinks. The draw is packed with corrals, outbuildings, and a house trailer. A big old campfire ring surrounded by stumps and makeshift board tables, cow pies all over. A huge stack of juniper and piñon indicates some serious wood hauling from up on the plateau and big, he-men fires. Several mangy horses stomp about the squirrelly stick corral. These aren't pretty trail horses; these are work-bedraggled horseflesh. Even though this is BLM land and it is illegal, somebody lives here. I call out. No one of my species answers.

Uneasy, I return the half-mile to my own exposed, out-there-with-my-mouth-hung-open campsite to think. Five hard, hard hours to drive out here to the end of the road. I am staying and hiking up the canyons tomorrow and the next three days, no matter how rough-edged these cowboys might be.

After the salad, I throw a hunk of lamb over juniper coals and eat cavewoman style—no utensils. The Grand Staircase–Escalante is known for its many endemic species so, for the evening's entertainment, I draw desert lupine, blackbush, *Eriogonum inflatum,* and scalloped phacelia.

At night, with a full moon, I have trouble sleeping. The dog is yipping now, as if someone were coming home late and opening cans of dog food and beans. I turn off my headlamp hoping, at least, to be invisible. Then turn it back on to write inside my sleeping bag. The temperature is dropping again.

I must have slept hard finally, because seemingly a moment later, a salmon light breathes the red rock to life. I hear no neighbors, so get up and fix cowboy coffee, a couple eggs, and black beans with salsa. The birds rev up so sweetly that I forget my fear of my unknown neighbors.

Sentinel buttes rise over hundreds of slickrock miles, casting mauve shadows against pink stone. I walk to the river canyon's edge and discover the Page, Arizona, power plant steaming away in the stiff distance. There's that dog yapping again.

I don a daypack, stick in one Granny Smith, string cheese and peanut butter, and 72 ounces of water—and set off across the desert and through bizarre canyons toward Lake Powell. My spirits are high. The creosote is aromatic with hydrocarbons. I love that smell. A small river runs under a wide line of damp sand through deeply eroding sandstone benches. Willows offer a rich habitat, a wet ecosystem in a dry land. Bird voices are loud and busy. I hear horses' hooves on slickrock.

Cow, I think hopefully. *Only cow.* But cows don't walk up on slickrock where there is no grass. The hooves are sharp and purposeful now. OK, he is about to sight my pickup, I think, so I must go up and say hello.

My heart is in my throat. I find where the dirt track exits the river canyon on the opposite side from the corral. It climbs up for two hundred feet, making sharp twists. Suddenly I am face to face with a tall horse. She bobs her head down then up in surprise catching me with a good clip below my chin. She knocks me backward. A small dog is dancing around my feet with a cacophony of trouble. His master astride the horse, unseen, is no doubt amused.

Knocked a little silly, I do not look up until I am sure I can pretend that there is no pain, not even a whisper of discomposure. To run headlong into an eight-foot-tall animal the color of coal in the middle of glaring white sandstone just doesn't look too bright.

"Are *you* alright?" exclaims a woman's voice. A woman!

I squint as best I can up into the sun and discover a stringy, 60-something cowperson tall upon a very tall horse. The horse rears up, and I am forced to dodge out of the way.

"Whoa, Delsy! Hey, she won't bite!" says the woman, "She's just damned high-spirited. Good horse, though, especially in open range. She won't bite."

The horse rolls her lips back and shows me teeth the size of stenographer's tablets.

I say brightly, "I'm not scared of big animals. We're just surprised, both of us."

"Shuddup, Kiki," she barks at the dog. "Whad'th'hell are ya doin' out here all alone?" she says to me.

"I'm camping." The horse is nervous, and the dog barks. "I'm drawing plants and identifying stuff," I explain, realizing these activities sound as absurd as walking smack into a horse.

"Well, ya shouldn'ta camped so close to someone's trailer and not come over to say hello, then."

It dawns on me that she is scared out here, apparently alone.

I apologize profusely, saying I didn't see anyone there.

"I git in pretty late after dark. You shouldn'ta oughta scare folks like that. I thought you was a rustler or some ATV riders," she snaps gruffly. "I'm Terry Virago. I got 133,000 acres to cover up here by myself. Lost my husband five years ago. People think I'm crazy, but I still gotta run these cattle by myself. When I'm not running my cattle up into the high country, I run horse trips up the Fifty Mile, as long as I git three or more rich folk. You ride?"

"Well, yeah, but I'm not rich."

"Yeah, I saw yer rig. I can't believe you're out here in that hunka cheap tin. Hey, when you goin' back in?"

"Soon, I'll be out of your hair soon," I say, thinking this a hostile question.

"Well, maybe we should tandem in together. I drove this cattle trailer up here and had a helluva time." Terry motioned to her corral. Behind one shed, blocked from my view last night, popped an immense cattle trailer and a substantial-looking pickup.

"And I thought I had a hard time on these roads." Suddenly it dawned on me that I was not the frail one in this little drama. I could reassure her.

"Yeah, I had trouble with that rig. Mighten be a wheel falls off."

"A tire? I change tires."

"I said wheel, dammit." On that Terry wheeled her horse away and down the track. Hardly pausing she shouted, "Drop over after supper tonight. Share some whiskey and stories. You got whiskey?"

"No, sorry I don't," I said. "When? I've got some serious walking to do tomorrow."

"*Walking!!!*" she snapped. "You cain't *walk* this country."

■ ■ ■

At 7:35, nervous and wanting to be alone, I saunter over to make quick hellos and leave. When I reach the rim of the little draw, a huge cedar fire blazes. Terry calls piñon "cedar." Out lunges Kiki like a vicious javelina, dangerous with a mouth full of tiny, sharp teeth. The elegant, five-year-old Delsy alone in her corral acknowledges my arrival with a neigh. Terry crouches out, not from the long house trailer, but a little wooden shack.

"The main trailer was trashed. Everything was trashed and stolen, gates left open, animals let loose. Cows all up Croton Valley. Horses scattered. I cain't git that trailer out on my own. Too big," she says sadly.

"So that's why you were so nervous about my presence last night. Who's doing the damage?"

She gestured abruptly toward a stump and I sat down.

"It's those wilderness folks that's doing this because they're trying to throw us cattle ranchers all off the land. But they don't pay a thing! They don't pay no taxes or fees. Is that fair?"

"No, but it's not them. I think it's just plain ol' roughnecks and hoodlums. Environmentalists don't trash. That's not our way."

She eyes me with hostility. "Djoo bring yer cup?"

I pull a Sierra Club tin cup from a daypack and hold it out.

"No, they are coming in and burning down all our places to chase us off. Somebody's gonna get shot over this. Just you wait."

I shift directions precipitously, rubbing my bruised chin. "Terry, I know you number your cattle, but do you name them?"

"My cattle don't have numbers! I know exactly who I got, and yes, they have names. Only friends I got. I have five of the original Escalante cattle. They're so smart, they know exactly where the quicksand is. You put in smart Escalantes, the rest learn. Now I wouldn't go down there on foot. You'd get into the quicksand."

"I'm real careful," I say. In spite of our differences, I'm growing to admire this solitary woman far out in some of the grandest open territory left in the West.

"You eat yuppie food, don't you? What would you say if you knew that cattle raised in stock pens are fed pig shit and chicken shit? Now my beef is all natural. They don't even know what hay is. All natural grass out there. I run only 150 head on 133,000 acres. Lloyd and I started with only 50 head when we lived in that trailer there. We were in love and runnin' cattle like proper partners. I would ride all day long. See, you don't get cattle of that quality if you kill the last of us cowboys off," she added.

"Well, my last husband was a real old-time cowboy. He just died five years ago and left me this huge operation. He was killed way out here. Got tangled up in his mule. Hit his head real hard on a rock. By himself, he made it all the way back into town but died a month and a half later. I wished he hadn' a gone that way. I wisht he'd just died and I'd found his bones."

"Quicker's better than slower." Death out here has a different meaning, and Terry seems adapted to its stark reality.

"I nursed him at home in the end. He was just trapped in his body. He'd open his eyes, but there weren't nobody there. Just gone."

"That's so sad. . . ."

"Yup, wouldn't even go to the doctors at first, but his concussion...mustuh burst a blood vessel. Whole right side of his head swoll up. Some folks suggest I killed him."

"I'm sorry. That must have been a very hard period for you. Some folks think you killed him?"

"Nah, I loved him. I loved him so much. He and I'd be out here all alone for weeks and weeks on end. He was the last of the real good cowboys. I'm run-nin' out of them."

"That's who you fall in love with?"

"Yeah, the young ones ain't no good. They're not worth a crap until they're over sixty. The young ones—they're so absorbed in themselves, big egos. No room for you and your ego. Women's lib just ruined men. Castrated them, don't know how to treat you like a real woman no more. We don't want them but we don't know what we do want. No, we sure screwed ourselves. We castrated the men—now what do we have? The last good cowboy up and died."

"Well, I loved poet-photographers," I said. "They're worse than cowboys in the opposite direction." I think to myself, *Here I sit forty miles out in the middle of nowhere with a crazy person who might have . . . nah.*

"How come they think you might have killed him?"

"Cuz we had bullets in us. He managed to crawl out, but I woulda died had not someone come out and found me."

"I thought you said he hit his head, and that you were back in town."

"He did hit his head, probably after a bullet hit him. Me, I don't know where I was."

Nervous with her story, I switch direction. "And what do you do now?"

"I take my comfort where I kin get it. I went on my first date in years just two weeks ago. It was a disaster. A complete disaster! He wants to play little mind games. I don't have time for that. I'm over sixty. He's a rancher too, and a good friend, but he don't know what he wants."

"Did he want a good little wife to settle in on the big ranch and run the . . . "

"No!" Terry declared angrily. "He don' know what he want. Men are scared of women who shoot straight from the hip."

"Whoa, don't I know!" I gazed into the enormous cedar fire, heat curling my side hairs into springs. Truly amazed by her ability to survive up here in such isolation, I ask, "So who do you care about? What sustains you?"

"I love my cows. Why, I sat down and had lunch with some of them today. I know them by name and personality. They're producing some really good calves: three dropped just in the last couple of days. Come June 1, I drive them right up here to the upper Fifty-Mile. I summer up there in a damn good cabin I love. Twelve by twelve, real whole-log cabin, dirt floor. I love that place. … but I expect it to burn down soon. Why, it was put there in 1937, a real piece of history."

"That'd be a tragedy to lose that. We environmentalists hate to lose that history too. That's terrible."

"The environmentalists want us outa here. They got a foot in the door with the new Escalante National Monument. Now, if they can just throw us all out."

"I don't feel that way, Terry. We just gotta share…."

"I don't mind taking people up into this wild country. I haven't had a whiner or a dud among 'em. I've met some fabulous people that way. Some days it's real hard and many days are really long, but they don't complain. They know the way it is. They don't complain about the heat or when the gnats get 'em.

"Horseback is the best way to see this country. It's too goddamned big to walk and there's a lot of places you just can't git to with wheels. I do all my own ridin' myself, and I can ride for days. Been out there diggin' out springs and checkin' on cows."

"You don't look dirty," I comment.

"Kiki and I had a long hard day yesterday. We rode up the Little Valley Creek. I rode the white mare you seen out there, and didn't realize she didn't have any shoes on. Shouldn'ta ridden her. Just sittin' in a vehicle now hurts my herniated disk. I live on painkillers. But that disk don't hurt to ride a horse.

"Those damn men, though," she says. "Just can't keep it straight and please a good woman. They wear out."

"Yeah, but you ride 'em hard and put 'em away wet," I say.

We both fall off our stumps laughing. After a grand evening, the cedar finally burning down, I excuse myself. Terry seems relieved, but Kiki raises a fuss.

"Shuddup, Kiki," we both bark.

"What time do you wanna git out of here?" asks Terry.

"Not tomorrow! I worked so hard to get out here, let me have one more day to hike. I want to enjoy my time out here and draw some more plants."

"Well come over the day after when you feel like it, but not too late. And remember, you cain't *walk* that…"

"Yeah, yeah, yeah…" I say.

■ ■ ■

Next morning I'm up at sunrise, make a great breakfast of refried beans and eggs, and climb up into Little Valley Canyon. I gain about 1,500 feet of altitude and find a beautiful hanging garden of maiden fern and gold columbine. I hike far out on Grand Bench, but never make it to the cliff overlooking Hole-in-the-Wall. Along the way, I discover petroglyphs, ancient stone toeholds pounded into the rock, but no condors. I take no time to draw, but hike all day long. By evening, I fall into bed with barely a snack for dinner.

The following morning, I find that I am looking forward to my time with this tough, timeless icon of the Old West, the cattle-producing West. I head down to Terry's about 8:30 A.M. I feel guilty, thinking that she's been up for hours. Instead, I wait for Terry to put on her face in the truck side mirror at 9 A.M. She does so very carefully and changes into an outfit of spiffy black jeans, black vest, long-sleeved shirt, and a belt with a mother-of-pearl buckle. I help Terry load Delsy and other horses into the trailer. We are both worried about the trailer's wheels falling off.

Only sixty-five degrees out with high mare's tails against a clear blue sky. Winds aloft. I feel gloriously powerful. I cross Croton Creek fishtailing, then park to wait for Terry. I cannot believe the finesse with which she negotiates the sharp turn and the creek at the same time. She pulls over behind me and gets out. After that maneuver, she deserves a hand-rolled cigarette. Below us sweeps a landscape of buttes and mesas, red and gold and blue, stretching forever.

"Look at this incredible panorama," I say. "Five miles out Sit Down Bench to a thousand-foot drop off to Lake Powell, and you live here! That's gotta thrill you."

"But I won't be comin' up here much longer."

"I'm sorry," I say. A camp robber jay lets off a streak of expletives deleted.

"I've got to go live with my relatives in Phoenix. I finally have to admit I cain't do this by myself no more. At sixty-two, I'm just too damn old. My people don't really want me there, but I s'pose they gotta have me."

"Phoenix! Well, I hope you rise again. Hey, you'll like Phoenix. There's tons of stuff to do. Cowboys there, too."

As we drive on, we round the head of Last Chance Creek, only twenty-nine miles to go. Lots of cows and a lame calf. Terry knows its owner's telephone number by heart. Stopping again, she shows me a grave marked "Rogers," an old sheepherder.

"He got himself killed out here," she says sadly.

"Seems to be a lot of that going around."

We pay homage. I am aware of the wind blowing and how short a time we each have here on the Grand Bench, Utah. Me, because I must go back north and work. Terry, because her work and way of life are coming to a close.

"My brother owns a bunch of sheep, so I thought I'd try sheep up here. But the smart-ass, meddlin' government, the BLM, wouldn't let me. Seems they pass on brucelosis to the bighorn sheep."

"Look!" I point up. "A falcon with a snake in its claws!" Terry follows it with her hawklike eyes. I say, "I came out here to find fossils and petroglyphs, and perhaps catch a glimpse of one of the newly released California condors. But treasure never comes on demand." Terry cranes her wrinkled neck and her sharp, leathery nose after the peregrine.

"Sure can say that again," she says.

Seven hours later, we reach the highway, complete with all our wheels.

"Come on back out to Grand Bench. Bring a bunch of dudes and I'll lead you all out over some of the wildest country you'd ever want to see. I'll even teach you to wrangle."

Terry's invitation is a ruse, not to fool me, but to divert us both from an overwhelming sadness. This, I know, is the Last Cowwoman of Grand Bench. Perhaps in protecting wilderness, I had a part in the demise of her way of life. Perhaps not. Perhaps this is just the way of the body, how all of us some day must cease doing what we love way out in solitary canyons. This is a day of endings.

As I shake Terry's hand, a ten-foot wingspan shadow slides over the cliff face in back of her. I wonder instead, is this a day of beginnings?

 **Women at Work**

SUSAN BISKEBORN

Thirteen years ago, my husband, Tom, decided to fix our leaky basement once and for all by installing a French drain around the foundation of our Seattle home. This complicated task took all summer (Tom was a teacher at the time) and entailed hiring and managing a few plumbers and many strong men. What's a French drain, you say? Well, I'll tell you. It's a twelve-foot trench, sloped toward the city sewer connection and braced in the deepest parts to avoid fatal slides, filled with fine gravel and pipe wrapped in filter cloth, and finally, more packed gravel and tamped-down earth.

We were surrounded by a moat! But all was not well in our kingdom. Every day, it seemed, a new desperado appeared on the job. Disreputable they may have been, but discriminating nonetheless, especially about coffee, this being Seattle—one homeless guy on the project sneered at Tom's fresh-brewed coffee, preferring to buy his own Starbucks latte.

Every day brought more tools: shovels, pickaxes, wheelbarrows. And then Tom rented the mother of all tools—a jumping jack—a gas-powered pogo stick that roared like a chain saw. The men gleefully used it to compact gravel and earth. One day, when the jumping jack had been going full bore for hours, skewing all the pictures on all the walls inside our house, our next-door neighbor called. "What on earth is making that racket?" she asked. "Have you got a helicopter over there?"

Each and every day, Tom and his crew quit work at "Beer-Thirty" (5:30 P.M.) to quaff a few and rehash the pit's progress while someone fixed dinner. (Reader, it was I.)

It was a man's, man's world that summer, and it was time for me to hit the road.

Fortunately, I had just signed a contract for my first book—*Artists at Work: Twenty-Five Northwest Glassmakers, Ceramists, and Jewelers*—and it meant traveling to artists' homes in Montana, Idaho, Oregon, and Washington for interviews. The perfect excuse to get out of town. My collaborator on this project was Kim Zumwalt, the photographer who was to take all the artists' black-and-white portraits for the book. We knew each other somewhat from our previous jobs at a weekly paper in Seattle, so to minimize expenses we decided to travel together.

A girls' road trip! We postponed our visits to artists in nearby Oregon and Washington until late fall and winter, and that sunny summer we headed east to the Big Sky country of Montana and Idaho.

Our route was this: east from Seattle on Interstate 90 to Ellensburg and Spokane; south on 195 to Pullman, Washington, and the adjacent college town of Moscow, Idaho; 95 south to 80 east to Boise; then 86 east to Pocatello and north on 15 to Helena, Montana. (Speeding north into Montana at dusk, so many dead insects piled up on the windshield of my 1981 Honda station wagon that we were forced to pull over and swab them off to continue.) From Helena, south on 287 to east 90 to Bozeman, then west on 90 to Missoula, north on 200 and 93 to the town of Bigfork near the head of Flathead Lake, and home weeks later on west 90.

We also drove into the Sawtooth Mountain Wilderness east of Boise on a dirt Forest Service road that bounced my station wagon around like an old buckboard for three hours, hugging hairpin turns to avoid gigantic logging trucks driven by wild men hell-bent on...but more about that later.

In my sturdy Honda wagon, Kim and I stowed all the necessities: her photographic gear as well as my tape recorder and notebooks, a cooler packed with soft drinks and Kim's indispensable string cheese, and creature comforts—her pillow and espresso machine and my teapot and smoky Lapsang Souchong tea.

We delightedly discovered that we had many habits and preferences in common, such as an aversion to eating breakfast in a restaurant and a fondness for clean, cheap motels of the AAA variety. We were thirty-nine years old and in our pre-snoring days then, and every evening we happily shared a modest room with twin beds. Our best find was an old nunnery outside of Helena, Montana, where we eschewed the pricey bed and breakfast rooms on the first floor for two dirt-cheap, cell-like rooms upstairs, complete with dorm bathrooms and glorious views.

Amazingly enough, neither of us much liked to listen to music in the car, so we read aloud to each other as we covered those long, lonesome Western miles. (This was before the boom in books on tape.) I know what I was reading that summer—*The Letters of John Cheever*—but I can no longer recall what book Kim brought along. All I remember is the sound of her low, laughing voice as she sat in the passenger seat and read when it was my turn to drive.

All in all, Kim and I were perfect work spouses and travel companions, in spite of the fact that we couldn't be more different. Although we are both the eldest of three daughters, and were both born in 1950, we had wildly dissimilar upbringings. Kim grew up on a farm in Oregon, while I was raised in suburban Pennsylvania and Maryland. Here's a telling detail: whereas Kim's parents bought her a Tennessee Walker horse to train and raise, my parents gave me such girly girlhood presents as an embroidery kit for placemats. Perhaps because she is a Westerner, Kim is an intrepid traveler; since our road trip she has journeyed solo to India and Nepal. Me, I still don't know how to change a car tire.

We differ physically, too. Kim is tall and lean, with a swinging dark ponytail; I'm small and round, short of hair and fair. Each of us resembles a movie star with the surname of Keaton—but while fine-featured Kim is a ringer for Diane, I'm as thin-lipped as Buster.

We soon settled into a routine when we were on the road. Every morning, we would breakfast in our room, then Kim would drive me to an artist's house or studio to interview him or her for the morning. At lunchtime, Kim would reappear with my car and I would go off, leaving her to photograph the artist. When I picked her up in the late afternoon we went out to dinner at some inexpensive place that—and this was important—had a liquor license. After dinner, we repaired to the motel to relax and review our day's work and get ready for the next day. Invariably we turned in early.

Of course, there were times we cut loose, too. For instance, we attended the annual summer "Brickyard Bash" in Helena at the Archie Bray Foundation, one of this country's foremost pottery schools. And what a bash it was. The band that night was the popular Big Sky Mudflaps, and they entertained a draft-beery, dance-happy crowd with rhythm and blues numbers such as "Mama, He Treats Your Daughter Mean." One of the band's members is Beth Lo, a ceramist I included in my book. Beth is a studious-looking, bespectacled woman, and it was a revelation that night to see her play the electric bass and croon on stage.

Kim and I also went shopping, of course. (Are we not women?) The best thrift shop I have ever encountered was in Helena. It was easy to see just how wealthy some of the citizens of this former mining town had once been by perusing the women's clothes, many of which boasted labels from New York and Paris. I bought armfuls, including feathered hats and elbow-length gloves and an elegant smoking jacket that (once) fit me perfectly.

And as women do, we talked. How we talked. Miles and miles of talk as we covered what were to me, a former East Coast gal, unimaginably vast distances. We talked about our mothers, of course, those titans of our childhood who even in our thirties still loomed large. Both our mothers had worked as teachers, the career path of choice for smart women of their generation. But my mom liked to stick close to home, whereas Kim's more adventurous mother loved traveling, a passion she obviously passed on to her daughter.

We skinny-dipped, or rather Kim did, with her friend, the jeweler Barney Jette, who lives on the land his family homesteaded in Montana's Swan Valley, just west of the Continental Divide. One of the best moments of my life was sitting on Barney's porch at dusk, eating a slice of his homemade huckleberry pie and watching the approach of two summer lightning storms—one moving toward us from the west across Flathead Lake, and one headed our way from the Bob Marshall Wilderness to the east.

On our journey Kim and I saw other amazing things, too, such as the ceramist Patrick Siler's domain outside Pullman, Washington. Patrick lives in an ordinary suburban development, but his lawn-free, sunflower-choked yard stood out among the manicured surroundings of the other tract houses like Van Gogh's *Sunflowers* on steroids. The inside of Patrick's home was a bourgeois nightmare, as well, for he had converted the entire shebang, save for bedroom, bathroom, and kitchen, into one big studio complete with a wall-to-wall carpet of paint-splattered cardboard boxes and old paintings lying face down.

But his art! Trained as a painter, Patrick can and does draw anything—from scroungy dogs and beer-swilling good old boys to a skeleton pushing a lawnmower—in an antic style that marks him as a true original. He has since given up clay to concentrate on drawing and painting.

Visits to other artists proved equally fascinating. Kim and I marveled over Sonja Blomdahl's luscious glass bowls and Flora Mace and Joey Kirkpatrick's toddler-sized, hand-blown pieces of fruit. We peered into one of Akio Takamori's porcelain vessels in the shape of a reclining naked man to discover the figure's internal organs lovingly painted inside the vessel's cavity. We ogled Richard Notkin's tiny clay teapots cunningly crafted into mordant memento mori such as nuclear cooling towers, skulls, and anatomically correct hearts. And we admired the witty, wearable sculptures of Kiff Slemmons, who uses everything from beach pebbles to Plexiglas to slate and old typewriter keys in her jewelry.

The most incredible part of our trip, though, was traveling to the old goldmining town of Atlanta, Idaho, which is 100 miles east of Boise. Remember the dirt Forest Service road into the Sawtooth Mountain Wilderness I mentioned earlier? Well, that was how we got to Atlanta, the summer home of the Boise-based ceramist Kerry Moosman. Three hours on that rutted road made Kim and me feel like pioneer women jouncing along in a Conestoga, but it was just as well, for it prepared us somewhat for a trip back in time.

Founded in 1864, Atlanta was once a boomtown of 500 to 600 people, but when Kim and I visited, the town had dwindled in population to about thirty people, many of whom worked for the Forest Service. Atlanta still supported (and how!) two bars, though. At the Whistle Stop Tavern, we heard, one barfly distinguished himself by his ability to leap onto the four-foot-high bar from a standing position on the floor while holding a mug of beer, but without spilling a drop. Kerry and his male friends, all wicked gossips, had dubbed this specimen "The Abdominals."

Other than modern amenities such as running water, electricity, and U.S. Mail service, little had changed in Atlanta in the last one hundred and some years, thanks in part to Kerry. When he was in college in the early 1970s, he drafted a petition to the Idaho State legislature, and now three acres in town are listed on the National Register of Historic Places. Kerry himself owned three houses in Atlanta, all meticulously and authentically restored—that is, without indoor plumbing, running water, or electricity.

Kim and I stayed in one of these cozy cabins for a few nights in early September, and we woke to the tolling bell of the town's two-room elementary schoolhouse, still presided over by Mrs. Inama, the same teacher who had taught Kerry there in the 1950s.

In Atlanta, it's common to hear other old-fashioned sounds, too, such as the squeak of water pumps and the crackle of kindling in wood stoves. At night, Kim and I drifted off to sleep listening to the roar of the Middle Fork of the Boise River behind the cabin, and the wild lullaby of coyotes yipping and elks bugling nearby.

The occasional bear still wandered into town, too. Kerry and his friends told us about the black bear who had recently ended up as bear steaks after he went on a rampage that began with swiping the townsfolk's hummingbird feeders and escalated into house break-ins. Even the Abdominals' dog, a huge half-wolf cur, could no longer scare him off. The bear sealed his fate, however, by getting into a villager's truck and accidentally throwing it out of gear so that it rolled down a hill and smashed into a tree. He escaped, but not for long; he met his fate at the end of a shotgun. In the West, you don't mess with somebody's truck.

For three heavenly days, Kim and I drank sweet water from Kerry's pump and breathed in the dry, high-mountain air of Atlanta, which smelled like crisp apples. We bathed in a hot-spring pool swarming with red dragonflies and facing 9,300-foot Greylock Mountain. Each night we ate dinner in Kerry's homey kitchen by the soft glow of kerosene lanterns. The night we arrived, two friends of his from Boise whipped up a feast of pork chili, hot sauce, rice, and refried beans on Kerry's woodstove. Another friend, visiting from New York, contributed homemade corn bread.

That same night, on my way back from the outhouse, I stood staring up at the stars spangling a sky as black of one of Kerry's burnished, thigh-high ceramic vessels. Turning back to his house, I peeked through the window into the lantern-lit kitchen where bearded Kerry and his three flannel-shirted friends sat talking and laughing with Kim, who was absentmindedly piling her long ponytail atop her head. It was like magic, this lamp-lit scene, like a glimpse back to a lost time one hundred years earlier, when bachelor miners entertained their occasional female guests.

How Kim and I hated to leave! When we reluctantly waved good-bye to Kerry and his friends, we vowed to return, but all these years later, we have never been back.

Much has changed since our trip, of course. My husband finally finished his project, I finished my book, and two years later, we adopted our daughter Mary from someplace even more far-flung than Atlanta, Idaho—the Fuyang Orphanage in Zhejiang province in China.

Kim had a knee operation last year for an old mountain-bike injury, the same year her adventurous mother succumbed to the ravages of cancer and the year my own mom turned eighty. Kim and I are in our fifties now, the same age as our mothers—those former titans—when they were in their prime.

My daughter is ten years old, and I'd like to think that maybe someday she and I would make our very own girls' road trip, back to Atlanta and some of the other places that Kim and I visited.

But what we'd see this time would be colored by what I now know of how the West was won. I'd like to show my daughter where hard-working men from her birth country lay railroad track across the desolate Western plains, and some of the towns where they slaved as miners.

The Chinese in Atlanta did the same backbreaking labor as the other miners, yet they lived in a ghetto, a Chinatown incongruously segregated from the other cabins in this village of fewer than 700 people. And if those same Chinese miners in Atlanta were unlucky enough to die so far from home, they were buried downhill from the other townsfolk, relegated to graves alongside the suicides and other outcasts.

Chinese women won the West, too. I'll tell my daughter the amazing story of Polly Bemis, born Lalu Nathoy in 1853 in northern China. She was sold when she was young to bandits and sent to America as a slave. There she was auctioned to a Chinese saloon keeper in Warrens, Idaho, a mining town in the Payette Mountains north of Atlanta. She married Charles Bemis, who reputedly won her in a poker game, and ran a boarding house in Warrens until they left town to homestead on the Salmon River. By the time she died, Polly Bemis was so well-respected in her community that members of the city council in the nearby town of Grangeville served as her pallbearers, and the creek running through her property was named "Polly Creek" in her honor.

Maybe someday my daughter, Mary, would like to see that creek, to visit the place where Polly Bemis lived, so far from the country where both she and Mary were born.

And perhaps Kim would even accompany us on our girls' road trip, especially if we went back to see Kerry Moosman in Atlanta. And some night, my daughter might find herself outside Kerry's cabin, peering through the lamplit windows at Kim and me. Squinting, maybe she will be able to imagine the two of us in our salad days, when we were young women at work, on our own and on the road.

How Tununak Came to Me

CAROLYN KREMERS

"This is your last chance to back out," Phil said over the crackling phone. Several days of clear, calm weather had lured many men in Tununak out into their boats to hunt seals. Now the wind had returned, sending the men home, and Phil, the school principal, had been able to meet with the village elders' council and with the Tununak school board. They had endorsed his recommendation that I be invited to teach music and English in their remote village.

"The job is yours if you still want it," Phil said, less crackling coming through the line now. I knew that he was only half-joking. "Congratulations."

■ ■ ■

"I don't know why anyone would want to build a village there," the personnel director for the Lower Kuskokwim School District had grumbled into the phone in Bethel, two weeks before. I had called to inquire about the position the day the job announcement arrived in my Boulder mailbox, on a sunny morning in mid-September.

"Tununak sits right on the edge of the Bering Sea, totally unprotected, no trees for 125 miles," the man's southern voice drawled. "The headlands at each end create a wind tunnel that funnels all the turbulence and weather right down into the village. The wind blows fifty miles an hour all winter, and half the time you can't even land a plane. Tununak is the foggiest, windiest village in the Delta—as bad as the Aleutians, I think. And wind means cold. Windchill can bring the temperature down to ninety degrees below zero."

I tried to say I was used to cold and that I liked winter, but he kept on talking.

"Your house won't have running water, you know. You'll have to haul water and dump your own honey bucket. There's a good oil furnace in that house, though. Forced air, if I remember right… Where do you live? Colorado? Well, think about it some more, and in the meantime we'll take a look at your file."

Competition for the job was stiff. The personnel director had over a hundred qualified applicants, most of whom had applied, as I had, through the University of Alaska Fairbanks Teacher Placement Center. He and the principal had narrowed the field to ten, then to three. Phil and the Tununak school board had made the final decision.

■ ■ ■

"Of course I still want the job," I said to Phil, my hand tightening around the phone. Perhaps, at last, one of my wishes had come true. I couldn't play high notes softly on my flute, and my fingers and tongue weren't fast enough yet to audition for a good graduate school, and I couldn't seem to connect with a man who understood me—but I *could* move to Alaska.

"Good," Phil said. "How soon can you get up here?"

I requested two weeks to extricate myself from my apartment lease, my part-time job as a high school orchestra teacher, and my schedule of twenty-six private Suzuki flute students. I gave away or sold all the belongings I could bear to part with and locked the rest in a Boulder storage locker. I packed enough dried and canned goods to last until I could send my first mail order to Anchorage for food. Then I scurried through stores and catalogs, purchasing on credit the long list of bush gear that Phil's wife, Ginger, had patiently described over the phone.

■ ■ ■

On October 21, 1986, a Twin Otter buzzed down out of the clouds, gently popping the ears of one *kass'aq* (white person, from the Russian word *Cossack*) and seven Yup'ik Eskimos strapped into seats behind the cockpit. A pile of freight, mail, and baggage filled the space behind them, secured with yellow nets of rope.

One wing tilted toward the gray sea, the plane banked left under gray clouds, and I caught my first glimpse of Nelson Island. I did not know, then, that during the next five years I would receive numerous gifts. Nor did I expect that my journey—the inner one and the outer, the journey I began making as a child—would begin to become so clear. I had had a premonition, though.

I had arrived at the Anchorage International Airport on a dark, sleeting Sunday, the only day of the week when buses didn't run downtown. Not looking forward to a four-hour layover before boarding the flight to Bethel, yet not wanting to spend twenty dollars on a cab, I had taken a walk around the airport.

A Kodiak brown bear, a snarling wolverine, a bald eagle, and several other animals and birds confronted me in silence from glass display cases. They reminded me of the one other time I had been in the Anchorage airport—with Michael, my former flute teacher, the man I had dragged to Alaska from Boulder five years before for a rainy three-week ferry-hopping, hitchhiking, train-riding trip that he would describe later as "nothing but a miserable nightmare."

Not everyone sees things the same way.

At the baggage-claim area, I decided to walk outside. I stepped out the door, turned left, glanced up, and stopped. Denali, the tallest mountain in North America, shone in the distance just beneath a thick band of gray clouds. The rounded summit, touched somehow by a ray of sunlight, gleamed white.

One of the reasons I had wanted so much to return to Alaska was my memory of the backpacking trip that Michael and I had made up Sunrise Creek, deep inside Denali National Park. We had surprised a grizzly in the willows, backed off safely, and watched her for two hours through our binoculars. Her twin cubs boxed and chased each other as she alternately napped and gorged on berries.

A few days later we had camped at Wonder Lake, eighty-five miles inside the park, and "the Mountain" had cleared off completely—a rare sight in summer. Cerise fireweed burned against centuries of snow.

Now Denali greeted me like a trusted friend.

Smiling, I walked down the sidewalk. The wet air stank with automobile exhaust fumes, though. I decided to go back inside and find something to eat.

I knew that prices would be high, but I bought a bowl of Manhattan clam chowder with oyster crackers anyway, for two dollars and fifty cents, and sat in the almost empty cafeteria at a table next to the windows. No view here. Sleet began to drum against the glass. I swallowed the soup slowly, enjoying the warmth and the salty fish taste, but doubt crept in. Maybe moving to Tununak wasn't the right thing to do after all. I could still change my mind.

Last chance to back out?

I was thirty-four years old. I had never been able to talk any of my "gentleman friends," as my father called them, into moving to Alaska with me. Not even Michael, who knew all the birds in Gregory Canyon by their calls and spent hours wandering the trails above Boulder looking at lichens and sedges, listening to leaves, breathing the butterscotch smell of ponderosa pine bark.

If I really wanted to live in the Alaskan bush—and I had wanted to ever since my first visit to Alaska in 1973—I should do it now. Especially since my progress with the flute seemed at an impasse. The job in Tununak could bring time to practice—summers at least—and money to pay for lessons. And anyway, I loved to teach. On the other hand, if I actually thought this wasn't what I wanted, then I should be honest enough to find a pay phone, call Phil, and tell him that I had changed my mind. It would be better to tell people now than later. I had seen the phone outside the cafeteria, and the number was right there in my pocket.

The next two hours passed slowly as I agonized over the decision I thought I had already made. I knew that I would be far from my family and friends. I would have no access to the world of classical music—no public radio broadcasts, private flute lessons, or master classes. No live concerts. No opportunities to perform or to rehearse with other musicians. I knew, from teaching in public schools and later as a Suzuki flute instructor, that teaching could consume all of my time and energy, leaving little or none for other creative work.

But I steered clear of the phone. I had always had too much pride to quit, even when quitting might have been smart. Besides, I was pretty sure that I could handle this.

■ ■ ■

An hour before flight time I walked to Gate A3, where the MarkAir jet for Bethel would depart. The waiting area was empty except for one overweight black-haired man slouched peacefully in an orange plastic chair, asleep. I sat as far away as possible, so I wouldn't have to make conversation if he woke up.

Within fifteen minutes, the waiting area filled with more black-haired people, plastic shopping bags under their arms, children in tow, elders leaning on canes. A tiny woman, slumped in an airport wheelchair, was rolled in by an airport attendant. The woman's wrinkled brown face looked out, like a peeled avocado seed, from a bright green parka trimmed with silver rickrack. A quilted hood, edged with a circle of black fur and a circle of white, bunched behind her head like a pillow.

People wandered into the area in ones, twos, and threes, looking as weary as I probably did. Almost immediately, though, they recognized someone they knew and were shaking hands, hugging each other, smiling, laughing, talking in a guttural language that I had never heard. The level of energy in the dead room shot up like a geyser. Even the woman in the wheelchair smiled. I realized that these people were all Eskimos and that they must be speaking Yup'ik. I couldn't understand a word they said, but I could guess what some of it meant. Suddenly I thought I had done the right thing.

■ ■ ■

The jet landed in Bethel in pitch darkness, broken only by red and blue runway lights. Inside the small airline building, I telephoned the woman whose number Phil had given me. She was the bilingual program administrator for the school district.

"I just got home a few minutes ago," Paula said. "Do you mind taking a taxi? Good. Tell the driver to come to the BNA Apartments—Bethel Native Association. He'll know what you mean. All these buildings are blue, so tell him to stop at the one closest to the antenna dish. My apartment is at the top of the stairs."

After introducing her two children, giving me a quilt for the sofa, and explaining that the stains in the toilet and sink were caused by iron in the water, Paula began cooking spaghetti.

"Phil sure is looking forward to having you in Tununak," she said, as she stirred the sauce. Her black hair showed glints of silver, and her complexion was darker than mine. I wondered if she was part Native.

"I'm looking forward to being there," I said, thinking of the sudden energy in the airport. "I hope I can live up to Phil's expectations.... Do you speak Yup'ik?"

"Oh, no!" she laughed. "My first language is Lakota Sioux. I grew up on the reservation in South Dakota."

This was interesting, but I wondered: How could a bilingual administrator not speak the language she was supposed to be administering?

At eight o'clock the next morning, Paula dropped me at the airport. Five other passengers and I walked outside in the dark to board the smallest plane I had ever been in. Having arrived in Bethel in the dark and now leaving in it, I had no sense of time or direction. Why hadn't I thought to bring my map, instead of mailing it?

We flew in bumpy darkness and dim clouds for an hour, all the passengers asleep in the cold plane except for me. Then we began to drop elevation over gray water dotted with ice. The plane landed in the middle of a frozen field of nothing, stirring up snowflakes in the faint light. I thought of the flat plains of Kansas.

When the back door opened, I could hear snatches of English and of what I would later discover was called "cowboy Yup'ik" by people in Tununak. This was Cup'ik, the dialect of Mekoryuk, the only village on Nunivak Island.

With another whirl of snowflakes and a roar, we were aloft.

I watched the water and ice below us in the dull morning light, hoping to see a seal. After perhaps fifteen minutes of no seals, the plane tipped suddenly, rounding the bend of a rocky cliff. At a crazy tilt out the small window, I spotted a string of wooden houses hugging the sea, then a river winding behind them.

"*Something something Tununermi*," the man in front of me said.

The plane circled the village—buzzing the local airline agent, I learned later—and I glimpsed several more houses clustered on a bald slope.

Phil said the school is on top of a hill. Then that big rust-colored building must be it. And that little gray house next door, beside those two huge tanks—fuel? water?—that must be mine.

I caught sight of a white door. Then there was nothing but gray sky, gray water. The pilot finished circling and the plane leveled. Noise in the cabin rose again to a roar and, my ears still popping, I felt the wheels touch ground.

We coasted to a stop near an orange windsock and a shiny brown pickup truck, and the pilot jumped to the ground. The copilot ducked his head through the cockpit opening and wormed down the aisle to the rear of the plane. I could hear him scuffling with mailbags and boxes, shoving things toward the open door as he had on our previous stop. I pulled ski mittens over my polypropylene gloves, gathered my camera and two flutes, and smiled at the woman watching in the seat across the aisle. Trying to look as if I knew what I was doing, I stood up halfway and hunched toward the rear.

"Welcome to Tununak," the pilot said, offering his gloved hand as my boot groped for the footstool he had placed on the gravel. "What brings you out here?" He handed down my navy blue duffel bag from the tail of the plane, but that was all.

"I'm the new music teacher. English, too, I guess. I came up from Colorado."

I wasn't sure that he had heard me very well. The wind whistled around the edges of the metal door. Above us, the copilot was rearranging boxes and crates, shoving and grunting, evidently trying to make room for outgoing mail and freight.

"Have you seen two boxes that say Colorado on them?" I yelled into the wind, aiming for the copilot's ear.

"Boxes? Colorado? Nope, no sign of them here. Did you check them at Bethel?

"No. I checked them all the way through from Denver. Denver to Tununak."

The two men looked at each other and laughed.

"You can't do that," the pilot on the ground said. His blue eyes twinkled, making me notice a Roman nose and a neat, brown beard.

"Your boxes are probably still sitting in Bethel by the conveyor belt, waiting for you to haul them to the counter. We'll take a look around when we get back, send them out on one of the flights next week. Don't worry, they'll turn up sooner or later."

"Okay," I said, trying not to sound concerned and not to let this man fluster me with his eyes. *I bet he knows he's good-looking. Those were my food boxes and my blankets and sheets. And my pillows.* "Thanks."

I glanced around for a man who might be the principal, but the only person I saw was a black-haired woman in tennis shoes. Bulky in a ripstop nylon parka and polyester pants, she leaned over the open tailgate of the brown truck. Slowly, she pushed cardboard flats loaded with red and green cans of pop toward the back. Then she straightened up. With one gloved hand on her hip, she waved me over.

"Good luck," the pilot called, winking.

"Get in," the woman said. "It's cold."

Thinking suddenly of the rustle of yellow aspen leaves against a deep blue sky, I heaved my duffel on top of two crates labeled POTATOES and CARROTS and opened the door. A blast of hot air blew in my face from the heater, and a little girl in diapers and black braids scooted closer to the steering wheel.

The woman put the truck in gear and steered over the frozen mud toward a narrow plank bridge. A fine dust of snow glittered against a brown hilltop under an overcast sky, and ice skimmed the puddles in ruts and potholes. No trees. I crossed my legs in my new jeans and felt the little girl staring at the pointed toes of my shiny brown high-heeled leather boots. I could see I was going to have to start the conversation.

"Hello. My name is Carolyn," I said over the noise of the heater. "Thank you for picking me up."

"I'm Sara." The woman kept her eyes on the road. "This is Robin."

The truck bumped over the wooden planks of the bridge. Still not looking at me, Sara spoke again.

"We didn't know if you came in today or not. It's very windy, last few days." She sighed. "Winter's coming. October already, almost November. I have still so much to do. Too much work. But winter comes, whether or not we are ready." At last, she smiled. "It always does."

All I can remember of the view out the window that day—inside the hot truck, with Robin's big black eyes, her thumb in her mouth, the smell of new vinyl seats—are the faces. Round, browned faces, most of them boys', behind the chain-link fence in the old BIA school playground, fists punching a tetherball. Then girls and boys running, running, and jumping, jumping. Chasing and laughing. And some of them stopping to stare at the truck, then waving, staring, and waving.

We wound up the hill and stopped in front of the rust-red building I had seen from the plane. Sara didn't look at me and she didn't turn off the engine.

Maybe she's going to park and come in later.

As soon as I pulled my duffel from the back, though, Sara drove off. I wasn't sure, but I didn't think she had said good-bye. I had, hadn't I?

I walked inside.

■ ■ ■

In a tiny office crowded with boxes and the green glow of a computer screen, a boyish-looking man with pale blond hair and pale blue eyes introduced himself as Phil and offered his sheet-white hand. His Yup'ik clerical assistant, Gabriel, also shook my hand. Gabriel was as handsome as the pilot, but with dark brown eyes, a clean-shaven face, and thick, shining black hair. It would be weeks before I would realize that I was taller than he and almost all the other people in the village.

Phil gave me some forms to fill out for the district office in Bethel, then took me to each of the three secondary classrooms. He introduced Mary, the only Native teacher on the faculty, and the eight members of her freshman/sophomore English class. The students were editing poems they had written and stapling them onto big sheets of colored butcher paper.

All I can remember of that first glimpse of the students—besides their dark eyes intent on me, "the new Teacher," all of them turning quiet when I walked into the room, their Yup'ik faces polite, curious, all looking alike to me, so that I couldn't remember their names—are the worksheets. Not in Mary's class, but in the junior high. The junior high did worksheets in English and spelling and social studies. Finish one, dutifully do another. I thought of Black Beauty, *how I read it as a child, startled, and cried at the way the bit slides easily into the horse's mouth. He discovers what it's for, but by then it's too late. I couldn't help it. I thought of bits and horses.*

Mary seemed younger than I—in her mid-twenties, perhaps—and very energetic. She had permed black hair, bright dark eyes, and a round face. She spoke with her class, sometimes in Yup'ik, sometimes in English, and she smiled a lot. But she didn't smile at me.

Next I met Grant, who taught social studies, jewelry making, and small-engine repair. He had blue eyes and a brown mustache, wore a T-shirt and jeans with a big ivory belt buckle, and stood half a foot taller than I. The eight students whom I had met in Mary's class now hunched over their desks, taking a test. At the back of the classroom, Grant flashed a big grin and shook my hand.

Ginger, Phil's wife, taught science and yearbook. She moved about the room, gathering dirty glass slides and petri dishes, as four girls pasted up photographs. Ginger's thick, frizzy brown hair exploded behind tight barrettes, and red wire-rimmed glasses slipped down her nose. She seemed confident, almost brash, but very friendly.

Scissors, rulers, colored pencils, bottles of rubber cement, and metal film canisters lay scattered on the two tables where the girls sat. They talked and teased in Yup'ik as they cut and pasted. They had pleasant round faces and wore makeup and dangling earrings. One girl's shiny black hair was cropped in a pixie style, while another had a kinky perm, her hair more brown than black. The other two girls had thick straight black hair that reached halfway down their backs. When Ginger introduced us, they each smiled and shook my hand lightly—my fingertips, rather. Then, seeming more interested in pasting than in me, they turned back to their work, still giggling.

Phil returned to his office to accept a phone call while Ginger showed me around her room. It contained a menagerie of microscopes, seeds sprouting in paper cups, a life-sized replica of a human skeleton, a jar of cow brains. Bright grow-lights illuminated a steamy glass case, crawling with purple and green plants and pink blossoms. Two white rats skittered in cages next to a napping spotted snake, and a solitary tarantula flexed its hairs.

As in the other two classrooms, the walls of Ginger's room were not walls at all, but movable dividers that reached only halfway to the ceiling. Voices from the other two classes filtered over, as well as laughter, shuffling, and— I would discover later—film soundtracks, music, scolding, and the beeps and loony tunes of computer games. Wafting over everything was the familiar school smell of freshly baked bread. A thunder of feet and of books closing signaled that it was time for lunch.

"Grant can show you the lunch line," Ginger said, putting on her parka. "Glad you're here. See you later."

I followed Grant into the gym and through the line, spooning oily lettuce into one compartment of my cardboard plate and canned peaches into the other. I had been a vegetarian for twelve years and preferred natural foods, so I passed up the hamburger macaroni, Jell-O with Dream Whip, and Hawaiian Punch. I took a piece of warm white bread, a glob of margarine, and a plastic fork and spoon and paper napkin. Then Grant led me to the "faculty lounge."

The place where the teachers ate had been intended as a shop room, Grant said, but was used mostly for supply storage. It had a cement floor and a metal grid staircase with steel railings that led up to the furnace room. A bright fluorescent tube, suspended from the ceiling two stories above, shone down like a searchlight. Crammed in the small space on the floor were a table and a few plastic chairs, a television and VCR on a cart, a band saw, some welding equipment, and various cardboard boxes.

Grant and I squeezed in at the table with two special education teachers, who introduced themselves as Brian and Judy. Judy said that they had moved to Nelson Island from Chicago six years before and had a son and daughter in the high school. Judy and her husband looked only a few years older than I. They described the self-contained classroom where they taught eleven junior high and high school students with special needs. The students had various emotional, mental, and physical problems, most caused by meningitis or by fetal alcohol syndrome. One, a twenty-one-year-old, was severely retarded.

"There are several guitars up in the attic," Judy told me. "Some are in better shape than others, of course." She laughed. "I think I've seen an old electric piano somewhere, too, and an autoharp."

I knew that I would have to scrounge instruments at first, even though Phil had hired me to help spend thirty-five thousand dollars to establish a music program. Phil played clarinet and wanted the school to have a band, partly because he thought the village would like it and partly because he and his wife wanted their sons to have music instruction. Now that the pipeline boom was over and the world price of oil had dropped, Alaska's economy was in a recession. The state legislature had begun cutting back its generous funding for rural schools, and Phil feared this might be the last year that money would be available in the district budget for "extras" such as music.

"In some respects, this school has everything," Grant said, flashing his big grin again. "Even a full set of gymnastics equipment—balance beam, parallel bars, rings, the whole bit. We knew we better not put it together, though, unless we wanted to risk getting sued. Who in the bush is going to know how to teach gymnastics, or want to? What would you do if a kid got hurt out here? But I swear, somebody in the district office must've been a PE nut, because when these schools got outfitted, every one of them got boxes of gymnastics equipment. And that stuff ain't cheap."

All three teachers lit cigarettes and continued talking, mostly among themselves. I was surprised that they hadn't asked me more questions than what state did I come from and had I been to Alaska before. Later I realized that both Brian and Mary, the Native teacher, were unhappy that I had been hired. Both wanted to teach English, but neither was certified. Mary, a business education major, had taught the high school English classes for two years, and Brian, certified in special education, had taught the junior high classes for one. Both teachers were popular with their students, but the district superintendent was pushing for school accreditation. When she discovered that Tununak had no certified English teacher, she told Phil to hire one.

I laughed when I found out later what Brian had said when he heard I had been chosen. "What we need around here is a Jeep, not a Rolls-Royce."

After lunch, I returned to Phil's office and we discussed my schedule. Phil had been able to convince the superintendent that it was best to wait until January to assign me to Mary's high school classes, since the semester was half over. The junior high students, though, had had three different teachers since August, due to scheduling problems.

"One more teacher isn't going to hurt," Phil said.

He decided that I should teach junior high social studies, English, spelling, and reading; high school yearbook; and two elementary music classes: first through third grade and fourth through sixth. He said he would show me around the elementary school in the old Bureau of Indian Affairs building at the bottom of the hill, the next day.

"Would you like to see your house now?" he asked.

■ ■ ■

I followed Phil across the narrow boardwalk, for about a hundred yards, to my new home. Forty feet below, the Bering Sea rolled to Siberia. The bay was clear, but I glimpsed blocks of ice far out on the horizon. Open space stretched as far as the eye could see, and the wind blew.

Yup'ik. The "real people." Later I would learn that, perhaps three thousand years ago, the Eskimos of Western Alaska had chosen this name for themselves. *Yuk*, their word for "person," and *–pik*, meaning "real" or "genuine," had been combined to make *Yup'ik*. Like the Inupiat Eskimos in Northern Alaska and the Inuit of Canada and Greenland, Yup'iks considered themselves the "real people," distinct from outsiders.

My house, a square frame structure not quite twenty-two feet by twenty-two, had been the contractor's shack when the new high school was built. The shack was not intended for winter occupancy. Various improvements had been made by previous tenants—most notably by Lois, a middle-aged spinster whose primary domestic concern, I would learn later, was peeping Toms; and by Todd, a counselor and special education teacher who had been involuntarily transferred to another village after five years in Tununak. Some people, including Phil, had accused Todd of selling marijuana and bootlegging whiskey.

"A joint costs ten dollars here, whiskey a hundred dollars a bottle," Phil said, as we stood in the kitchen. "People who get into drug dealing and bootlegging in this village can make a pile of money. Todd was smart to leave. He was very popular, so you'll probably get some of his old visitors."

Lois had insisted that an arctic entryway and an attic be added to the shack for more insulation, and Todd had built the kitchen counters and shelves and had installed a sink. He had run a length of thick rubber pipe from the sink's drain down through a hole cut in the floor. Since the house sat on blocks several feet above the tundra, the pipe could drip onto the ground below.

Todd had also caulked the windows and the cracks between the floor and walls with red and green modeling clay that he had gotten, apparently, from the elementary school. He had submitted a request for the freestanding forced-air furnace that I had heard about in Boulder over the phone. An old iron pot-bellied oil stove as big as an electric range still squatted in the kitchen beside the doorway to the living room. Someone had scratched a big smiling face on the soot-blackened damper.

"Those things are smoky and impossible to regulate," Phil said. "You're fortunate that Todd requisitioned this furnace and that it actually came in on the barge this year."

He pointed out other amenities: a thirty-two-gallon gray plastic trash barrel for water storage, a two-burner hot plate, and a large electric refrigerator. The L-shaped living room/bedroom seemed crowded with a brown and white striped sofa, a gray Formica table with chrome legs, four tan vinyl-covered chairs, a mustard-yellow swiveling easy chair (who could need so many chairs?), and a laminated fake oak desk, bureau, and double bed. Instead of a closet, a line of four-inch nails stuck out of the wall across from the bed.

"Stock BLM furniture," Phil remarked. "You'll find this stuff all over the Delta. The district must've gotten a good deal at one time, from Sears or Monkey Wards."

"Well, here's the new honey-bucket room," he continued. "How do you like it?"

He pointed past the head of the bed to a space adjoining a set of shelves. I laughed, wondering what I was supposed to see. Stepping closer, I noticed unpainted lines where the shelves had extended before.

Phil told me how he and Charlie, one of the school maintenance men, had decided to create a space for the honey bucket. An hour before my plane landed, Charlie had sawed through the middle of the shelves and had removed the right half of each. He hammered a plywood box together to fit around the rusty, five-gallon paint pail that had been Todd's honey bucket. Then he hinged a square of plywood over the box to make a lid, sawed a hole in the middle, and nailed a black steel toilet seat and cover on top. He positioned the paint pail and the lidded box in the new space and ran a long length of rubber pipe, like the kind in the kitchen, from a hole in the box, out the drywall and plywood framing to the outdoors, and up the outside wall almost to the roof. This would vent odors above the snowdrifts.

"Todd kept his honey bucket out in the entryway, where it didn't smell much in winter because the porch was unheated," Phil said. "But he was a bachelor. I always thought that a little rude, not to mention how cold it must have been to sit out there. Everybody had to walk past the thing when they came to visit. You know, the roll of toilet paper hanging on a nail, everything. Todd didn't seem to mind. But Charlie and I thought you might prefer something a little more civilized. You can hang a curtain or something across here. Did you bring all the things my wife suggested?"

I had. In addition to the two boxes that I hoped were somewhere in the Bethel airport, eight others were in the mail.

"Good," Phil said. "One last thing: fire escape. As you probably noticed, there's only one entrance to this house. That means if there's ever a fire in the kitchen, you'll have to bail out the window."

He nodded toward the furnace and the only window in the room.

"I'd keep something heavy nearby—a walrus bone or something—so you could smash the window quickly if you had to, without cutting yourself. I don't mean to scare you. This house has two ceiling smoke alarms, and Charlie just put new batteries in them yesterday. But it's important to be prepared."

I nodded.

"You'll want to get some candles, too. The village generator goes down every now and then, especially in winter when it gets overloaded."

I told him I liked candles, and that several were already in the mail.

"Good," he said, reaching for the doorknob. "Oh, and I'll have Charlie put a padlock on your door. Looks like Todd took the old one with him. You're lucky to have been assigned to this village. There are problems with drugs and alcohol, but they're nothing compared to what teachers encounter in much of rural Alaska. Most families here keep their problems to themselves. It's unlikely that anyone will bother you, especially up on this hill. You're pretty isolated from other houses."

I nodded again, just glad to be in a house instead of an attic or a condominium. Now I could play my flute any time of the night or day, and no one would notice. Especially if it was windy.

Phil opened the inner door to leave. "This is a very traditional village. I think you'll find you like it here. Well, see you at our house tonight for dinner."

I fluffed out my down sleeping bag, spreading it over the blue and white mattress ticking, and plugged in my alarm clock. I had seen two stainless-steel shower stalls in the girls' bathroom at the school. No one had told me to wedge a piece of wood between the hand railing and the shower button in order to keep the button down, then let the water run for ten minutes until it got warm. It would be a few days before I took my first cold shower, and several more before I mentioned it to Mary and discovered the secret.

I finished unpacking the rest of my duffel bag, wondering what I had gotten into this time besides thirty-two thousand dollars in starting pay. I dropped my high-heeled boots on the ratty brown carpet and pulled on my new felt-lined Sorels. It didn't seem cold enough outdoors for such heavy gear, just muddy, but the knee-high rubber boots that Ginger had told me to buy were lost somewhere in the Bethel airport.

Then I remembered the words of the Buddhist watchmaker. I had read them in *The Way of the White Clouds*, a book that a friend had given me two years before. The book had been a beacon for me during my nine months of private flute study with Geoffrey Gilbert in Florida, at his home in DeLand.

I thought of our weekly lessons in the ivy-covered studio on peaceful East Oakdale, how Mr. Gilbert—who was seventy, balding, and six inches shorter than I—wore brown polyester slacks and a yellow polyester shirt that smelled of cigars. His British English sounded regal, but he often had a twinkle in his eyes. His best-known student was "Jim" Galway, who had grown up in a working-class neighborhood in Belfast, Ireland. Galway's flute teacher, Muriel Dawn, had studied with Mr. Gilbert in England. When Galway was only fourteen, Mr. Gilbert came to Belfast to give a concert, and Muriel arranged for "Jim" to audition for lessons.

Galway played a Mozart concerto, and later Mr. Gilbert asked Muriel, "How did you teach that lad to phrase like that?"

"I didn't," she said. "He's phrasing differently today because he heard you play last night. He always picks up the best out of everything he hears."

"I've never come across anything like it," Mr. Gilbert said. "I want to teach him."

I smiled, remembering my own circuitous journey to the flute and to the opportunity to play for Mr. Gilbert and be accepted as his student.

Surely it is the right wish, the watchmaker had said, *that draws us to the right place. Nothing of importance happens accidentally in our life.*

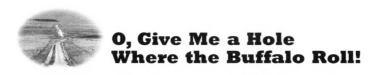 **O, Give Me a Hole
Where the Buffalo Roll!**

JESSICA MAXWELL

"I hope no one can see my Tweety Bird underwear through these."

So spoke Rande Lisle as she zipped up a new pair of khaki slacks in preparation for the first golf lesson in her life.

A Seattle high school art teacher by profession (hence her creative personal effects), Rande has about as much interest in golf as Tiger Woods has in… well, probably Tweety Bird underwear. But being best friends, we've supported each other through more than twenty years of assorted obsessions. So, since I had taken up golf, Rande had to take up golf. Besides, it's a social game. I needed girl golf buddies the way guys need guy golf buddies. The royal and ancient game, however, seemed to push the edges of Rande's tolerance envelope.

"GOLF?!!" she hollered when I called to confess my new passion. "I thought golf was for Republicans… and dorks!"

So far, I agreed with the dork part. In fact, I resembled that remark. Nonetheless, I tried to convey to her the exhilaration of the game, the joy of a golf ball well struck.

"But, I'm dyslexic!" Rande wailed. "That makes me *un*coordinated. I'd probably kill someone if I started hitting hard little balls all over the place. Maybe I'd kill *you*."

She sounded serious. There was, I knew, only one sure course of coercion.

"Well…," I said in a voice like a greased weasel, "you know, Rande, in a couple of weeks I'm going on a golf tour of MONTANA… and I thought, you know, maybe you'd like to go with me."

I counted the beats: one, two, three… FIRE!

"MONTANA!!" Rande yelled into the phone. "You're going to MONTANA!?"

Some people love Paris. Others love Hawaii. Rande loves Montana with a passion that borders on geographic dementia. Dangling Montana in front of her was the only way I got her to go on a fly fishing adventure with me the summer before, even though she considers catch-and-release "torture-and-release." I reckon I could persuade Rande to take Limburger cheese-making lessons with me, or study the history of parasite removal, as long as it took place in Montana. To her, the whole state is infused with an energy so ecstatic that she goes into a kind of spiritual stupefaction when she's there. The problem as I saw it was going to be how to get my artiste compadre to keep her eye on the ball and *not* the Big Sky state's big sky.

"*Look* at those clouds!" Rande rhapsodized as we aimed our little sky-colored rental car in the direction of the Flathead Valley. It was almost summer, and Montana had already turned on its famous cloudworks, massive high-rise cumulus humilis coiffures that appear to have recently escaped from the court of King Louis XVI.

"They're nice," I allowed. "But clouds have nothing to do with golf."

"Well, that one looks like a golf ball," Rande countered. Then she frowned. "What does Montana have to do with golf anyway? I mean, when you think of Montana you think of mountains or horses... even fly fishing. But *golf??*"

"Oh, there's been great golf here for sixty years," proclaimed Mike Dowaliby, head golf pro at Whitefish Lake Golf Club. Whitefish Lake was our first stop on the Montana golf marathon I'd put together. My plan was to hook Rande on the natural beauty of golf courses *before* we took our first lesson. From the look of it, Whitefish Lake was a great start.

"We built our first nine holes in 1936," Mike explained. "The second nine in the early sixties—that's our North Course. Our eighteen-hole South Course was built between 1980 and 1994."

It's a very pretty place, Whitefish Lake Golf Club, slugged up like it is in the far corner of the Flathead Valley in Montana's northwestern hill country.

"Is this golf course named after those lawn decorations?" Rande asked.

Mike's eyebrows went north. His eyes followed her gaze to a set of white-washed wooden fish resting in the grass near our feet.

"Those are tee markers," he explained. "Traditionally, men use the white, ladies use the red, and your better golfers use the blue. The club is named after the lake, which is named after the town of Whitefish, which is about a mile south of here.

"There's our clubhouse," he added, waving toward a vintage varnished log building as we squished ourselves into a golf cart.

"Wow," Rande said, her Art History Radar on red alert. "It looks like a WPA project."

"It was," Mike confirmed. "Built in 1935. It houses the Whitefish Lake Restaurant, one of the best around. Okay," he began a little farther down the cart path, "we're on the North Course now, and this is our fourth hole, our signature hole. It's a par three, a hundred ninety-four yards from the blue. The big fountain there is the most photographed feature we've got."

"Any fish in it?" I asked.

Mike looked at me coolly. "I doubt it," he said, then drove us to the South Course in silence. Soon we were among houses. Very nice houses, but some seemed awfully close to the fairway. One appeared to have been vandalized.

"Why does that one have so many broken windows?" Rande asked.

"It's on the fifth hole, a long par four, three hundred eighty-nine from the back tee. Guys try to cut over the house."

Our cart labored uphill. On the other side, the landscape opened into something out of a Sierra Club calendar. Birch trees were everywhere, their new green leaves strobing wildly in the sun, their trunks burning white lines into Montana's blue sky. To the left, ducklings followed their mothers in panicked caravans across a surprisingly long pond filled with half-submerged cattails. Wood ducks and mallards posed with great nobility beside the shorter grasses.

"Is that Whitefish Lake?" Rande asked.

"No," Mike answered ruefully. "That's a marsh that flooded and became a lake. We've had a lot of rain—a hundred one inches used to be the record; we've had a hundred forty-three already this year."

"Sounds like Seattle," Rande commiserated.

Our next stop was the 18th hole, the club's championship par 4.

"That's a big mountain!" Rande noted.

"That *is* Big Mountain," Mike replied. "Snowcapped until June. Makes a good championship hole. In April here you can downhill ski in the morning and play golf that afternoon."

"Oh good, break your leg *and* a window in the same day!" Rande replied, giggling until I elbowed her.

Wishing to make short work of the soggy end of Whitefish Lake Golf Club, and probably of our tour, Mike drove us swiftly back to the North Course, stopping at its 3rd hole to greet an elderly golfer.

"How you doin', young man?" Mike called.

"As I please," the gentleman practically spat back, then he took a mighty swing with his driver. His ball vanished. "We'll see when you get to be eighty-three if you can still do that."

"What's his name?" Rande asked Mike. The man overheard her.

"You know, when I was a singer and comedian I went by the name of Yasihavenjokeshagkavovitch ... but you can call me Eddie."

Our first vaudevillian golfer.

"See, Rande," I said, "all kinds of interesting people play golf."

At the 12th hole Mike stopped again. There, finally, to the right of the fairway was the real Whitefish Lake.

"Oh, it's beautiful!" Rande sang, and took a photograph.

"That's Jim Nabors's house up there on the hill," Mike said.

"Sha-zam!" Rande and I replied in unison.

"And there's our glass guy," he added, hailing a walking golfer.

"Whose window are you replacing today?" Mike asked him.

"Mountain side," the golfer answered. "You know which one."

"Yeah," Mike replied. "That's why they're moving."

Our last stop was the 10th hole, which Mike pronounced "a little dogleg."

"Is that because dogs like to lift their legs on that tree out there in the middle of the wayfarer?" Rande asked.

"*Fairway*," I corrected.

"No, but a lot of guys would like to," Mike confessed. "You can see it's in the way. About ten years ago it was hit by lightning and everyone said, 'Great'… but it came back twofold. Grew two new trunks and now it's bushier than ever."

"I heard of that happening to a guy's hair after he was struck by lightning," Rande said solemnly. "He lost it all, first, then it grew back like Einstein's."

"Just like learning to play golf," I muttered. "You think you've mastered something, then you completely lose it and it's twice as hard to learn it again."

"I can't wait," Rande groaned.

She didn't have to wait long. We had a quick but impressive lunch at Grouse Mountain Lodge, a handsome place overlooking the south Course's 18th hole. We shared a feast of hot duck potstickers, smoked quail salad, and a sampler of grilled buffalo steak, broiled antelope, and venison in a blackberry demi-glace.

"I feel like I just ate a Montana zoo," Rande moaned happily. "So far, golf is pretty fun."

So far, my plan was working.

Our first lesson was scheduled at Meadow Lake Resort, just northeast of Whitefish in the town of Columbia Falls. The entrance is all but invisible—we passed it three times, then learned that this is part of Meadow Lake's admirable attempt to blend into the landscape.

"The course really is carefully cut through the woods," Meadow Lake golf pro Kyle Long told us. "The owner, Peter Tracy, is very ecologically minded."

"That's just like the Robert Trent Jones Trail in Alabama," I said to Rande. "You'd be surprised how many golf courses are enlightened these days."

I felt a little like a golf brochure. Beautiful Scenery! Fun Golf Carts! Interesting People! Fabulous Food! Environmentally Friendly! PLAY GOLF!! But the truth is that it's often true.

Meadow Lake goes so far as to apply the high-minded principles of Integrated Pest Management to all of its 330 acres, keeping the use of toxic chemicals to a minimum.

"That really reduces water pollution and protects wildlife," Kyle instructed. "The water trap on the fifth hole is full of little brook trout. [I held my tongue.] We're one step away from being an Audubon-certified golf course."

Which explains why a wide selection of migratory songbirds exploded out of the bushes when I shanked the bejesus out of the first drive of our golf lesson.

"Line the club up with your target, not your body," Kyle offered.

Now that was a new one. How many golf swing concepts *are* there, anyway?

I tried it. The ball straightened out all right, but it skittered along the grass as if I were bowling. Kyle told me to keep practicing while he inspected Rande's grip. He was a fast-moving fellow, and he had an intensity about him that made you pay attention. It also made me nervous.

"The most important thing is the grip with the left hand," he told Rande. "Gals tend to do this ..." He slid his left palm to the left. "You want your left hand all the way on top of the club."

Rande regripped her club—a three iron, on my recommendation—then took a mighty swing. Her ball squirted a few inches up into the air.

"Ever hit a golf ball before?" Kyle asked.

Rande shook her head.

"I thought so."

"I'm dyslexic!" Rande cried in defense, as if the notion of being good at anything mechanical was impossible. Kyle didn't seem to hear her.

"My feeling is that if you can't hit the ball to there [about three feet], then you can't hit it to the green. Practice that a while ... you get to look at the Rockies while you do."

I couldn't have paid him to be a better golf mascot. Rande was so taken by the extravagant landscape, she didn't care that her golf balls spewed forth like popping popcorn.

"Oh [zing!], the mountains are just [zong!] *beau*tiful!" she agreed. Then she spotted something at the edge of the woods.

"Look! A buffalo! Rolling on its back!"

"That's an elk," Kyle corrected. "They bed down all over the place in the spring. We also see black bear and moose, especially around Meadow Lake. The lake attracts animals. Pretty soon there'll be baby turtles out there, too, sitting on their parents' backs. The lake also makes golf more interesting," he added. "Our eighth hole has a great peninsula green, for instance; you putt surrounded by water. And holes 16 and 18 actually cross the lake."

"Dyslexics don't swim very well," Rande said anxiously. I reassured her that we were just hitting a few practice balls, not playing the course.

Meadow Lake, it turned out, is fed by Garnier Creek, which eventually joins Trumble Creek, a tributary of the Flathead River where Rande and I had fished the summer before. Once again, I lamented our lack of fly rods, especially given the local brook trout population, but didn't dare say anything to detract from Rande's budding interest in golf... or, at least, golf courses.

We spent about twenty minutes hitting golf balls. Rande continued to make a mess out of each drive, and so did I. I *tried* to read the ball. I *tried* to trust the club. I *tried* to keep my head in the club head. I *tried* to be one with the Tokatee Coyote. I *tried* to line my club up with the target (though, on the driving range, I wasn't sure what it was). And I *tried* to keep my left hand on top. But my faithful three-iron felt like a foreign object in my hands. My swing had no form at all. And every shot just zigged or zagged with heartbreaking regularity.

"I've got Golfheimer's disease!" I finally wailed to Rande. "I've forgotten everything I've learned!"

"Oh," she sang back between frighteningly erratic power-swings, "it doesn't matter." [Zing!] "Golf is a *spiritual* sport! Just look at the sky!" [Zong!] "Just look at those *trees*!" [Zap!] "Just look at that buffalo rolling around happy as a pig in mud!" [Zowie!!]

"Elk," Kyle said. "But you're right about the scenery. With the trees and the wildlife, the lakes, mountains, streams, and with the course itself cut through all this natural beauty... well, to me, that makes Meadow Lake a real Montana golf course."

We left Meadow Lake in a real Montana summer storm. The northern sky looked like it had taken a beating. Monstrous cumulonimbus clouds rose above us like tarnished silver belt buckles. Soon raindrops covered the windshield with massive welts. Rande was driving.

"We're hydroplaning!" she cried. "I can't see the line between the lanes."

"That's because there isn't one," I answered.

One thing all girl golf buddies know—when the weather gets tough, the tough go shopping. So, when we spotted the "Annual Boot Sale" sign in the window of Kalispell's Western Outdoor store, we didn't even have to discuss it. Two hundred dollars later we sashayed back to the car like a couple of golfing rodeo queens. The skies, we noted, had cleared.

"Works every time," I confirmed. "Hey, maybe we should have bought a pair of those baby cowboy boots as a golf god offering."

"Aw, let's just leave 'em some Tweety Bird undies."

"Then what would *you* wear?"

"Tweety Bird undies. They were ten pair for a dollar. I've got tons of 'em."

"Well, I'm glad you told me or I would have thought you never changed your underwear."

"You *can* see them through my golf pants, can't you?"

"Only when you bend over."

"Which is every time I swing."

"Well, just think about golf," I counseled. "Graham says we should keep our head in our club head, anyway."

"Your grandma played golf?" Rande asked, amazed.

"Of course not," I answered.

"Then who's 'Gram'?" Rande inquired.

"I really don't know," I replied.

"What do you mean you don't know?"

"Oh, he's just this guy who keeps showing up when I practice hitting balls back home."

"A golf stalker!" Rande breathed.

"He's not a stalker. He's...sweet."

"They always are," Rande cautioned. "At first."

"Well, why would he be stalking *me*?"

"Breasts."

"RANDE!"

"Well, you can see them through your golf clothes."

"He's not that kind of guy."

"Every guy is that kind of guy."

"No," I replied. "Graham is different. Maybe he likes breasts—I don't know. But he's...thoughtful."

"He *thinks* about breasts."

"Oh, stop it."

"Okay, so why is he stalking you?"

"He's not...oh, I don't know."

"Well, how many times have you 'run into' him?"

"Twice. But it was just a coincidence. There are only four golf courses to choose from back home, and one's private."

"And he just happened to be at both places at exactly the same time you were. Okay, so, where's he from? What does he do? What do he daddy do??"

"I didn't ask him."

"Well, what did you talk about?"

"Golf."

"Golf?"

"Golf."

"You only talked about golf?"

"Rande, that's what people *talk* about on golf courses. GOLF. Actually, Graham really has helped my golf swing."

She eyed me sideways. Then she dropped her Best Girlfriend Bomb.

"He's cute, isn't he?"

I didn't answer.

"He's CUTE, right?"

"Okay...YES! He's cute! Okay?"

"How cute?"

"Very cute."

"Shoulders?"

"Yes."

"Thighs?"

"Oh yeah."

"Hands?"

"Perfect."

"Wedding ring?"

"Nope."

"Bald?"

"Blue jay."

"Blue jay?"

"He's got one of those spiky new crew cuts."

"Cool."

"I know. He even fly fishes."

"So, when are you going to see him again?"

"I don't know."

"Just whenever he shows up?"

"I guess."

"Do you think he will?"

"He has so far."

(One-Minute Unconvinced Girlfriend Silence)

"I don't know," Rande said slowly. "This game has a lot of sex in it: shafts, heads...holes."

She was just trying to get back at me for telling her that fly fishing was sexy because it was full of "rods, flies, and shooting line."

"I'll be careful," I promised her.

"Well," she said with a strange little flamenco hand gesture as we parked in front of the Northern Pines Golf Club, "safe golf!"

 # Coming Home

KAREN JETTMAR

I peer out of my tent into dense fog; a lone caribou passes, stepping soundlessly, its curved antlers piercing the mist. Only a gentle trickle of water in the creek and the low rumble of the Kongakut River tumbling over boulders break the silence of early morning. We're camped at the portal of a traditional migration path. Countless trails crisscross this broad, low swath of tundra, where the Porcupine caribou herd has trod between northeast Alaska and northwest Canada for millennia. My mother lies in a hospital bed in Takoma Park, Maryland, more than 4,500 miles away, and I need to get home.

■ ■ ■

Last night, as Connie, Page, and I lay in our tents in the last foothills edging the Beaufort Sea in Alaska's Arctic National Wildlife Refuge, we heard the drone of a single-engine bush plane approaching, then landing. The pilot hiked south along the river until he found us. "Karen, is that you?" he called gently from outside the tent. Connie and I sat straight up in our sleeping bags. "I got a call; your mom's not doing too well. We're gonna get you out of here first thing in the morning."

Connie and I talked after he left. I think she knew I was in shock. She coaxed out memories of my mother, the community activist who'd kept encroaching developers at bay, the woman who had been my Girl Scout leader for ten years, she who'd driven me to winter swim-team practice throughout my teens, the one who'd let out a long tether for an adventurous daughter, wandering far beyond the perimeter of suburban creeks and woods, and out into the world, finding refuge in the northernmost landscape on the continent.

"Are you scared?" Connie asked.

"No, I'm just going to get there," I responded.

I couldn't imagine the chain of communications that had located me here. In the summer, few people know my exact whereabouts, possessing only a vague notion that I am "up north, somewhere in the Brooks Range." Arcing east to west across the top of Alaska like a huge scythe, the 600-mile-long, 150-mile-wide Brooks Range lies entirely above the Arctic Circle. These are the northernmost mountains in the world, a range scored by ice, wind, and time, and pretty darn far from any reliable airport. I'm a long way from my child-hood home of Adelphi, Maryland.

I later learned that my dad had called Anchorage from Adelphi; my sum-mer roommate had gotten the call. She had found a folder in my file cabinet containing names of charter air companies. A couple calls later, she had located the pilot who'd flown us into the Arctic Refuge. Though Alaska has a vast land area, its small population is closely linked. The pilots know me. But how quickly could I get back East to be with my mom?

■ ■ ■

We pack up our bags and the tent and walk to meet the pilot, each lost in our own thoughts. I climb a hillside and crouch to dig a cathole latrine. On the tundra beside me, perfectly intact—neither a feather out of place, nor a mark on its body—lies a dead golden eagle. I cradle it in my arms, admiring its golden hackles and bright yellow beak, feeling its strength, the power of its talons. A spirit messenger, the eagle represents illumination and an acceptance of personal power. Eagle medicine reminds me to take heart, gather courage, and soar beyond the horizon. Courage? I fear my mother is dying. The tears I pushed away last night now stream over the dead bird.

I return the eagle to a clump of mountain avens and climb back down the hill to the plane. Connie and Page are waiting beside the river. We load, and with a roar the four-seater rises above the rough cobble airstrip and heads into a stiff north wind. Then, banking a turn above the river and climbing several hundred feet, our pilot pulls us out of the fog bank and heads south.

■ ■ ■

We had planned a two-week journey on a remote river in the Arctic Refuge as a gift to ourselves. A wilderness guide who's been taking small groups to arctic rivers and mountains for fifteen years, I am familiar with the territory. But this trip would be different. Without clients, I could push my own limits, be free to explore at my own pace or just relax and absorb everything, without the pressure of being responsible for every aspect of the expedition.

Each of us had been recently touched by cancer. I'd spent a week with my mother at the end of May, after her first round of chemotherapy. She had fallen ill in late March, losing energy and weight. Shuffled from doctor to doctor, she'd been diagnosed first with sarcoidosis, then with non-Hodgkin's lymphoma, while my father had insisted that she "looked great" with her weight loss. When cancer had been mentioned by the doctors, he'd been in denial, until she had collapsed and had to be rushed to the hospital. Perhaps our entire family had been in denial. None of us could believe she could ever get cancer. When I had left her on Memorial Day, I had promised my mom I'd spend two weeks in July with her, and we'd celebrate her seventy-third birthday, the day before Independence Day. In the twenty-four years since I'd moved to Alaska, I'd never been back East in the summer. Mom had prepared to leave the hospital, and we had both eagerly anticipated our time together.

Connie, veteran of many northern river trips, has paddled three arctic rivers with me. She loves rivers; the longer the river, the better. In the 1970s, she had been part of a couple pioneering all-women's river explorations in northeast Canada. Connie's idea of heaven is logging miles and days gliding through vast, unspoiled northern wilderness. At fifty-five, she was experiencing the bodily mysteries of menopause, and during her work day divided her time between a private psychotherapy practice in Anchorage and fund-raising for The Nature Conservancy. For more than a year, Connie had been steadfastly caring for her partner, Susan, through the labyrinth of breast cancer chemotherapy and radiation. She had longed to explore a river, and Susan, now well, had urged her on.

Page, lifelong Alaskan, accomplished bush pilot and ecologist with the National Park Service, had never been to the northeast corner of the state. Her father had piloted sorties in the proposed Arctic Wildlife Range for the U.S. Fish and Wildlife Service in the 1950s, while managing the Kenai National Wildlife Range in South-central Alaska. Page and I ski all winter; we live to telemark in the Chugach Mountains or skate-ski the extensive network of groomed trails around Anchorage. Page is of Olympic stock; both her younger sister and brother had competed in Nordic skiing. Page would say that her "Olympics" was achieving a Ph.D. in ecology, but she is so physically strong, I have no doubt she could have competed internationally if she'd set her mind to it. Lynne, her sister, even after competing in three Olympics, says that Page is the strong one. "When we go moose hunting in the fall," says Lynne, "we always count on our big, tough sister to haul the meat."

The previous fall, Page's father, Dave, had been diagnosed with prostate cancer, and her family had spent the winter nursing him through chemotherapy. Much improved, Dave had gotten back to splitting firewood and working on his cedar strip canoe. Page had been eager to dip her paddle into a clear, snow-fed river, scramble up a mountain, and drink from a mountain freshet. Connie and I were, too.

■ ■ ■

From Anchorage, it is a 385-mile drive to Fairbanks, Alaska's second-largest city. Small commuter planes, such as a nine-seater Cessna Chieftain, carry passengers to remote rural villages beyond the road system. Arctic Village is an hour and a half north, over the Steese and White Mountains and the Yukon Flats, a vast wetland punctuated by myriad lakes, ponds, and ancient oxbows, and pierced by the mighty Yukon River. Our flight paralleled the Chandalar River, its meandering bends spread across a wide valley, and we landed in Arctic Village, rural in the extreme. Just a couple miles of gravel road connect the airstrip to a scattering of handcrafted log cabins with no indoor plumbing, where one hundred Gwich'in Athabascans actively pursue subsistence hunting, fishing, and gathering. Beyond that, all is wilderness.

Our bush pilot arrived. Into the plane went our tiny raft and paddles, our food and personal gear. Three lightweight women and a well-planned load, we easily fell below the 900-pound load limit on the small plane. We were off, soaring northward, the lake-dotted valley below us a mosaic of textures and hues, wetlands and forest-encircled mountains. Reaching like tendrils up the valleys, spruce forests gave way to rolling hills engraved with caribou trails. Beyond, a procession of rugged peaks piled up seemingly without end. Rivers glinted in the sun, twisting like a woman's French braid. Soon we crossed over the snow-covered backbone of the range, northernmost extension of the continent's great divide, where the rivers change direction—south to the Yukon River or north to the Arctic Ocean.

Circling over the headwaters of the Kongakut, we saw caribou drifting along the edge of the mountains, and we dropped down onto a small gravel bar. We unloaded, then waved to the pilot as he disappeared over a ridge. Surrounding us, precipitous peaks rose above a green velvet valley, while puffy clouds drifted across a cerulean sky. High above, a small column of Dall sheep climbed single file along a limestone ridge. In the stillness, a covey of rock ptarmigan glided low over the tundra. Between their low-pitched calls, I heard their wing beats.

After setting up our tents, we began a routine that served us well: eat dinner around midnight, wander over the tundra in the soft, suffused golden light as the sun dipped low across the northern sky, and collapse in the wee hours of the morning, sleeping till the sun baked us out of our tents. Some days we spent paddling and other days we spent afoot, moving camps every second or third day, so we'd have time to settle in and get to know a place.

The next day, Page and I set off hiking in shorts and tank tops over hillsides lavish with Lapland rosebay, a miniature rhododendron, and mountain avens, a low, showy, cream-colored flower. It was the peak of wildflower season in the mountains. Flowers—yellow, purple, pink, magenta—splashed across the tundra like a painter's palette. Our routes were not hiking trails in the traditional sense. Instead, we followed the traces of brown bear, sheep, and caribou. We climbed, crossing tumbling creeks fed by snowmelt, and reached sheer limestone towers. Amid the dark gray rock, brilliant magenta moss campion and pink phlox bloomed. Orange, white, black, and yellow lichens clung to the rocks. Below, the river glinted like strands of tinsel. We became sheep, climbing for the sheer joy of it, absorbing the views. For hours we didn't talk, content to wander sentiently, smiling constantly. And when the beauty got to be too much, we'd just stop and embrace.

Connie took a less strenuous approach, taking on the job of camp organizer. She liked planning the meals and packing lunch. She spent her day by the river, walking the gravel bars and low tundra banks, observing rocks and animal tracks. "I'm staring and learning to see," she said over dinner. "You can just feel the movement, feel that life is on the move, with all the tracks and scat in the area. Even when the caribou are not around, you can feel them." Long after midnight, we crawled into our tents. With the mountains looming overhead, we fell asleep immediately.

Our boat for the journey was a ten-and-a-half-foot-long raft named *River Beauty*, after dwarf fireweed, a brilliant magenta wildflower that graces gravel bars throughout the north. Small, maneuverable and, yes, magenta, the raft was perfectly suited to our load of three women, six dry bags, three food buckets, three daypacks, a camera case and tripod, and a tiny cinnamon-colored stuffed bear, riding high atop the load with her own hand-carved cottonwood paddle. Cinnamon, the bear, was the eyes and ears for my mom, who couldn't be here. The raft also served as a windbreak for our kitchen, with a tarp tied above it in case of rain. Completely mobile, it could be repositioned if the wind changed.

Our third day out, we loaded *River Beauty* and pushed off. The boat bounced over rollicking, spirited water, riding high through swell and trough. I steered from the rear, while Page and Connie took the brunt of the breaking waves. Prior to the trip, Page had told me she was afraid of white water. She quickly overcame her fears. "This is so much fun!" she beamed. We relaxed while the river poured through a corridor of emerald mountains and past great walls of *aufeis* (shelves of overflow ice). Layer upon layer of turquoise blue ice rose, illuminated by sunlight. We climbed atop the six-foot walls. Streams cut sinuous channels into the ice and poured over the edge, cascading into the transparent river. Dull white calcium carbonate, leached from the mountains, lay in circular piles. Rapidly disintegrating, the crystal ice walls collapsed into jeweled prisms beneath our feet.

Caribou (Page affectionately called them "'bous") were everywhere; hillsides shimmered as they poured down the valleys and swam the river. We pulled the raft to shore constantly, tucking ourselves down behind the tubes, our telephoto lenses in hand. Occasionally we surprised a loner, dark antlers dancing above the willows. Vulnerable to predators, he pranced haltingly, bolting from us as soon as he caught our scent or running toward us as if to join our little herd. *Che yaa t'ok*, the Gwich'in call him—a young, foolish male. Hoofed tracks marked every gravel beach. Whitened, sun-bleached bones and antlers lay scattered upon the land. Brown and white hollow hair hung from bushes and pooled in eddies on the river.

Dall sheep clustered on the ridges or paraded down to the river to lick calcium off the *aufeis*. Tiny lambs scrambled at the feet of ewes, surefootedly crossing steep precipices. One afternoon a tawny grizzly ambled our way across a broad gravel bar, his humped shoulders and huge head rippling in the afternoon light. Sensing us, he veered off a few paces, rose on his hind legs and sniffed the air with forepaws raised. Dropping back to the ground, he suddenly bolted away and up onto a steep slope. In less than a minute, he galloped halfway up the slope, then paused in the alders to look back at us.

Mornings were sunny and warm. We basked on smooth river stones, with robins our constant camp companions. Many people come to the Arctic and are surprised to encounter robins, but *Turdus migratorius* has a circumpolar range. I am always comforted by this bird of my childhood, both of us adapted to a land of endless light and space.

Time became meaningless as the days passed. We slowed down and could finally listen again to subtleties in the silence: the cry of a rough-legged hawk; the clicking of caribou anklebones; a murmur of water over stone; the beating of our own hearts.

My mother's presence remained strong. I photographed Cinnamon as an alpinist, climbing *aufeis* crystals with avalanche cord draped over her shoulders. Later, she posed on a bandanna by a quiet pool, her tawny body reflected in the water. On the tundra, she reclined in a cluster of purple cranesbill geraniums or amid a fragrant patch of artemisia. Each vantage point I climbed, she viewed from atop my daypack.

Though I'm not much for naming features, Page introduced the idea and, like the Gwich'in and Inupiat have done, we imbued our landscape with meaning—*place of the wolf tracks, place where the porcupine roams, valley of the caribou*—to remember what we'd seen there.

The river changed character, first spreading into dozens of channels, then pinching back together as it swirled by the bases of twisted ramparts. Slowly the river gradient increased; we were approaching big white water.

Mergansers rode the current just beyond our paddles' reach. Sandpipers danced along water's edge. As we stroked by gravel bars, arctic terns and gulls dive-bombed us in an effort to protect their nests. A couple of musk oxen grazed on slopes studded with lupine, lousewort, and glacier avens. We camped where the river constricted, carving through a deep mountain gorge with striated rock. The mountain sheared off on our side, its flanks rising above 6,000 feet, so caribou headed north needed to swim to the opposite shore to avoid the white-water canyon just a mile below us. We were in a perfect spot. Small groups of velvet-antlered bulls wandered near as we ate breakfast. A small porcupine with light gray fur trailing off its back waddled by. Curious, the caribou approached the porcupine, trailing it down to the river. Then they swam across, single file, leaving the porcupine to continue resolutely down the beach. "Now I know why it's called the Porcupine Caribou Herd," I laughed. "They follow the porcupine!" Actually the herd is named after the Porcupine River in Canada, but we celebrated our own version of its origin.

Page and I hiked up a slim side canyon lined with thick alder and willow shrubs. Bear tracks led from its mouth into the narrows. We followed the tracks, traversed a roaring creek, then climbed high to avoid the brush. Matched in pace, with shared interests, Page and I were perfect hiking companions; our energy and enthusiasm fueled us to crest many a height, and we'd gaze out from our perch at golden eagles and hawks soaring above us, or sometimes below. The encircling landscape was virtually unaltered by humans. "This is where I feel most free," I whispered.

Page added, "No sense of time, no responsibilities. No worries. Just living each moment."

The smallest discoveries delighted us. We found *Eritrichium aretioides*, the minute purple-hued arctic forget-me-not, growing in jumbled slides of maroon and gray shale. We wandered amid the willows in the footsteps of a musk ox, picking downy qiviut from the branches. We watched a merganser shooting through the river horizontally, spearing fish.

On Page's forty-seventh birthday, June 20, we dodged boulders and skirted rock walls as the river seethed through a white-water canyon, creating huge standing waves. *River Beauty* punched through the swells, bouncing like a duck, while waves exploded over our heads. We made an early camp and pre-pared for a party. I cooked pasta with pesto, Connie made a cabbage–sorrel leaf salad, we steamed a side dish of *Mertensia* leaves (Page had collected mountain sorrel, and I had collected lungwort), and I baked a pineapple upside-down cake. The well-hidden cabernet sauvignon came out of my bag. "Shall we have the dessert first? " Page queried. "While it's warm, of course." After the candles were extinguished, we ate the cake, then polished off the rest of the meal. The sun stayed out all night and, like salmon returning to spawn, the caribou kept moving steadily north.

Days later, the paddling over, we reached ancient Caribou Pass. Climbing to the top of a bluff, we found the horizon filled with the silhouettes of antlered bodies. I hiked up into another pass, my own *valley of the caribou*, and discovered thousands of animals covering the slopes, most of them lying on the ground with their heads down. Here was an Eden, where cows, bulls, and baby 'bous blanketed the tundra, resting. I sat quietly, unmoving. An hour passed, maybe two. Caribou rose and drifted up the hill, surrounding me; the air filled with low grunts. They nibbled at the tundra, ignoring me. Then, with a whim that only the wind understands, they poured back down the hill, join-ing the brown mass below. As the clouds dropped down to envelop the land, I returned to our creekside camp, joining Connie and Page for hot supper. A penetrating cold mist sent us to bed early.

■ ■ ■

My heart races and my stomach churns as our bush plane lands in Arctic Village. There's no room on the commuter plane. Connie speaks up. "It's an emergency."

"Other people have emergencies," replies the pilot.

"Yes, but this is her mother," she says. "She's trying to get home."

Somehow an empty seat appears; someone must have given up a space. We land in Fort Yukon and I call my father from the pay phone. He answers. "Karen, she's going fast. I don't know what I'll do without her." I tell him I'm on my way home.

Once in Fairbanks, I use Page's airline ticket to Anchorage; then I go home for a few clothes and return to the airport. When I try to explain to the ticket agent why I need to go to Washington, D.C., I can only sob. Twenty-three hours from Alaska's northeast edge, I reach my mom's side.

Eagle medicine; though riddled with cancer, my mother holds on long enough for her four children to get back home. Heavily sedated, tubes taped to her arms, she can no longer swallow or speak, but she gazes at each of us long and hard with clear blue-gray eyes, smiling, while tears stream down her cheeks. We gather around her hospital bed, with all our attention focused on her: embracing, holding hands, stroking arms, massaging feet, singing, telling stories, weeping. According to Mom's wishes, the nurse removes all life support, and for eight hours we witness her transcendence as she gradually releases her physical self. The moment comes when she no longer breathes. Free now, she soars into pure spirit.

■ ■ ■

Two years later, I return to the ancestral pass with a couple of friends. We are here in late May, hoping to observe the vanguard of the Porcupine caribou herd—arrival of the pregnant females. I secretly wish to see a calf born, though chances are slim that a cow will wander near and just drop her newborn. I'm content simply to hang out and watch spring arrive in the Arctic.

In our days here, snow flurries and fog obscure the sun for days; yet slowly the land is warming; snowfields melt into lakelets and rivulets race to the river. Pussy willows emerge, red catkins reaching to the constant sun. Ptarmigan drop their white plumage feather by feather, even as they sit on snowdrifts. Their variegated plumage will soon blend completely with the tundra. Buds swell and flowers burst open to the sky, each a tiny heat-gathering parabola. Waterfowl wing in by the thousands. The land explodes with life.

I climb a hill to admire clumps of pale lavender anemone—the same hill I climbed that foggy morning two years earlier, when my mom was still alive. Amid the clusters of flowers, near the opening to an arctic ground squirrel burrow, lie scattered bones—long delicate wing bones, smaller leg bones, scythe-shaped talons, and a skull with a hooked, pale yellow peak. Olive-brown feathers are strewn about. Cupped in my palms, the skull feels nearly weightless. Long wing bones are smooth and sun-bleached. My eyes drift upward to a blue-gray sky, the color of Mom's eyes. High over a distant peak, a golden eagle soars, its broad wings held horizontally. Vision clear and spirit soaring, I see her again. There is an unbroken circle in life and death—the herd and flocks migrate, the sun and planets circle—the ancient rhythms continue. I am home again.

Contributors

KIM BARNES is the author of two memoirs: *In the Wilderness: Coming of Age in Unknown Country,* which was a finalist for the 1997 Pulitzer Prize, and *Hungry for the World.* She is editor, with Mary Clearman Blew, of *Circle of Women: An Anthology of Contemporary Western Women Writers.* Barnes's first novel, *Finding Caruso,* is soon to be published. She teaches creative writing at the University of Idaho.

SUSAN BISKEBORN is the author of *Artists at Work: Twenty-Five Northwest Glass-makers, Ceramists, and Jewelers.* Shows at the Boise Art Museum, the Cheney–Cowles Museum in Spokane, and the Mia Gallery in Seattle resulted from that book. In addition to working as an editor, teacher, and reporter, Susan Biskeborn has also published numerous poems and essays in regional and national periodicals. She lives in Seattle with her husband and their daughter, Mary.

For the past two decades, MARLENE BLESSING has worked in book publishing in the West and is currently the editor-in-chief at Fulcrum Publishing. She is a published poet, essayist, and cookbook author. *A Road of Her Own* is the first collection of women's writings that she has compiled. She is also a contributor to the anthology *Face to Face: Women's Stories of Faith, Mysticism, and Epiphanies.* She lives in Denver.

MARY BRUNO is a biologist turned journalist. She studied sleep patterns in rats, the diatom communities in bogs, and the uptake of carcinogens by stream algae before going to work for *Newsweek* magazine. She has since been a writer, editor, and boss for various publications, including *Newsweek, Seattle Weekly, New York Woman,* Mr.Showbiz.com, ABCNEWS.com, and OnHealth.com. She is now a freelance writer based in Seattle. She travels to New Jersey at least twice a year.

SUSAN EWING's books include *The Great Rocky Mountain Nature Factbook, The Great Alaska Nature Factbook,* and *Lucky Hares and Itchy Bears,* a children's book of animal verse. Her nonfiction has appeared in numerous anthologies and in such publications as *Gray's Sporting Journal, Sports Afield,* and *Big Sky Journal.* She lives in Montana and is currently working on some short stories.

NATALIE FOBES specializes in photographing people, places, and wildlife. Her first book, *Reaching Home: Pacific Salmon, Pacific People,* was the culmination of over ten years of reporting around the Pacific Rim. She was a finalist for the Pulitzer Prize in a writing category, and received the Alicia Patterson Fellowship and the Scripps Howard Meeman award for her salmon work. Her exhibit of the same name has been shown at museums throughout the West and Alaska, including The Burke Museum, The Alaska State Museum, and The Birch Aquarium at Scripps Institution. Natalie's photographs have been published by almost every major magazine, including *National Geographic, Smithsonian, Natural History,* and *Audubon.* Natalie is co-founder of Blue Earth Alliance, a nonprofit corporation dedicated to helping photographers document endangered environments, threatened cultures, and social issues. She lives in Seattle.

LINDA M. HASSELSTROM writes, ranches, and conducts writing retreats on the ranch homesteaded by her grandfather in 1899. Her published nonfiction books include *Windbreak, Going Over East, Land Circle,* and *Feels Like Far.* Her poems are collected in *Dakota Bones* and *Bitter Creek Junction,* and she has edited or co-edited numerous other books. She writes, "I am a perpetual student of American Western history, culture, and ecology. I write to learn. My primary job is writing about the territory I love, including not only the land but its inhabitants, human and otherwise, and their stories." She lives in Wyoming.

TERI HEIN lives in Seattle, where she teaches high school students receiving cancer treatment at Seattle Cancer Care Alliance. Her traveling life has included places as disparate as northwestern Pakistan, the Arctic, and the Amazon jungle. Her first book, a memoir, *Atomic Farmgirl,* was selected for recognition on the BookSense 76 List.

LINDA HOGAN is a Chickasaw poet, novelist, essayist, and author of ten previous books. *Seeing Through the Sun* received an American Book Award from the Before Columbus Foundation; *Mean Spirit* won the Oklahoma Book Award, as well as the Mountains and Plains Booksellers Award, and was a finalist for the Pulitzer Prize; and *Book of Medicines* was a finalist for the National Book

Critics Circle Award. Hogan has been the recipient of a NEA grant and a Minnesota Arts Board Grant, a Lannan Award, a Colorado Writer's Fellowship, a Guggenheim Fellowship, and the Five Civilized Tribes Museum Playwriting Award. She lives in Colorado.

After a summer of hitchhiking across the West during college, **KAREN JETTMAR** permanently took the road Northwest from Maryland when she was twenty-one, and has called Alaska home since then. Writer, naturalist, and wilderness guide, she is the author of two guidebooks: *The Alaska River Guide* and *Alaska's Glacier Bay,* as well as a forthcoming book of photography and essays, *Arctic Refuge: The Last Great Wilderness.* She directs Equinox Wilderness Expeditions, an adventure travel company specializing in taking small groups on extended expeditions to the North's most remote and spectacular wilderness areas. She lives in Anchorage and Vancouver, British Columbia.

PAULETTE JILES was born and raised in the Missouri Ozarks and now has dual citizenship with Canada. A critically acclaimed poet, she is a past winner of the Canadian Governor General Award, Canada's highest literary honor. Her previous books include *North Spirit* and *Cousins.* Her acclaimed first novel, *Enemy Women,* was recently published. She lives in San Antonio, Texas.

BHARTI KIRCHNER is the author of seven books, three of which are critically acclaimed novels: *Darjeeling, Sharmila's Book,* and *Shiva Dancing.* She is also an award-winning cook and author of four popular cookbooks, including the best-selling *The Bold Vegetarian.* She has written numerous articles and essays for magazines and anthologies. She lives in Seattle.

CAROLYN KREMERS writes literary nonfiction and poetry, and teaches at the University of Alaska Fairbanks. She has also served on the faculty at Eastern Washington University, Spokane. She is the author of *Place of the Pretend People: Gifts from a Yup'ik Eskimo Village.* Her essays and poems have appeared in numerous anthologies and magazines, including *American Nature Writing 1999, Brevity, Creative Nonfiction, Manoa, Newsday, North American Review,* and *Runner's World.* Currently she is completing a second book of nonfiction and a collection of poetry.

A nationally known adventure travel and conservation writer, **JESSICA MAXWELL** wrote Esquire's travel column for a decade and is a former columnist for Audubon magazine. Her books include *Femme d'Adventure: Travel Tales from Inner Montana to Outer Mongolia; I Don't Know Why I Swallowed the Fly;* and

Driving Myself Crazy: Misadventures of a Novice Golfer. Bill Bryson included her *Audubon* feature on Bhutan in his anthology, *Best American Travel Writing 2000,* and she contributed an essay to *September 11: West Coast Writers Approach Ground Zero.* She is currently the West Coast editor of *Love Magazine* and continues to write for publications as varied as *Forbes, Departures, Islands,* and *Audubon.* She lives with her husband and part-bobcat kitty in Eugene, Oregon.

DIANE JOSEPHY PEAVEY is the author of *Bitterbrush Country: Living on the Edge of the Land.* She lives on a sheep and cattle ranch in southcentral Idaho and writes stories about that life, its people, history, and the changing landscape of the West. Many of these pieces air weekly on Idaho Public Radio. Her writings have appeared in numerous magazines and journals, including *Boise Magazine, Talking River Review, Range Magazine,* and *Northern Lights.* She has also contributed essays to the following anthologies: *Shadow Cat, Written on Water,* and *Woven on the Wind.* She is the Director of the October Trailing of the Sheep Festival in Ketchum, Idaho.

BRENDA PETERSON is a nature writer and novelist, author of over fourteen books, including the award-winning memoir, *Build Me an Ark: A Life with Animals,* which was selected as a "Best Spiritual Book of 2001." For the past two decades, she has studied and written about marine mammals and the environment. Her acclaimed essay collections include *Nature and Other Mothers, Living by Water,* and *Singing to the Sound.* Her third novel, *Duck and Cover,* was selected as *New York Times* "Notable Book of the Year." She and Linda Hogan are the editors of the bestselling "Women and the Natural World" three-volume series, including *Intimate Nature, The Sweet Breathing of Plants,* and *Face to Face: Women's Stories of Faith, Mysticism, and Epiphanies.* She lives near the shore of Puget Sound in Seattle.

PEGGY SHUMAKER's books of poems include *Underground Rivers, Wings Moist from the Other World, The Circle of Totems,* and *Esperanza's Hair.* Her essays have appeared in *Under Northern Lights, A Year in Place, Prairie Schooner,* and *Ascent.* She is professor emerita from University of Alaska Fairbanks, where she taught for many years. She lives in Fairbanks, Alaska, and travels widely.

JANET THOMAS is a playwright whose work has been produced nationwide. She is the former editor of *SPA* magazine and the author of *At Home in Hostel Territory,* a guide to hostels throughout the West. Her most recently published book is *The Battle in Seattle,* an insider's account of the WTO demonstrations in Seattle in 2000. She lives in the San Juan Islands in the northwest corner of Washington State.

Award-winning author and columnist SUSAN J. TWEIT began her career as a field ecologist studying wildfires, sagebrush, and grizzly bears. She now writes on how the wild nearby teaches us about being human. Tweit's seven books for adults and children include *Seasons in the Desert: A Naturalist's Notebook*, a nominee for the Western States Book Award, and *City Foxes*, a picture book named Outstanding Science Trade Book for Children in 1998. She contributes to *Audubon* and other magazines, as well as the *Denver Post* and Writers on the Range. A popular speaker, Tweit teaches creative writing and natural history workshops around the country. She is co-founder of the Border Book Festival, and a member of Women Writing the West, PEN West, and the Society of Children's Book Writers and Illustrators. She lives in Colorado.

SUSAN ZWINGER is the author of *The Last Wild Edge*, one woman's journey from the Arctic Circle to the Hoh River; *Stalking the Ice Dragon*, winner of the Washington Governor's Author's Award in 1992; *Women in Wilderness*, co-edited with Ann Zwinger; and *Still Wild, Always Wild*, a Sierra Club book celebrating the newly protected areas of the California Desert. A talented artist and teacher, Susan has written for a variety of literary and art journals. She has been a fine artist and museum curator in Santa Fe, New Mexico, an environmental activist and natural history educator in the Northwest, and an interpretive ranger for the National Park Service. She haunts the woods of an island north of Seattle.

Credits